LEADERSHIP TO **LAST**

LAST
LEADERSHIP TO

How Great Leaders
Leave Legacies Behind

GEOFFREY JONES
TARUN KHANNA

BUSINESS

An imprint of Penguin Random House

PENGUIN BUSINESS

USA | Canada | UK | Ireland | Australia
New Zealand | India | South Africa | China | Singapore

Penguin Business is part of the Penguin Random House group of companies
whose addresses can be found at global.penguinrandomhouse.com

Published by Penguin Random House India Pvt. Ltd
4th Floor, Capital Tower 1, MG Road,
Gurugram 122 002, Haryana, India

First published in Penguin Business by Penguin Random House India 2022

10 9 8 7 6 5 4 3

The views and opinions expressed in this book are the authors' own and the
facts are as reported by them which have been verified to the extent possible,
and the publishers are not in any way liable for the same.

ISBN 9780670096589

Typeset in Adobe Caslon Pro by Manipal Technologies Limited, Manipal
Printed at Replika Press Pvt. Ltd, India

www.penguin.co.in

This is a legitimate digitally printed version of the book and therefore might not
have certain extra finishing on the cover.

To our families

Contents

Introduction

Society tends to glorify the get-rich-quick entrepreneur—build a company and go public, then (maybe) give to charity. Nothing wrong with that, but here we are more interested in iconic leaders in India who have demonstrated leadership to last. We have also included selected examples from elsewhere in South Asia and other emerging markets to illustrate that the ideas the Indian entrepreneurs speak about have echoes in the views of their compatriots in the so-called 'Global South'. All these stalwarts have built, to general acclaim and acknowledgement, organizations that are seen as forward-looking and innovative, subscribing to a code of ethics, and generally contributing to the betterment of societies. To our minds, this is the trifecta that is a lot harder to achieve than unicorn status. Nothing wrong with unicorns, but it's not what we're after in this book.

This book draws on a large set of in-depth interviews with business leaders across Africa, Asia, Latin America and the Middle East conducted by Harvard faculty as part of the Creating Emerging Markets (CEM) project. The last three decades have been transitional in much of this emerging world.

The idea behind the project was to capture the memories of the men and women who built transformational organizations in this era. The high-level contacts and the financial resources of Harvard Business School (HBS) enabled the project to access the most important and impactful people in many countries. One promise made to all of them was that the database of interviews would be available to everyone free of charge and without restriction for research and teaching. They were giving back by helping build a collective memory about how iconic organizations were built.

The project started with a few audio interviews of top business leaders in Argentina and Chile. The business leaders of these two countries were traditionally highly discreet, so starting here was a test of whether Harvard's name, along with a generous dose of enthusiasm, would open doors. It did. From 2012 the geographic scope of the project was expanded, with a particular focus on India, where HBS had strong and enduring connections and a robust local research presence. The project expanded by mid-2021 to 152 interviews, each at least one hour long and frequently much longer, in twenty-eight countries, conducted by twenty-five Harvard faculty members. The video archives continue to grow even as we write.

Any curious reader sees that there are tomes written on leadership daily. As academics teaching in a management school, we are of course aware of, and informed by, much of this incredible work. For example, the work that distinguishes personalist from situationist perspectives reminds us to pay attention to both the attributes of the individual leader and the circumstances within which he or she works. The work on leadership being both embodied in a person and being the cultivated result of a process is similarly informative.

What, then, do we bring to this leadership discourse? First, is the obvious variation in settings. The leaders that our Harvard colleagues and we have had occasion to engage with are from across the developing world. The countries in CEM account for 43 per cent of the world's population; perhaps more importantly, the challenges that these leaders have navigated are emblematic of those faced by 82 per cent of the world that lives outside the Organization for Economic Co-operation and Development (OECD) nations. We leave aside the much more extensively profiled leaders, mostly from the US and other OECD countries, as scholars and pundits have trawled over those examples extensively. Any social scientist knows that 'sample variation' is a driver of insight, so prima facie, accessing vastly more varied data points such as ours on leadership journeys is bound to be informative. Our submission in this book is a small first step, we hope.

Second, is our focus on the longue durée. We are focused on lasting institutional change, triggered by individuals over multiple decades—an intrinsically historical exercise—not on episodes of individual CEOs as saviours. It has become a cliché in some circles that 'history matters', but it really does matter in many ways. A little history stops us from reinventing the wheel, an all-too-common phenomenon among management scholars on the lookout for the new and exciting. There are patterns, waves and ebbs and flows in history, which are ignored at one's peril and understood to one's advantage.

A little history also helps differentiate a fad from a trend and enables a much deeper understanding of the here and now. In the context of this book, for example, we can see how resilience is built into cultures represented by many organizations in this book. We can ask whether this resilience is newfangled, or the result of these organizations having navigated near-existential crises, or capitalized on unique opportunities, over past decades.

Third, we focus on the power of narration, of storytelling. We present but a lightly edited narrative, straight from each proverbial horse's mouth. It is the unvarnished sense-making of people widely admired by their brethren for having achieved lasting institutional change in challenging milieus. Of course, there is a sample selection issue here—by design we do not learn from the failures of other would-be entrepreneurs—but that is not the exercise here.

To see why storytelling matters, just consider these two alternative stories of the texture of US society within which both of us work, as immigrants. French diplomat Alexis de Tocqueville's narration in *Democracy in America* (*De la démocratie en Amérique*) of a year of his travels in 1831 conjures up the idea of America as the home of individualism, liberty and democracy with a healthy dose of free-market principles. In contrast, Left-wing historian Howard Zinn, in his *A People's History of the United States*, offers a narration from the view of the marginalized—they neither experience liberty nor have the freedom to express individual creativity—in the same American society. They're as different as chalk and cheese!

So, what do we take away from these hundreds of hours of fascinating narrations in CEM, only a few highlights of which can be shown here?

The first is that the featured entrepreneurs lead with ideas and actions. Some organizations started with a clear long-run vision that has been actualized, others had an emergent animating idea. In all cases, the leaders nurtured a coalescing of organizational energies on an idea, a theme, that drove things forward, that acted as the entity's economic and moral compass. Significantly, this nurturing always entailed action, not just thought. We see throughout that actions speak louder than words.

Second, they lead from within the organization, of course, but equally also lead in shaping the context. In a country—India—and other environs—South Asia and other emerging markets—where investment in public goods is sorely lacking, it is insufficient to focus on the ensemble of individuals who comprise the organization in question. The ecosystem must be catalysed to compensate for institutional inadequacies as well. We see the leaders recognizing the intertwined nature of economic and social problems in these settings. It's hard to address one problem without being bedevilled by another, and it's hard to rely on the absent institutional foundations that normally propel creativity when societies have under-invested in them for a long time.

The diversity of settings is an exciting feature of the book—we have companies that some would consider too traditional—but it's their very stability that provides a base for the innovation and creativity on which we want to shine a light. In any event, almost axiomatically, if one wants to examine leadership that 'lasts', you're inevitably going to look at entities that have been around a while. As you'll see, their existence is anything but inimical to the even flashier forms of entrepreneurship.

Equally, we have newfangled 'tech' industries represented here. Kiran Mazumdar-Shaw's Biocon brought the life sciences movement to India; several software entrepreneurs put India on the world software map some decades ago, and their skill sets have in turn over subsequent decades permeated many of the interstices of society. The mobile revolution in Africa was unleashed by Mo Ibrahim's Celtel (the descendants of that entity are now part of Bharti Airtel in Africa).

Truth be told, we find as much to learn from incumbent enterprises, if you will, and newer ventures, as also from social entrepreneurs. Gujarat's Self-Employed Women's Association (SEWA) and Dhaka's BRAC are emblematic of some of the best examples of social entrepreneurship anywhere in the world.

Our overall takeaway is simple. We are just humbled by the combination of audacity (of intent), humility (of demeanour) and steadfastness (of purpose) displayed by the giants whose life lessons are narrated here.

1

Managing Families

We start the book with a chapter on how family structures are the crucibles within which 'leadership that lasts' is forged. It's true that, in emerging markets across the world, one can find the occasional non-family (that is, purely professionally owned and managed) entity that has exhibited lasting leadership, but, as an empirical matter, family ownership is ubiquitous enough to demand attention as a proponent (or detractor) of an entity's candidacy for leadership status.

In the selections in this chapter, one of the constructs that is referred to in every instance is that of a set of rules by which the family agrees to abide by as it pertains to the nurturing of the business in question. Adi Godrej of the Godrej Group is explicit in itemizing three rules that his family has lived by for decades, having to do with the rights and expectations of whether a next-generation family member will have an operating role in the business and, if not, the rules by which they will nonetheless benefit from the fruits of their predecessors in a way that is fair. Rahul Bajaj of the Bajaj Group also evocatively tells us that 'the five fingers of a hand are not equal in size', correctly noting that not everyone in the next generation is likely to have the

1

capability to steward the business. Sanjay Lalbhai of Arvind Limited notes that his predecessor generations explicitly thought through the rules by which the women in the family— generally not favoured in Indian society—were empowered to be creative and take on significant roles that suited the social fabric within which they operated.

The importance of rules is also apparent in their breach. Bajaj points to the importance of strong leadership in each generation, that must hold things together when disputes arise, as they inevitably will in the rough and tumble of modern business.

And when rules prove inadequate, values matter enormously. This comes through loudly in the Lalbhai interview as well as in Dubai-based luxury retailer Patrick Chalhoub's description of his family's robust support for the values of respect, excellence and entrepreneurship in the Middle East. Though not explicitly stated in so many terms, it seems to us that an abiding value through all these interviews is that of fairness towards all family members. We imagine that it is difficult to build an organization that lasts unless most key family members do not feel disgruntled. Lalbhai is clear on this, and it's apparent in the Godrej family's decision to split revenues somewhat evenly across different branches.

Finally, the 'lasting' part of our key construct, 'leadership that lasts', is perhaps most important in this chapter than in the subsequent ones. There are two attributes of well-run families that make them candidates for longevity, in our view. The first is their ability to take the long view. Chalhoub says this explicitly. It is also apparent in M.V. Subbiah's evocative interview of the intergenerational perspective that his predecessors took, spanning multiple countries and the reengineering and ultimate dismantling of the British Empire in South and South-East Asia. Perhaps it is even more apparent in the interview of Ayala Corporation CEO Jaime Augusto Zóbel de Ayala on how his family has lasted seven generations through their commitment to building lasting organizations in the Philippines.

Zóbel de Ayala's interview also displays another reason for longevity of an organization, that is committed to values that transcend only making profits. The Zóbel de Ayala family is credibly committed to the development of the Philippines and is therefore rightly seen as a reliable partner in setting the rules of the game when new opportunities arise, new technologies make their appearance on the stage and so on. Zóbel de Ayala refers to how the rules for real estate were co-created, in a way that probably benefited them but also did right by society, and elsewhere we note that a similar story played out in their involvement in telecommunications and other sectors.

In subsequent chapters, we will look at how the foundation provided by these family-run enterprises has enabled these exemplars of 'leadership that lasts' to innovate, be inclusive of society's myriad segments in sharing their gains and to fight corruption, among other salubrious achievements.

1(a)

Adi Godrej

Adi Godrej is the chairperson of the Godrej Group, an Indian multinational conglomerate that was founded by his grand-uncle, Ardeshir Godrej, in 1897. The company began with making locks, before moving into soap manufactured from vegetable oils at the end of World War I. Adi Godrej joined the family business in 1963 and was successful in growing the group during India's licence raj. The Godrej Group's activities now range from chemicals and agriculture to consumer goods, and it is the largest locally owned home and personal care company in India. Adi Godrej has a long history of philanthropic giving to support education and healthcare.

Interviewed by Tarun Khanna in Mumbai on 2 May 2013.

Interviewer: I wonder if we can go back to the formative years of your company and indeed the Parsi community, which has had such an enormous role in the development of Mumbai and India?

Adi Godrej (AG): Well, our family business was started by my grandfather's elder brother, Ardeshir Godrej, in 1897. He was very motivated as an Indian to start a business to help India gain independence. He felt that without economic independence, it would be difficult to get political independence from the British. He was very nationalistic. He supported the freedom movement. He donated to the Indian National Congress. He was an inventor. He was a lawyer by profession, but an inventor. So that led him to get into several businesses. Some of them failed. But he succeeded in making locks, and from that our enterprise grew.

My grandfather, Pirojsha Burjorji Godrej, was much younger than his brother and joined the business later—not much later—and he was the builder. My grand-uncle died at a relatively early age. Then my grandfather built the business over the years, helped by my father and my two uncles.

The business grew considerably, starting with locks, and then organically grew into many other areas like safes, security equipment, then furniture, and then from one product to the other. And my grand-uncle also started a soap business in 1918. He was motivated to make soap from vegetable oil. In those days, soap used to be made from animal tallow, which posed problems for some Indian consumers. So, he decided to try making soap from vegetable oil; he succeeded, and from there our soap business grew.

And from the locks and the soap business we went into other areas—to engineering products from the lock business, and to fast-moving consumer goods from the soap business, and that's how the business expanded. But it was very strongly motivated by seeking economic independence for India from the British.

Interviewer: The origins of the soap business are very interesting. So, was that a first in the world—making soaps from vegetable oil?

AG: That's difficult to say. There used to be some soaps made from olive oil in Mediterranean countries. But olive oil was not available here. So, it had to be made from Indian oils.

Interviewer: So, it is a nice example of something that you see a lot of now.

AG: Yes. There are many things caused by raw material restrictions and many issues caused by consumer acceptance. The bottom-of-the-pyramid products have become of great advantage in India and have now taken off across the world. We have done that very successfully, so that's working very well.

You mentioned the Parsi community. The Parsi community has always been very entrepreneurial, so I think that helped. In fact, my grand-uncle was financed by others in the community and that also helped. The community always paid attention to entrepreneurship and to, of course, professionalism, so overall I think that helped the origins of the business.

Interviewer: So, let's switch to the talent side. I think of the Godrej Group as being a home for professionalism. Can you speak on how your views about talent, and in the group, have evolved over time?

AG: Yes, we've changed tremendously in our human resource development [HRD] approach. Early on, we had some strong HRD practices but after our joint ventures, learning from GE Appliances (a subsidiary of the American multinational conglomerate General Electric Company) especially, and recently with my children joining the business, they've brought tremendous, both strategic and HRD, practices into the group.

We've hired a lot of excellent talent from outside. We've changed incentive systems very strongly in the group. We've changed our evaluation systems very strongly in the group. In the old days, people joined our group as youngsters, as management trainees, and retired from our group. Now that's a little different. We have very strong selection systems. We always categorize about 5 per cent of non-performers at the bottom of the ladder and we work towards having them leave the group. With the top 10 per cent performers, we work towards giving them much more responsibility at a young age, etc.

So, our entire human resource approach has very successfully changed. Our strategic practices have changed greatly. And I think we have a fair amount of talent from the best business schools in the world, including Harvard Business School, Wharton and MIT-Sloan School of Management [the business school of the Massachusetts Institute of Technology], etc. I think that's helped a lot.

The other thing I must emphasize is that we are still a family-controlled business, but we insist that anybody in the family who joins the business must be at least as professionally qualified as our external talent. So we don't divide it between family members and professionals. We always insist on everybody being professional, be it family or non-family professionals running our business. Today, a lot of our businesses, most of our businesses, are headed by non-family professionals.

I have three children in the business and I am by far the oldest in my generation, so the other children have not fully joined the business. One of my nephews is in the business, but he is currently studying abroad, doing his master's degree. My two daughters who are in the business have very strong strategic roles. My daughter Tanya handles marketing and the Godrej brand across businesses. So, family members are much better equipped to handle things across businesses than non-family professionals. My daughter, Nisa [Nisaba], handles strategy, innovation and human resource development across businesses. Now she has been appointed as an executive director of Godrej Consumer Products. My son, Pirojsha Adi, has been the executive director of Godrej Properties, the real estate company, since 2012, and is now also the managing director.

Interviewer: You are such a good example, your family is such a good example, of a family business, which is a ubiquitous feature of many developing countries and many developed countries as well. I wonder if you could help us understand the evolving role of this generation, you and your cousins and siblings and so on, and how the transition is happening from them to the next generation.

AG: Well, we followed two or three things in our management of the family business. One is that we have divided our ownership in my generation equally between five owner cousins, if you will, including my brother of course. That avoids any disputes in ownership within the family. The other is that we have a very strong family council which meets regularly, exchanges notes, discusses issues, and we have set an important rule that only professionally qualified family members can join the business. The others can of course be shareholders.

So, I have a cousin who is a wildlife photographer. He has not joined the business; he likes what he does very much. There could be others who do wish to join the business, but unless they are qualified, we would not permit them to join the business. That works reasonably well.

Interviewer: And that's a philosophy that is transferring over to the next generation?

AG: Yes, . . . very strongly. Now I think even the youngsters who wish to join the business clearly realize that they will not fit in if they are not well educated; they will not qualify. In the old days when the taxes were very high, it was difficult to survive just as a shareholder, and so if you joined the business, you could at least enjoy some perquisites from the business. Now of course that's not necessary at all.

Learnings from Adi Godrej: Family members seeking to be involved in the business should subscribe to clear rules. The rules, in turn, should be applied fairly.

1(b)

Rahul Bajaj

Richter Frank-Jurgen/Horasis

Rahul Bajaj is the grandson of Jamnalal Bajaj, an industrialist and prominent supporter of Mohandas Karamchand Gandhi during India's independence struggle. Rahul Bajaj took over in 1965 and is the chairperson emeritus of the Bajaj Group—one of India's largest multinational conglomerates, which grew to include more than thirty businesses spanning consumer care, energy and sugar. In 2001, Rahul Bajaj received the Padma

Bhushan. From 2006 to 2010, he was a member of the Rajya Sabha, the upper house of the Parliament.

Interviewed by Srikant M. Datar in Pune on 8 July 2014.

Interviewer: How do you balance the inevitable tensions between family members and professional managers?

Rahul Bajaj (RB): It is a very important subject and there is no one answer as far as I am concerned. Each case is different and has to be treated differently: what kind of family, when did you start, how many people, their temperament, their competence, their capabilities, their educational background, etc. Starting with what is family management versus professional management: what is a professional manager where he is not an owner? Then, why do you give him stock options? He becomes an owner. Well, he is a minor one, but why did you give the stock options to him? To provide an incentive, to recruit him and retain him. To provide continuity, that is what an owner does. He is born with that incentive, meaning he's got equity, and he won't normally leave his company for a higher salary. A professional manager, not for 20 per cent maybe, but for a 100 per cent increase in salary or for a much bigger company, may leave you. It happens every day. The owners have their wealth invested in the company. If you have the incentive of ownership—your wealth and reputation—you get the motivation, you maintain continuity. Because of your ownership, you have long-term thinking; you are not concerned with quarterly results, you're not going to buy shares, you are not going to sell shares, and you don't have stock options. I don't either. None of our Bajajs in the group have ever had stock options. We have large numbers of shares, probably 50 per cent or more, in each of our companies.

So, what is a family company; what is a professional company? Take Bajaj Auto. We employ about 9000 people top to bottom, and we have a sixteen-member board. Below the sixteen-member board, there is no Bajaj. Among the 9000 people, there is no Bajaj, there is no relative of a Bajaj. On the board, the family is represented, but who are the full-time directors? At Bajaj Auto, non-executive directors are not in management. There are only three full-time directors: the chairman, me; the vice-chairman, my cousin—not brother— Madhur Bajaj; and my elder son [Rajiv]; not even my younger son. Sanjiv [Rahul Bajaj's younger son] is in the financial services companies and the same story repeats there; in their board level, only one full-time director is a Bajaj. I'm not . . . I am the non-executive chairman. At Bajaj Auto, I am non-executive chairman, and my elder son Rajiv is the managing director. No other relative is a full-time director or a manager in the company. Is this a family-managed company or not?

Interviewer: How do you assess the capability of family members who wish to enter management? How do you avoid bias in the selection process?

RB: If one is not qualified, is not capable, then such a professional manager will be sacked. The family guy—an example is Rajiv Bajaj, and I have said this on TV at the cost of being challenged, not once, but two or three times. I would like to know the names of three people in this country of 1.2 billion people, three people who can be better CEOs—managing directors or CEOs—of Bajaj Auto than Rajiv Bajaj. I know many managers in India. They could be as good, but my point is, who could be better than him? I don't know of any. He has lived his life in Akurdi [in Maharashtra], he now lives in Pune, he graduated in first class with distinction in BE in mechanical engineering and got a first class with distinction in his master's at Warwick University in the UK. You can see how he writes about marketing, brand-building as well as engineering. He happens to be a Bajaj—is he a family manager or is he a professional manager? The ideal is a family manager who is qualified. By qualified, I don't mean only having a degree, but qualified for that post; he may have a degree or he may be like a Dhirubhai Ambani [founder of Reliance Industries] with no degree.

Problems happen in family management when there are three or four brothers. We say in India, the five fingers of a hand are not equal in size. All brothers may not be of equal capability and commitment. If somebody doesn't want to work in the company, they should simply go. You should hold the post for which you are not just okay, but among the best. Then the fact that you happen to be an owner is an advantage. It provides you with an automatic incentive and continuity. Problems happen when the person is not very qualified and he says, 'but I want this post—why does my brother have it, who says he is more qualified?'

Each case is different. Who is the head of the family? Do they listen to him? In my case, I happen to be the head, and they listen to me, so what I say goes, it is accepted. This puts a lot of responsibility on my shoulders. Now, if they don't accept, that is where the family breaks. One alternative is a brother who wants a break. 'I want to do my business my way. You say that "I'm no good"—we will find out after ten years. I want to

separate; maybe I will become better than you.' It is fine; that is
a good solution. The best man should manage the business at
whatever level, including at the CEO level. If they are equal in
competence, according to me, the family or the owner-manager
has an advantage. The problem that people are referring to is
when the family members start fighting. And at that time,
whoever is the leader should ensure the fighting stops and
does not affect the company. That's what I have done with the
Bajaj Group. One needs a great deal of communication among
family members, a lot of give and take, and maybe, sometimes,
outside help.

*Interviewer: If everything else is equal, then an owner-manager
has the advantage for economic reasons, they get a lot of incentives,
they have continuity, long-term thinking.*

RB: Yes. The trouble in family management, as I said, is
when members start fighting. It happened in my group. We
are five brothers, including cousins. The son of one, he is very
ambitious, he wanted to do business in another manner and so
we decided to separate. It is a good example. The Bajaj Group
didn't suffer at all; now he is managing his companies, and we
are managing our companies.

But some other groups where family members separated
suffered. We had very good groups, and where are they now?
They say that's why the third and fourth generations often
disappear. It's not necessarily that the guy is not competent.

*Interviewer: Before your wife's passing in 2013, I know Rupa
Bhabhi's role with each of these brothers was critical.*

RB: They respected and loved her tremendously. I don't think they respect me like that, but they respected her always. She was on the phone frequently with my brothers and their wives; her health was bad towards the end, she couldn't move, but she was on the phone every day with each of them. Nobody would oppose her.

Learnings from Rahul Bajaj: Not all family members are well-suited to run a business. There are major difficulties when the rules by which the family governs its involvement in the business don't keep pace with changing aspirations.

1(c)

Sanjay Lalbhai

Sanjay Lalbhai is the chairperson of Arvind Limited, a leading manufacturer of cotton shirting, denim, knits and khaki fabrics based in Ahmedabad, India. The roots of the Lalbhai family business can be traced back to medieval times but the modern group began modestly in 1897 when Lalbhai Dalpatbhai, a Jain merchant, opened a cotton mill in Ahmedabad. Following his early death in 1912, his seventeen-year-old son, Kasturbhai

Lalbhai, and other family members took over. The group grew as a major textile producer in Ahmedabad in the period between the two world wars, while Lalbhai was a prominent supporter of India's independence struggle. The group diversified during the decades after Independence, starting India's chemical industry, and is now a leading producer of denim. Sanjay Lalbhai joined the family business in 1977 and during the 1980s introduced domestically made denim into the Indian market, causing the jeans revolution. He has been managing director of Arvind since 1985.

Interviewed by Sudev J. Sheth in Ahmedabad on 6 February 2019.

Interviewer: What were your aspirations at such a young age growing up and what are your early recollections of the business itself?

Sanjay Lalbhai (SL): The family did not have any kind of expectations, so that was the most wonderful thing. I lived in a joint family with my grandfather, my mother, my father and my sister. There were three generations staying together, but there were no expectations at all. We were allowed to be ourselves. We were told to do what we were passionate about; do what your heart tells you. At that time, I didn't really think about anything at all except that I was happy, I had a core set of friends, and I was spending a very normal childhood. I was only pursuing things that interested me, like playing cricket, listening to music, going for movies and reading comics. So, very normal things. I had no clue as to what I was going to do, and I had never even thought about it.

Interviewer: What was the business like at that time? Can you tell us a bit more about that?

SL: Dadaji [Kasturbhai Lalbhai] had a game plan. He believed in a joint family. He had two brothers and four sisters. One of the sisters was unmarried. So, he built seven textile units. He had inherited one, and then he acquired the other one, but he built five new publicly listed, completely composite textile units, so [he] started from making yarn all the way to fabrics. When I was born, there were around nine companies in the family, all listed: seven textile units, one dyes-and-intermediates company called Atul Limited and one starch company. These two companies were almost manufacturing auxiliaries for the main textile business. So, he [Dadaji] had nine publicly quoted companies and the logic of having seven separate textile mills was that he wanted to give four companies to the brothers and three companies to the sisters, because one sister who was unmarried was treated as a brother. So, there were four companies with the brothers and three companies with the sisters. He wanted to keep everyone together, but at the same time, he gave them the autonomy to operate their own units.

Interviewer: So now let's go to 1977. This is the year that you returned from Mumbai and joined the family business. You joined as a manager of materials. What was that like and what is a manager of materials?

SL: So, at that time we were a joint family. We had twenty owners for these nine listed companies. We all used to get together and discuss everything about these nine companies. My father was responsible for the finances of all the nine companies, and also the HR policy. I think that for succession there were around nine people from the family—from my father's sister's family and my father's cousin's family. We had in total twenty-four people because every listed company had three members from the family in the company. So around twenty-four people from nine companies, less than three on average. So, my father had to decide for me along with my six cousins when they joined. We were second cousins joining the business, and each cousin was assigned either with his father or with his uncle. I was the guy who got assigned with my uncle rather than my father. My father was in Anil Starch and he, along with my grandfather, decided who should go into which company of ours. I was assigned to work under my uncle Arvind at that point in time. But when I came back after studying, I had no job. They had not decided where I should be, and I wanted to join the family business. I sat around for a while and kept asking which company I could go to out of these nine companies. He [my uncle] had no answer because he had not worked it out. My father didn't have an answer. So, my mother went to my distant cousin in Anil Starch to say that Sanjay is not doing anything, he is getting frustrated. He has come back from Mumbai with his MBA degree, and he has nothing to do.

My cousin gave me an assignment in Anil Forgings, which was a division of Anil Starch. It was a small forging company, and no one was really paying any kind of attention to it. I was given a free hand to go and make sense out of it. I had the perfect playground, where there was no interference from anyone because the company was making losses, and because it was not part of the core business of Anil Starch, it was ignored. I went into that company and I had complete freedom to turn it around. So, I learnt my business in Anil Forgings; it was making flanges at that time for piping and all that. With my MBA education, I realized that this did not make sense. I completely changed the product mix and went into automobile forging components, and at that point in time, the company saw one of the worst disruptions in the labour force. They went on a major strike, and I had a very militant leader of the union to deal with. I learnt a lot about how to negotiate, how to bring back industrial peace, how to address the issues raised by the workforce. By that time, my father, along with his cousins, had figured out where to place their sons or nephews. I ended up in Arvind, and Anil Forging had turned around. I had brought in a professional to run it, and so I was pretty much done there, and Arvind was a much bigger platform. I joined the materials department. I was given profit and loss responsibilities and I thoroughly enjoyed that, whilst the functional responsibility did not excite me. There were two of my uncles and one of my cousins with me, so we were four people in management, and there were professional managers.

Interviewer: Can we talk about the role of the female members of the Lalbhai household? So could you tell us a bit about the wisdom that your forefathers have passed on to you when it comes to thinking about the female members of the household and how that might have changed over the years?

SL: My grandfather very clearly thought of the entire family. He created independent identities or business entities for each of his sisters and his unmarried sister was a managing partner. She was managing director of one of our listed companies. So

Lilavati Lalbhai, until she died, was associated with Raipur, one of our publicly quoted textile companies, and she ran it. Every woman in our Lalbhai family was allowed to pursue whatever she desired and was even allowed to come in and run the business. But this was for unmarried daughters. The married daughters were given separate entities. There would never be joint management of those entities. By the time I came into business, it was categorically decided that my sister and my female cousins would not get into the business unless they were unmarried. That was a very clear understanding the family had arrived at. Only the male child would be entitled to get into the business, but every female child was allowed to pursue whatever she wanted to pursue. So they ran institutions or went wherever their passion took them; they were allowed to do that and were empowered, and they were given enough capital to pursue that. That has been the kind of freedom the whole family has enjoyed.

Interviewer: How does that play into longevities of business families in South Asia?

SL: I think this longevity is explained by a combination of professional management, owners, majority shareholders, the ability of an enterprise and their ability to network with the government, external agencies, and a key focus on vision and strategy and the long-term future of the institution or of a business identity. When you combine these, I think you have much more dynamism and energy in the company. It gives you a better chance of surviving in the long run because you bring the long-term vision and the rigour of management together by this combination.

Learnings from Sanjay Lalbhai: When next-generation family members are empowered to pursue their aspirations, group dynamism is enhanced. Making a special attempt to include female family members and to be more inclusive generally pays off.

1(d)

M.V. Subbiah

S. Kumaran/Sri Krishna Video Studio

M.V. Subbiah is the executive chairperson of Murugappa Group, a large business conglomerate owned by the Subbiah family, with activities in sectors including sugar, agribusiness, bicycles and insurance. The family business can be traced back to 1896, when his grandfather started a moneylending business in Chettinad in south India. In 1948, the Subbiah family established a joint venture with Britain's Tube Investments (TI), making parts for bicycles, and subsequently the family remained in manufacturing. Subbiah joined the business in 1961 and became chairperson in 1996. In 2012, he was awarded the Padma Bhushan.

Interviewed by V.G. Narayanan in Chennai on 28 April 2016.

Interviewer: *What was your family's first foray into the business world?*

M.V. Subbiah (MVS): My grandfather is the one who started it. Our community of Nagarathar Chettiars was a mercantile community that claimed Chettinad in south India as its home. They were moneylenders and traders. My grandfather went to Burma [Myanmar] at the age of fourteen to learn the trade from one of his uncles and was there between the ages of fourteen and eighteen for a very important period of training. At the same time, he also learnt the Burmese language. He came back and got married. And with the money that his wife had got as streedhana—not dowry, as streedhana [literally translates to 'wealth of the women', it is a gift a woman receives at the time of marriage over which she has total ownership]—and the money that he had saved during the four years in Myanmar, he went back and started, along with another partner, a moneylending business, which is what all Chettiars did in those days, and he did exactly the same thing. So that's the origin of it. In 1896, he started the business of moneylending with a partner in a place called Moulmein in south Burma, where there was a lot of deforestation and development of rice fields. In 1900, he split from his business partner and continued his moneylending business on his own, under the name AMM Firm. From then onwards, it was the moneylending business that continued in the family . . . his sons came up one by one, at least the first two . . . the third one was quite young as he was born in 1917. First two sons were there, then they joined the business, and he slowly developed the business. So that is the origin of the whole thing in the family.

Interviewer: And how long did the business continue in Burma?

MVS: Well, until World War II, and the way the community developed in Burma was fantastic. We were always moneylenders here first in India but then we went along with the British to Burma from Calcutta. There were six people from Calcutta who went to Burma and then my grandfather went later, much later, almost twenty-thirty years later. But the way they trained the young people in the Chettiar community itself is so interesting; you joined at the age of about eleven or twelve as an office boy, even if you were the son of the owner of the firm you went and started with the agent as an office boy— and that was to teach you humility. Humility, piety and self-confidence is what they trained you for in the first three to four years, and you started off literally as an office boy or as an errand boy. And then slowly, after the first three years you came back home and then you went back from the age of fourteen to seventeen, when you were really running as an assistant or as a cashier, both the jobs were learnt. You stayed with the agent's family because they had to be very frugal. It was very simple living. So that was the system everyone in the family followed. My uncles, my father and I had a little bit of that training in the family during the summer vacations and things like that; I was probably the last one to have it and other members unfortunately didn't have the benefit of that. And I think it's a sad thing because I personally think if I am what I am today, it's because of that training I got from the agent of ours in Colombo.

Interviewer: Let's go back to the Great Depression and World War II. What happened to your family business in Burma around that time?

MVS: My father was very, very active, and from whatever little I have read and whatever I've heard from my uncles, he was very active in Burma. He was the president of the Nagarathar Chettiar Association. Between 1937 and 1939, he went around the entire area and told all the Chettiars, 'Please do not reinvest'. I mean, all of us were doing so well that we kept on reinvesting the money in Burma or moved it to Malaysia or Saigon and places like that. But he said, 'Don't ever do that. Take the profits every year and send them back to India and do something in India.' And my family did exactly that. That's why my family was one of the very few families that did quite well after the war, also because profits kept coming in. And he said, 'Cash in whatever you can and send the profits to India.' He foresaw the economic troubles ahead, I think because he was very close to the British in those days. He was a 'club-able' person and he went to the club, played tennis, and so he mixed with them. None of the other Chettiars did that. Therefore, he had some insight, a gut feeling, and grandfather agreed to whatever my father wanted to do. That's exactly how our family had a fairly substantial head start here in India on the industrial side. And he said no more moneylending, and when he repatriated the profits, they were always put into buying either a rubber estate or factory because the British were selling things here. The first thing that he bought was a parachute silk factory in Bombay and then the second thing was a rubber estate in Kanyakumari. So those were the kinds of things that the British had gone into . . . in Singapore and in Malaysia and Burma. So, he started putting money into them and where the British were selling here and going away, he was buying them here. Then the other brothers took care of it here. The brothers were interested in stockbroking, so they also started a stock brokerage firm. Our family did that but none of the others did . . . money was tight. Immediately after the Great Depression, people wanted to borrow money, so more and more people in Burma, more and more Chettiar firms in Burma lent money against the paddy fields. And what happened was that when World War II came and the Japanese took over, the currency collapsed, and the Chettiar firms had all their money there and the only thing they had was land. And the government confiscated the land, I mean, when Burma became independent, they confiscated the land, and the Chettiar firms had nothing left. So that's how the entire community collapsed.

Interviewer: And after your training in Colombo, how did you enter the family business?

MVS: That was during my studies, see, it was always during the study period that the families got you into business . . . I was the last one, after that they never did that. After me, everybody went to public schools. They didn't have time to go for the kind of training that I did. But we always went and worked. By the time India got Independence, we had a joint venture with TI. That was the first joint venture, with TI to make bicycles . . . Sir Ramaswamy Mudaliar, a good friend of my grandfather [Dewan Bahadur A.M. Murugappa Chettiar] and my uncles [A.M.M. Murugappa Chettiar and A.M.M. Arunachalam], introduced them to Sir Ivan Stedeford, the chairman of TI. They [the Murugappa Group and Sir Ivan] decided that bicycles had a tremendous opportunity in independent India, so they started TI Cycles in 1948. The sandpaper company, Ajax, was also looking for an opportunity and found Carborundum in the US and Universal Grinding Wheel in the UK, and they came together [with the Murugappa Group] as a tripartite agreement in 1948 to form Carborundum Universal Madras India, which is CUMI, and then formed those two companies [TI Cycles and CUMI]. So my uncles started running those two companies. I lost my father [A.M.M. Vellayan Chettiar] just after the war. He went back to Burma and was assassinated there, so I lost him at that time.

Interviewer: How old were you at that time?

MVS: I was seven years old; it was 1946. And my grandfather said, after he lost one son, he said, 'I am going to withdraw', and he withdrew more or less as patriarch of the family and my two uncles took over. My eldest brother had just graduated. In fact, he was in his final year of geology in Presidency College in Madras. So he joined the family business and the uncles trained him. Thereafter, we were always on the industrial side of grinding wheels, abrasives and bicycles. And all of the businesses went into backward integration for the next fifteen years; from making the grinding wheel, we started mining, right down to mining of bauxite—we did everything for the next fifteen years; it was always backward integration. Similarly with bicycles. From making bicycles, we shifted to tubes and then steel strips, roller chains. So every three years, there was something that was coming up.

Interviewer: Can you talk about how your group is structured?

MVS: As a family, we have a very clear rule. We don't have many rules, but one of the rules is that at sixty-five you have to retire, but initially none of us knew about it. My uncle, when he reached sixty-five, he called all of us one day—all the senior executives and the family—and said, 'I am handing over to my nephew M.V. Arunachalam because I am sixty-five' and my father had suggested that my uncle retire at sixty-five. So that's how it happened: only then we came to know that the retirement age is sixty-five. So my brother also retired at sixty-five and handed the company over to me at that time.

The managing director's position is always with the family in all the companies. Professionals could come up only to a certain level; but that changed with my brother agreeing to change the whole thing and he called in all the senior executives to the meetings. The finance head and the head of human resources were two professional people but they were not sitting on the boards, so we brought all of them slowly on to the boards when my brother was there. And he had what's called the Murugappa management committee of senior executives, at that time mostly family but for two or three professionals. Then slowly we changed. One by one the family started moving away and

we had a more corporate board, but my brother was there . . .
had suggested we have three members from the outside on the
corporate board and some of the family members should join
them. And also, the head of finance would always be a non-
family member. So that kind of corporate board was formed
and the family started meeting with them.

*Interviewer: You know in India we have the Hindu undivided
family and the karta who takes decisions. How does that relate to the
way you used to function? Does it still play a role in some context?*

MVS: It doesn't play a role any more but it did in the old days.
See, unfortunately the British tampered with the original karta
thing. None of us really know the original karta. The karta was
the most acceptable person, he is not the head of the family,
he was the person who was acceptable to the whole family—
anyone, young, old, brother, nephew, everyone accepted him.
I have seen a little bit of that in operation with my eldest uncle
and my younger uncle when they were still alive. See, for
example, when it comes to union negotiations, they will call
me. I lost my second brother, Muthiah, he died fairly young;
he was an excellent finance person. When it came to public
relations in Delhi, it was my eldest brother, M.V. Arunachalam.
So whichever company, both my uncles would send that person
for that job. That was the role of the karta, to send the best
person for that job irrespective of which company he belonged
to and what his designation was. So that is the way it worked.
If there is an issue in the family, if I am being a difficult person,
who is the best person to tackle me? They would send him and
my eldest brother was very, very good; Arunachalam could deal
with Delhi, he could deal with the family and he did everything

with a smile. Even though my uncle was the head of the family, when it came to these kinds of issues, whether it was Delhi or the family or whatever, it was he who used to send my brother to deal with it and sort it out and then finally go and get the blessings of the uncle. So that's really the karta's role, to nominate the best person for that job . . . or the most acceptable person . . . who would be able to get the job done and that was the kind of thing that happened. Those things are all, I mean thanks to Western education and the West, falling to pieces now and I think it doesn't happen any more.

Learnings from M.V. Subbiah: Communication within—and between—generations predispose a family business to continued adaptation, allowing it to develop an intergenerational arc. Traditional practices can be adapted to modern times. For example, the karta is the individual—not necessarily the eldest—who everyone agrees is best suited to decide who, from across the family's often myriad businesses, is most suited to address particular challenges.

1(e)

Patrick Chalhoub

Chalhoub Group

Patrick Chalhoub is the CEO and group president of Chalhoub Group, which is based in the United Arab Emirates, and currently the largest luxury retailer in the Middle East. The family business began in 1955 under his parents, who opened a small business in Syria which slowly developed to become the leading luxury retail group in the Middle East. The group grew from selling products directly to consumers, to opening brick-and-mortar stores, to developing large distribution networks and later opening department stores and one-of-a-kind concept stores. The family moved to Lebanon in order to reach a larger market, and then to Kuwait after the outbreak of the civil war in Lebanon in 1975. The business remained in Kuwait after the Iraqi invasion in 1990, but Chalhoub and his brother also began to diversify their business elsewhere in the Arab world, including opening an office in Dubai. In 2001, Chalhoub and his brother became joint CEOs. In 2018, Chalhoub became the sole CEO of the group following the death of his brother.

Interviewed by Geoffrey Jones in Dubai, the United Arab Emirates, on 21 March 2018.

Interviewer: Can I ask you about the decision of your parents to hand over the business to the next generation. It's 2001, and the decision is taken that you and your brother will be joint CEOs. Can you talk me through how this happened?

Patrick Chalhoub (PC): After the Iraqi invasion of Kuwait in 1990 and the subsequent liberalization—when my brother and I decided to open locations in Dubai and other countries—already my parents had started to step a little bit away from the daily operation of the business. At that time, we felt it was important to start putting in place a stronger governance of the family business. And during this period—between 1992–93 and 2001—we probably put together the initial governance structure of the group, which was a way for them to let go. Initially, my parents took a step back from day-to-day decisions, and then between 2001 and 2006, they started stepping back from strategic decisions. After 2006, they completely retired. So, there was this preparation period—putting together a governance structure through which decisions could be taken by the management, and which would be reviewed by the board, which at that time was only the family itself. It required a novel look, handing over some of the operational activity of the group. And I think it was good preparation for my brother and I to be able to hand decisions over with much more assurance, and even a security for us to know that we had a certain framework within which we could work. We also had a certain obligation towards the board, but at that time, it was mainly a family board. So this was a very interesting period. Now, I would say that it took us three years in total to put our governance structure in place. There were already quite similar views about many decisions, because we lived very close to each other—my father, my mother, my brother and I. So even if it wasn't any more an autocratic, one-person decision, we were still living in harmony together. And this was even true retrospectively, because then we reworked our documents, etc., and I would say we have still maintained a lot of decisions where we had a kind of consensus or agreement among ourselves to do it.

From my parents' side, it was also to make sure that things would not go out of control or in a different direction. And then for us, by taking certain decisions that had a positive impact for the evolution of the group, we were reassured— and at the same time, it helped us create another level of empowerment within the organization and the structure. So 1991 to 2001 was a long period of handover, but a successful one. And then there was a second period, I would say, from 2001, when we had two different challenges—one, how to co-manage a company. So being co-CEO has some advantages, but also it could have certain challenges that we had to meet. And two—how to take it to the next level of governance, where we were not only within a framework—quite a closed environment—but we were moving ahead into a more corporate and institutional way of doing business, even if we were a totally family-owned business.

So, in terms of being co-CEOs, there was a first period where we had more defined roles, dividing activities among ourselves either by territory or by centre of interest of activity. Very importantly, we respected each other's decisions, but each one, I would say, operated within his territory or his area of expertise, rather than necessarily working together. And there has been a second period, in the last five to seven years, where we are co-CEOs in all our activities, but always with this kind of respect—consulting each other. If one of us took a decision—and we have different styles and different ways of treating a problem—the other would respect the decision taken by the other co-CEO.

In terms of governance, we moved from having a family board, I would say, to having a mix of family, non-family and non-executive board members. And at the same time—since 2001—we put in place an executive committee, which was designed to really support the CEOs in their decision-making. But it's a very interesting question—how to transform a family business into a professionally managed business. Probably, we are still very much a family business—through the values, through the culture of the family, and the way of doing business. At the same time, we have implemented quite a strong governance structure to take decisions objectively and with professionalism.

Interviewer: *What are the values of the family?*

PC: We went through the exercise of defining our values clearly in 2001, but retrospectively, everybody feels that these are the values that have existed within the organization since 1955. Probably they did—they just were not articulated. When we speak about our values, we speak about respect, we speak about excellence, and we speak about entrepreneurial spirit. And we walk the talk. When we speak about respect, it's really about genuinely having this respect for other people, and having respect for any commitment we undertake, being loyal—doing our business with very strong ethics, etc. When we speak about excellence—we always try to outperform ourselves in the quality of work and make no compromise on the quality because of the quantity of work or because of quick buys that we want to do. And when we speak about entrepreneurial spirit, it's always to take new initiative, being quite entrepreneurial, taking some risk, but at the same time planning for a sustainable long-term. It's true that today any of our 14,000 employees would totally remember our family values and feel genuinely that it has been there since the inception. And it was, but in the back of our mind. We only articulated it fifteen years ago.

Interviewer: *How do you keep the values so strong and cohesive when you're growing a lot and growing across quite different countries? How do you keep these core values alive?*

PC: For me, it's one of the biggest challenges we have, but it's also one of the biggest obligations we have as a family to our business. So perhaps one day our family members will not be in the management. But if they still own this enterprise, our expectation from them is really to be ambassadors of our values, making sure that those values are really in the DNA of the company. I would say it starts with the recruitment and induction of new team members, who go through a reviewing process and are assessed on their values. And then it happens by making sure that in terms of processes, of behaviours, we always walk the talk, and exemplify the way of doing business, always remembering those three pillars that are part of our values. So, all the way from recruitment to induction, to the way of doing business, to assessing the performance of our team members—there is an evaluation of how each member of the team is applying and living by the values of the group. And of course, a lot of communication of values happens internally, by example.

But it's still very complicated, because today we are much more numerous, and employees don't have as much direct contact with the leadership team. But it is quite an interesting challenge, because when we ask our teams what they like within our group and organization—how satisfied they are—they rate the fact that it is a business done with strong values very highly as one of the reasons why they are so attached to our group and to our family.

Interviewer: What are the advantages of a family business, in your view?

PC: I mean, for me, the biggest advantage is being able to think long term before short term, and this, again, is part of what we need to maintain. Because obviously when you are focused on the financial result, it gives you a certain discipline, but at the same time, it often leads to taking certain decisions that have a very short-term impact. So for me, the biggest advantage is being able to create a long-term view, which is most important (although the short-term is important, because if you cannot generate revenue and profit, you die). But thinking long term more than short term.

The second advantage—it's the values themselves. Those values, that culture unites all the members of the team. One member is in legal, one is in IT, one is in Saudi Arabia, the other one is in Egypt or in Lebanon, one is in sales, the other one is in another activity—but what would pull us all together?

Now, in many cases, in many corporations, they give a certain importance to the company's values, but the fact that they are coming from a family that really promotes them gives them much more authenticity and reality. Now thirdly, there is a certain emotional attachment. It has inconvenience as well. You have a certain emotional attachment to your partners, to your clients, to the team members who are working together. So, it's not only about being performance-driven or result-driven, but also there is emotion that enters into it.

Interviewer: How hard is it to integrate professional managers into that?

PC: Honestly, it hasn't been hard at all. Sometimes, some of the professional managers—because of the history that they have lived—would tend to be only results-driven. So if they cannot behave that way in our company—they adapt. But it's not because they are a professional that they need to adapt—because we find this at many levels. If they cannot integrate into the whole expectation that comes with joining this family business, then they feel disconnected—but not because they are professional or not. It's because they are not integrating those different, other aspects.

But most of the time, we really see people who really love it—even very professional managers who have had different jobs and sometimes a much more important portfolio than what they have when they join us. Or the reverse—people who have lived in the company and the group and then moved on in their career and who still have very strong memories and attachment to the family firm. So I haven't really found it difficult to attract professionals. I have had more difficulties, but for another reason, with attracting millennials to the company. They need much more freedom in the way they do things—they would like to have much more empowerment at any level. To me, that seems a good thing, but then we need also to review some of our ways of doing business and transform some aspects of the organization to be attractive to them. But otherwise, I only have seen advantages of the integration in a family business.

Some of the disadvantages could come if there is too strong an influence from the family, rather than letting the management take decisions—which might happen perhaps one day if and when the CEOs are non-members of the family. This is why I am already telling the third generation—we are trying to really make sure that the third generation understand their role as owners compared to the role of managers.

Learnings from Patrick Chalhoub: Transition of governance arrangements from one generation to the next is gradual, often taking a decade or more, and involves considerable experimentation. Family values provide the foundation for this transition.

1(f)

Jaime Augusto Zóbel de Ayala

Jaime Augusto Zóbel de Ayala is the chairperson and CEO of Ayala Corporation, also known as Ayala, the largest and oldest conglomerate in the Philippines, with interests in real estate, infrastructure, insurance and banking. The group's founding is traced back to the 1830s, as a trading house specializing in agricultural products. It is now a seventh-generation family business. When Zóbel de Ayala became the chairperson in 1994, he entered at a moment of change both within Ayala (undergoing major restructuring from a real estate company with other scattered investments to a holding company) and in the Philippines, more broadly with President Fidel Ramos initiating widespread privatization efforts. In 2017, Zóbel de Ayala became the first Filipino and South-East Asian to be named by the United Nations Global Compact as one of the ten Sustainable Development Goals pioneers.

Interviewed by Meg Rithmire in Manila, Philippines, on 8 November 2016.

Interviewer: What kind of company was it when you took over leadership in 1994? What did you see as the greatest challenges and how did you feel about its future at that moment?

Jaime Augusto Zóbel de Ayala (JAZA): Well, when I took over, we were a diversified group—what we continue to be today. And we were hitting actually a very interesting time in Asia. There was a great deal of expansion taking place. We had a progressive president in the country. And we were really at the early stage of the 1990s, which were actually boom years in Asia. It was only after 1997 that we had our first Asian downturn. It was an exciting time . . . because there were a number of opportunities on a variety of fronts, and it was really a good time to be taking over an institution that has had a long history in the country. So in some ways it was a concern at the time, taking on a responsibility of this magnitude. But at the same time, from a macroeconomic environment point of view, it was an exciting time in the country.

Interviewer: In 1994, what was roughly the layout of the business?

JAZA: We had just managed to come through with a fairly large move. You know, Ayala Corporation—if you just go back to our more recent history, post-World War II—we evolved into an important real estate company. So Ayala Corporation was not exactly the holding company you see today. It was really more of a real estate company with other investments.

And after World War II, we had an opportunity—my great-uncle and my grandfather looked at Manila. It had really gone through a very difficult period during World War II. Most of the city was destroyed. And they had the foresight in a very difficult time to see an opportunity, which was the possibility for the centre of gravity of the city to move . . . We had a large estate, farm estate, here in this Makati area, which is now the central business district, but at the time . . . there were open fields, there were cows grazing, there was nothing here. And they had the foresight to say, 'Look, Manila's been destroyed. There is an opportunity here to create a new centre of gravity for the city . . .'

And so, the company began to evolve. We started to develop the area following many of the things we had learnt from the US at the time, such as proper zoning of properties, turning them into business districts, residential areas and commercial areas. We came up with the first legal document describing condominium ownership in the Philippines and started to create a much more organized structure than existed in the country at that time. And real estate started to evolve. It now became, over time, the central business district of the Philippines. That created a lot of new cash flow and wealth for the company that then began to be invested elsewhere.

But real estate was such a big component that it was really in the 1990s we decided it might be time to separate all the real estate assets and put them under a separate corporate shell, now called Ayala Land, and turn Ayala Corporation into a holding company.

So I was indirectly involved in that process. It was a big transaction for the time. And as we turned Ayala Land, as it's now called, into a listed company, we created a new large, listed entity for our group aside from Ayala Corporation, the holding company. That was the period when I came in—when we were really starting to formulate a whole new sense of being and a reason for being for the holding company itself, which had been primarily just a pure real estate company with other investments. It was an exciting time in that sense to be at the helm of the institution.

And at the time, we also had a very progressive new leadership. We had President Ramos, a former military man, who came in with surprisingly—well, I say surprisingly—I should have known better at the time—progressive ideas. And he started privatizing a number of public utilities and liberalizing a number of sectors that had been quite tightly held in our country, and that gave a massive new impetus for us to invest in some non-traditional areas for our group.

Interviewer: So one interesting thing about your leadership at Ayala has been the involvement of the company in public infrastructure and utilities and public-private partnerships. I understand that one of your first large undertakings was the privatization of water in Manila.

JAZA: Very much so. Well, first and foremost, I work very closely with my brother. When I took over a position of leadership, my brother, who's just a year younger than me, we talked through how we would manage the company. And essentially, we decided we wanted a team-based approach, I guess, to how we tackled the disparate investments of the group. So both Fernando, my brother, and I worked very closely in formulating the strategies. And he actually took over the chairmanship of the water company. I became his vice-chair. And I took the chair of the bank, the holding company, and the start of a telecom business that we started to move on. So we worked hand in hand.

As we looked at the situation, a lot of the impetus really came from a macroeconomic point of view, from the political leadership at the time. And I can't emphasize how important that framework that the government put in place was to our movement. As a side story, more of an amusing anecdote, when I was handed the reins of leadership of the company, my father talked to me about a number of issues. And he said, 'Look, for what it's worth, I know you're interested in expanding, but my father'—which would be my grandfather— 'said to me, "Whatever you do, don't get involved in public utilities or any regulated industries." That's the only advice I can give you. It comes with significant headaches.' And so I listened to him. Then fast-forward, my brother and I do exactly the opposite, which is to expand quite exponentially in regulated fields.

But the reason we did it—despite the potential risk profile in an emerging market of getting into regulated industries— was, we really wanted to build . . . Also, we wanted to be part and parcel of the development cycle of the country . . . and to be relevant as an institution in a country that needed a lot of growth, a lot of development and a lot of institutional support.

That public utility space and infrastructure space was an area where we could really be a relevant institution.

Interviewer: Ayala is quite famous for its corporate culture. I think it's interesting to see a seventh-generation family-led corporation with a kind of modern corporate culture, recruiting global talent but also—in an environment like South-East Asia, like the Philippines, with political turmoil and a fair share of corruption—a clean corporate culture. So how has that been maintained?

JAZA: In 1976, we were one of the first family companies to go public. In 1973–74, we brought in a major partner at the time, the Mitsubishi Group. They came in and, out of a family partnership, they bought in and became an industrial partner of our group. And then we took the company public, took it to the stock exchange and brought in, I guess, institutional investors into the community. And at that point, we had to start transitioning into a professionally run company and not the family partnership that we were. That was very significant.

And I'd like to say, in that period, there was another interesting component that I think is underappreciated. We were really a partnership. We were not a corporation in the modern sense. The old name of Ayala in the 1970s was Ayala Corporation. And when I came in, I kept wondering, why do they keep emphasizing the word 'corporation' so much? I mean, a corporation's a corporation—why do we actually have it as part of the name? Eventually, we took it out. That's why we're called just Ayala today. But I realized that my great-uncle and my grandfather at the time felt that we had to evolve from a partnership into a corporation—a limited liability institution—and really create a vehicle that could raise capital and go to the public markets, issue securities, and create a whole new level of dynamism that didn't exist under a partnership structure. A lot of the modernity that you see in the Ayala of today really came from that first move as an institution. And I think that's not fully understood.

But fast-forward from then—I guess under my father's term, he believed in decentralizing the company, creating independent CEOs, not having a centrally-run institution. And both my brother and I followed a similar model. We're the only two family members working in the company at this time. We have redefined our roles on the governance side and really have just a first-class grouping of CEOs running the different businesses. In my opinion, each of them could be a minister in this country or run a whole portfolio for the government. They're that good. And we created an incentive structure and a framework for governance that gave them an independent leeway to manage as they saw fit, subject to board governance structures, and created an environment where people with talent could come in and realize that they could build a career for themselves in the group.

My brother and I generally like to bring in people with global standards. Many of the executives you see in our group have worked either for multinationals or in a global setting prior to joining Ayala. And we like that. We wanted to institute global standards into an institution that we wanted to basically be able to ride out into the future and continue a legacy that had been around for a long time. And for that, you had to build a culture that was progressive, that followed global standards. If we were going to go to the capital markets in a significant way and build trust with it, you really had to have standards in an increasingly transparent environment that were understood by the broader investing public. And those were the drivers.

Learnings from Jaime Augusto Zóbel de Ayala: Successful generational transition in family firms depends on a shared understanding of leadership roles and a commitment to professionalization at global standards. The family needs to transition from operating roles to governance and empower professional CEOs.

2

Committing to Values

A major challenge of business leadership is how to profitably navigate constant change and turbulence in a way that demonstrates honesty and integrity. Success in this endeavour requires careful balancing. Vast profits can undoubtedly be earned through underhand and unscrupulous tactics, but at a huge cost to society and, in most cases, to the long-term viability of a business. Conversely, a stellar commitment to integrity that lacks business acumen will provide a clear conscience, but little else. A striking feature of business leadership in India has been the ability to manage this balance well. Profitable and sustainable businesses have been built around strongly held values, sometimes passed down between generations in family businesses discussed in the first chapter of this book.

The importance of values comes out strongly in the first interview with N.R. Narayana Murthy of Infosys. In reflecting on the role of fairness in business decisions, Murthy asserts his desire to do to others what you want them to do to you. This matters in individual relations, but also, according to Murthy, on a large scale. He believes in leadership by example, and in the merits of self-restraint by leaders in their remuneration and other matters.

Prathap C. Reddy, in his account of the struggle it took to get Apollo Hospitals started in the context of the obstacles posed by the licence raj, the period of extensive state planning in India between 1947 and 1991, also stresses the importance of values. He talks of the three P's—purity, patience and persistence— which enabled him to navigate challenges and build a successful business. His mention of the 'Divine Doctor' reminds us of the huge importance of religion influencing values in India, which also comes out either implicitly or explicitly in many other interviews in this book.

Nalli Kuppuswami Chetti of Nalli Silk Sarees describes how his family and he have built their textile business over generations by employing Gandhian values of truth and honesty. What stands out in the interview is the intense attention to detail at every stage of the business. Quality and service stand out as characteristics of the business, and a key to success as customers stayed loyal to the firm.

The same values of quality and service, and going the extra mile for customers, emerge in the excerpt from the interview with Pakistan's Seema Aziz of Sefam, another reputable textile business. Aziz is particularly insightful in showing how the values of a business leader permeate down the hierarchy in the company and become the basis for a corporate culture. The attention to quality at her firm is such that flaws in embroidery are pointed out to salespersons even if they are not visible to the naked eye, so that customers have all the information.

Our final interview with a personality from South Asia is with classical dancer, actor and social activist, Mallika Sarabhai. She talks in a compelling fashion about her belief in social justice and equality, and how she uses the business of the arts to convey her values to broader audiences. Distressed by what she perceives as the loss in modern India of the very Gandhian values that so inspired Chetti, Sarabhai describes her creative endeavours. These include developing hard-hitting solo theatrical works, beginning with *Shakti: The Power of Women* (1989), and creating a fifty-two-part television series on Indian folk tales using puppetry, which aimed to celebrate the ethnic and cultural diversity of India.

Shinta Kamdani, who became the head of the Indonesian family-owned Sintesa Group in 1999, identifies the close connection between family values and corporate values in her business. She explains how she built a corporate culture based on the family values she learnt growing up and early in her career. Just like Reddy stresses the three P's, Kamdani institutionalized what she identifies as the four E's: family values of empowerment, entrepreneurship, excellence and empathy, and diffused them across the highly diversified business.

Robert Brozin, the co-founder of South Africa-based restaurant chain Nando's, explores how the business puts employees front and centre to deliver a good experience. 'For us to inspire you as a customer,' he notes, 'we need inspired people.' Having such inspired and engaged employees, in turn, allowed the company to remain true to its values by finding locally contextually appropriate means for their expression.

2(a)

N.R. Narayana Murthy

Catamaran Ventures LLP

N.R. Narayana Murthy co-founded Infosys in 1981. Infosys became a leading multinational corporation with activities in outsourcing services, business consulting and information technology. Murthy has been described as 'the father of Indian IT'. He became an advocate for social responsibility of business with his concept of compassionate capitalism. In 2001, Murthy stepped down as the CEO of Infosys and became the executive chairperson till his retirement in 2011. In 2013, he briefly returned to Infosys as the executive chairperson and additional director and in 2014, he became the chairperson emeritus. He has won many awards, including the Padma Shri in 2000 and the Padma Vibhushan in 2008.

Interviewed by Joseph B. Fuller in Bengaluru on 6 November 2019.

Interviewer: Could you talk a little bit about how you think about fairness in taking business decisions?

N.R. Narayana Murthy (NM): Well, the way I have measured fairness is through the golden rule: 'Do unto others what you want them to do unto you.' As long as two people conduct a transaction agreeing to follow the golden rule, then you are likely to see fairness in that transaction. That is the way I have defined fairness: following the golden rule.

Interviewer: So, you would be able to say to a colleague that rule applies to me as equally as to you.

NM: Yes, exactly. I think that is where I am a great fan and admirer of Mahatma Gandhi, whose greatest virtue was leadership by example. Whatever values he wanted his colleagues to follow, he first demonstrated those values in action himself and did not preach to others to follow it. His followers realized that what was good for Gandhi was good for them too and automatically followed and mimicked Gandhi's actions. If I want people to come to the office on time, then I should come to the office on time. If I come to the office on time, then I do not need to preach it to anybody. If they see me coming to the office on time, the employees will come to the office on time. Similarly, if I want my younger colleagues to be honest, I don't have to tell them to be honest, I have to be honest in every one of my transactions. Every employee carefully watches his or her leader. All eyes will be on the leader. Therefore, leadership by example is the best way to communicate values in a profound way.

Interviewer: How do you think broadly about the role of business in society today? Do you still hold firm to that notion of capitalism being the vehicle for human empowerment and improving society, and how has that vision changed over time?

NM: Well, I still believe that compassionate capitalism, which is capitalism in mind and socialism at heart, is the best way for a country to solve its problem of poverty. I am convinced of that. This is the time in India when leaders in all spheres of our life should embrace compassionate capitalism. The first thing for the corporate leader to do is to ensure that there is a reasonable ratio in the compensation between the lowest level and the highest level in his or her corporation. I understand that there should be incentives but we cannot have an obscene ratio between the highest and lowest levels of compensation. Second, whatever the rule the lowest level employees are to follow should be applicable to the highest level too in issues like coming to the office on time and using the company's resources for personal use. In other words, corporate leaders have to lead by example. They cannot say I will come to the office three days a week, but you come five days a week. That will not work. As long as the leaders of capitalism follow leadership by example and as long as they show a certain amount of self-restraint in accruing for themselves a disproportionate part of the benefits of the corporation, then I believe that kind of capitalism will succeed even better than what has already succeeded. That kind of capitalism is the one that will be welcomed even in developing countries.

Learnings from N.R. Narayana Murthy: Leading by example is the best management practice. This includes exercising restraint in compensation and wealth accumulation.

2(b)

Prathap C. Reddy

Prathap Reddy

Prathap C. Reddy is a cardiologist, and the founder and chair of Apollo Hospitals, a multinational hospital chain headquartered in Chennai. Founded in 1983 as the first corporate healthcare provider in India, Apollo Hospitals brought world-class healthcare to the country. Apollo Hospitals is now one of Asia's largest healthcare providers with a network of hospitals, clinics and pharmacies. Reddy was awarded the Padma Bhushan in 1991 and the Padma Vibhushan in 2010.

Interviewed by Tarun Khanna in Mumbai on 29 April 2014.

Interviewer: You have described how your back and forth with Prime Minister Indira Gandhi and then Prime Minister Rajiv Gandhi led to their becoming aware of some of the bureaucratic obstacles facing the Indian healthcare system. What is it that made you stick with running from pillar to post from Chennai to Delhi every weekend to try to get the roadblocks removed?

Prathap C. Reddy (PR): What drove me was the need to relaunch the healthcare of the country. The simple truth is that we all need to realize there is something within us that tells us we can do whatever we think should be done. In my thing, I call it the three P's. First, purity in thought, patience, and in India you need persistence. If you have all these three, you will not fail, provided your first P is right. So, I think this is where all of us, if you keep that focus, that's what we did. I didn't leave it with Rajiv Gandhi.

Year after year, I have made representations to various governments through industry associations such as the Confederation of Indian Industry (CII), Federation of Indian Chambers of Commerce and Industry (FICCI), Associated Chambers of Commerce and Industry of India (ASSOCHAM) and Indian Medical Association (IMA) to support healthcare through whatever representation that we give. We got a few things done. Pranab Mukherjee [minister of finance, 1982–84] gave me steel to build that hospital and then he gave the finance.

Interviewer: You continued this running back and forth to build a case for your efforts in Delhi even after Prime Minister Rajiv Gandhi? I'm still struck that the others were not focused on this.

PR: I think it's the inner call . . . the inner call, you know . . . when there are so many times you feel, oh, I wish I could have done this and I should not stop there. Then if you think that's a good thing and that we should do this . . . it's one of those. There are many things that I did not do. As a cardiologist, you help many people, but I also saw cases where I could not help. I have recounted many times that I was inspired to act to reform healthcare after a young man died, leaving two children behind, as heart transplants were not possible in India. I felt so miserable, and said to myself, 'Doctor, somebody who came to you, he's been lost.' So that is where I think such a thing is within all of us. When you have that feeling, saying you must do something about it, you need to bring that change; that is where I think I got the first P of purity. How you do that, is what I said about the other two P's. You need patience because you need to work with a number of people—in this case, a number of government officials; then the ministers; then the prime ministers and so on and so forth and finally the patients because that's our habit. But in any case, I think there are so many people who have done so many wonderful things—it's not just me. It so happened that it struck me then that there was something which was very valuable to life, which was not available for our people, and I thought we should do this. I experienced it when I was a cardiologist in the US and when I came back here and saw this, I said we must change it. I am glad we did change and changed the healthcare in the country.

Interviewer: I find the three P's are very instructive as a way of navigating challenges in many developing countries. I want to focus on the purity part. A lot of students at HBS complain about potential downsides of corporatization of healthcare and certainly if you look at the Indian environment of the last ten to fifteen years, there are a slew of private hospitals that have popped up and one is always struck by how they balance profit with clinical excellence. Can you reflect on your observations at the industry level and how this has changed over the last ten to fifteen years?

PR: Well, I cannot deny what you said. Of all those who started hospitals with a good intention, saying that they would provide the care that was not available for our people, some have deviated. They have deviated because they put importance on returns for themselves, rather than on returns for the patients. So what is necessary in healthcare is the intention Vaidyo Narayano Harihi [the Divine Doctor]—that it's always a sacred thing to help another person. I think as long as we keep this goal . . . there are a few people who do this. Unfortunately, sometimes I think the media exaggerates this. Tell me another profession where a doctor gets up at 3 o'clock in the morning, saves a life or manages a delivery at 4.30 in the morning? Or an accident takes place and four doctors—an orthopaedic surgeon, a neurosurgeon, a general surgeon and an anaesthetist, and nurses, all of them go help the victims. What other profession does this? Only healthcare. But unfortunately this is not reflected. The only thing that is highlighted is the one wrong person doing it. We accept that's wrong; we should condemn it as all of us must condemn it, saying that you are in a profession here to do good. You must be able to give the very best possible to a person who walks in to see you. I think it's a few people who are spoiling the entire good that is being created in healing people. We should go back to our ancient history where they did good and took no returns at all.

Learnings from Prathap C. Reddy: Values provide inner strength to persist in the face of challenging circumstances.

2(c)

Nalli Kuppuswami Chetti

Kalaimamani 'YOGA'

Nalli Kuppuswami Chetti is the chair of Nalli Silk Sarees, commonly known as Nalli and Nalli Silks, a family business he inherited in 1958. The family's history in textiles dates back to a group of weavers in the fifteenth century. Nalli built its unique national brand by emphasizing innovation, customer-centric practices, quality and honesty across its operations. Chetti is also a prominent philanthropist, with interests in the arts, culture and education. He was awarded the Padma Shri by the Indian government in 2003.

Interviewed by V.G. Narayanan in Chennai on 28 June 2014.

Interviewer: You have been much more successful than your competitors. What are the reasons for this?

Nalli Kuppuswami Chetti (NC): When I was in the ninth standard, my Tamil teacher was Narayanaswamy Iyer. On the very first day, to improve our vocabulary, he told us to go to the library to read books. It could be in Tamil or English. So I went to the library. But I couldn't identify what to read. When I explained this to the librarian, he selected two books for me. The first was Mahatma Gandhi's *Satya Sothanai* [*The Story of My Experiments with Truth*] and the second was Ramakrishna Paramahamsa's *Amutha Mozhigal* [*Thus Speaks Ramdas*].

Once I finished reading them, I thought to myself that Mahatma Gandhi had adopted two principles when he was fighting for the nation's freedom: truth and ahimsa [respect for all living things and avoidance of violence towards others]. I decided that I would adopt truth and honesty as my guiding principles when I joined this trade. And when I started working in Nalli, I realized that this shop was already operating with these principles. My grandfather and father both believed that we should not lie. Even today many people do not believe that it is possible to run a business without lying. But that is how we have been doing business. As a result, our customers have faith in us; if Nalli states something then it must be correct. Secondly, even during my grandfather's time, when we did not have many sari varieties, we always labelled our saris. Now, with many varieties—silk, silk-polyester, pure zari (an even thread traditionally made of gold or silver, used especially as a brocade in saris), German zari, half-fine zari, etc.,—we still use computer-printed labels for each of them so customers can understand the reasons for variations in price. They have faith in us and pay the price, but we want them to understand why they are paying a higher price for a specific sari.

The best principle is to be truthful. And on quality, my grandfather would never compromise on that. Now we refer to weight in grams, but in those days we used to refer to it in *palam* or *veesai*. My grandfather used to say that the actual weight of the zari in the sari could be in excess, but not fall short of what we were telling our customers. The third was price. We need a nominal profit, so our prices were set in such a way as to deliver a minimum profit. And my grandfather was satisfied with that minimum profit. Then, it was innovation in manufacturing. If there was anything new, my grandfather would come forward to try it first. I want to tell you about one incident. Until 1921, only vegetable dyes were used in India for cotton or silk. Or maybe there were chemical dyes for cotton. Then Ciba introduced chemical dyes for silk. Their managing director from Switzerland, a chemical engineer, and their dealer from Govindappa Naicken Street in Chennai came to Kancheepuram. They went to a big sari shop, P.S. Kandhaswamy Muthu. The owner of the shop directed them to my grandfather. He told them, 'If you want to try such things, there's a person called Narayanaswamy who may be able to help you; I'll introduce you to him.'

They were introduced to my grandfather. In those days, people would not typically disclose details about their dyeing department, though in those days we also did not have that many colour options. For instance, to get crimson, they would add a particular seed to the dye. Nonetheless, they wouldn't allow anyone to see the dyeing process.

The Ciba representatives had developed a new method. They requested us to show them our dyeing system first. And we agreed. We showed the dyeing process for one particular colour. This process began in the morning and it took half a day. The Ciba people waited patiently. They are used to certain climatic conditions and despite that they sat next to the stove throughout to observe the dyeing process. Even we find it difficult to sit there for more than fifteen minutes. We took the silk yarn out, arranged it to dry, and then showed them the colour after it had dried. When they saw the colour that we wanted, they mixed and measured some powder and then completed the dyeing process. Our process took half a day, and their process took half hour. Once they completed it, they asked us to check if the colour matched the colour we wanted. It was acceptable to the person who was responsible for dyeing. Now we had to check if it was acceptable to the weaver. They left the silk to dry in shade and then came back the next day. They asked the weaver to set the dyed yarn on the loom. Usually, the weaver can weave about nine to ten inches in three hours. The Ciba representatives asked the weaver if there was any difference in the yarn. And the weaver confirmed that it was exactly like the yarn from the earlier dyeing process. So both matched and it was over. Everything was okay.

This was the first time that this process was introduced in India, by my grandfather. Then in a few weeks, everyone

switched to the new process since it was easier. He was open
to trying out new things. It was in his nature. This was in
manufacturing.

*Interviewer: What about similar issues that you faced in other parts
of the business system?*

NC: On the marketing side, saris bearing new names are
introduced every year during Deepavali. In 1911, we were not
the proprietors. We were only weavers. And what we had woven
was named 'Durbar Border'. In 1947, India became independent.
To mark the occasion, we designed a sari border that resembled
the Indian Tricolour. It was named 'National Border'. It was
very successful. Then with the arrival of sound film [talkies] in
1934, one of the sari borders was called 'Thyaga Bhoomi' [Land
of Sacrifice] after the famous Tamil film. I came in 1956, and
in 1961, they named a sari 'Paalum Pazhamum Kattam' [Milk-
Fruit Checks] and 'Thennilavu' [Honeymoon] border. There is
a thirty-year cycle. The designs that were prevalent thirty years
ago are back in vogue now. That's because this generation is
new. The designs that were popular during their mother's and
grandmother's time may not have been seen by this generation,
so they appear new. So the 'Paalum Pazhamum Kattam' that
was introduced in the 1930s came back in the 1960s. It didn't
return in the 1990s but it has come back now, as before. In this
manner, we have been pioneering the process of branding or
naming of new designs.

The next thing is yardage. Typically, the length of a sari
is nine yards. But if you look at our saris, they will be nine
and three-fourth yards or even ten yards. My grandfather
insisted that the sari should not fall short even by an inch. He
did not want the shop to gain a bad reputation. So often our

nine-yard saris were nine and three-fourth yards. This was a standard procedure for us. But now many shops do this and call it 'premium yardage'.

At one stage, when we could no longer manufacture everything that was needed, we gave contracts outside. We were particular about the type of silk and zari that was purchased and used in our saris. There's a village called Sidlaghatta that has the best silk in the whole world. Similarly, when it comes to zari, there's a brand of zari called Napoleon in Surat, which is the best in India. You could also say that it is the best in the world. Essentially, people who initially manufactured and sent zari from France could not compete with Surat in terms of prices. So Surat zari can be called the best in the world. So we specifically purchased a particular type of silk and a particular type of zari. And the weight of the zari had to be 12 palams or 420 grams; it could be 425 grams but not 415 grams. We had such conditions, and we checked these before accepting the consignment. On a daily basis, even today, a supervisor visits all our weaving centres. Even if a minor difference is observed, measures are taken to rectify it on the spot.

Since we concentrate so much on this, our quality never differs. Each and every sari is checked by me before it is sent to the sales counter. This was the case when even my grandfather and father were running the business. We are in business because of our quality. And we do not want to jeopardize this, so we insist on checking every sari.

Interviewer: What were your experiences with retaining customers given this attitude of going the extra mile?

NC: Around 1935 or so, when there was a wedding at a judge or doctor's house, then they would say, 'call Narayanaswamy'

[Chetti's grandfather]. In those days, the *muhurtham* sari [a sari worn by the bride during the most auspicious time of the wedding day] would be selected by the family. This might seem really detailed, but I want to explain how our business was established. At the time of purchase, they would bring their family members. If they approved the muhurtham sari, then they would buy the rest of the saris for the wedding from us. This process can be quite tense; similar to when you're awaiting the results of an examination. We don't know whose sari they will select. But once they select the main sari, then they will buy the rest from the same person. And it is not necessary that we have to take the saris to their house; they will directly come to the shop to see the saris.

After they visited the shop to purchase saris, my grandfather would attend to all their wedding needs from A to Z. There were no marriage halls in those days but houses used to be large—almost on half-acre or three-fourths acre of land. My grandfather used to bring the person to erect the pandal [marquee]. He used to arrange the wedding caterers. There was a specific chef, Appasamy Iyer, who was considered the best at that time. My grandfather used to bring him. There were special flower garlands just for weddings. They're called muhurtham malai [a wedding garland]; they are different from regular garlands; the fresh flowers in wedding garlands are strung together much more closely. There was a famous flower shop called Ambika Flowers in Jam Bazaar in Chennai. My grandfather used to purchase the garlands from this shop for our customers. Similarly, in those days, there were no foam or Dunlop pillows. There was a shop called Marriage Beds in T. Nagar in Chennai; they were located in the same place that Lalitha Jewellery now sits. They were specialists in manufacturing beds. That way my grandfather was entrusted with full responsibility for all the wedding arrangements. The head of the customer's family would tell my grandfather that he would have to take similar charge for future weddings too. The head of the family would instruct that all wedding saris be bought at the Nalli shop and then Narayanaswamy would take care of the remaining arrangements.

Those additional services that we offered brought us many more customers. Nowadays there are wedding or event planners; but in those days, the customer would be a doctor, but he wouldn't know anything about wedding planning. If they had a prior wedding in the family, then they might have some knowledge. So that's why they would entrust my grandfather with all the responsibility. My grandfather became well known in this way; he would also attend the wedding reception; all the wedding guests were mostly his customers. This service helped our shop acquire a set of 'permanent' customers.

Interviewer: Did your competitors not offer this? Was their quality different? How and why were they not as successful?

NC: As for silk saris, in my opinion, I don't think they were as concerned about quality. They generated a lot of designs. 'Designer saris' as a term didn't exist thirty years ago. I think the competition has been only focused on designs. However, even when we created new designs, we still ensured that quality was not compromised. When giving orders to weavers, we insist that the product has to be of a certain quality, then we ask them for designs; only if they meet these two conditions do we accept the product. I think this system only exists in our shop.

My grandfather used to state that it was okay if our product was priced higher, say even by one rupee; and it was okay if customers felt that prices in Nalli were more. There is no harm in that. But they should not have a reason to say that they don't like our quality. The product is priced in such a way that we make a profit and you cannot blame us for that. But if the quality is inferior . . . customers have confidence when they buy at Nalli. We sell at a fixed price. Irrespective of who the shopper is, be it an adult or a child, they will pay the same price. We guarantee the same price to all our customers.

In the past, there were only code words to indicate price. The salesmen would quote the price according to the code. And then sometimes they would also offer a 5 per cent to 10 per cent discount. But none of this existed when I came on board. In fact, this practice wasn't there during my grandfather's time either. My grandfather instructed that we should price according to what was absolutely necessary for a profit. Nothing more and nothing less. Customers were also happy with the fixed price. My customers once told me that they typically would spend a half hour to select a sari and then forty-five minutes bargaining. With fixed prices, they could now use that time to select saris. They found it more convenient. So, we introduced fixed prices in 1965. It became successful.

Learnings from Nalli Kuppuswami Chetti: Truth and honesty bring a business success as well as serve society.

2(d)

Mallika Sarabhai

Yadavan Chandran/Darpana Archive

Mallika Sarabhai is an Indian actor, classical dancer and social activist. In 1976, she became the director of Gujarat-based Darpana Academy of Performing Arts, which was founded by her parents, Mrinalini Sarabhai and Vikram Sarabhai, in 1949. In 1980, Mallika Sarabhai founded Darpana for Development, which uses live performances to promote discussions about development and social change. From 1984 to 1989, she toured the world with the stage adaptation of the Mahabharata, in which she created the female lead role, Draupadi. She reprised the role in the 1989 filmed version of the epic. In 2009, Sarabhai unsuccessfully ran for Parliament against L.K. Advani, the Bharatiya Janata Party prime ministerial candidate. In 2010, she was awarded the Padma Bhushan for her contributions to the performing arts.

Interviewed by V.G. Narayanan in Ahmedabad on 15 December 2016.

Interviewer: *Can you talk about how your social activism started?*

Mallika Sarabhai (MS): Politically, I was naïve for many years, very naïve, in fact, until I finished *The Mahabharata*. I was a fighter for justice even in school. I remember leading a dharna against my aunt, who was the principal, when I felt that one teacher was being unjustly treated and so on. So fighting for justice was something that was deeply ingrained. But politically I was very unaware, I mean I lived through the Emergency [Indira Gandhi's two-year suspension of democratic rights in 1975–76] and I was doing my MBA at Indian Institute of Management [IIM] Ahmedabad and PhD at Gujarat University, and I was completely blinkered. People look at me today and say, 'How could you have been so unaware?'. First of all, IIM is a cocoon, and you don't even realize that you are living in Ahmedabad. And IIM was basically, as far as I know, unaffected by the Emergency or by what was happening around politically, or perhaps it was just us students who were unaffected. The workload was such that I could barely come home though I lived in the same city.

So I was completely blinkered, but activism started very early, in *The Mahabharata*, and feminism came because of the shock when I got to St Xavier's College in Ahmedabad to study economics and realized that women were supposed to behave differently, women were supposed to act differently, think differently, dress differently and that somebody had an authority over you in what you did. It was also when I realized that one of the first questions asked is: What caste do you belong to? And what religion do you follow? And having been brought up in a family where there were Buddhists and there were orthodox Greek Christians and there were Jews and there was nobody who wore religion on their sleeve, it was all very private, very personal. Papa was not religious, Amma was very religious but in her own way. We never went to temples or Jain derasars or anything like that, it was a very personal relationship. When I started realizing that people were treated differently because of their caste or their community or the colour of their skin, it used to anger me, and I would have long arguments with people. But it wasn't as an activist; it was just as a person who was deeply troubled by it and deeply concerned.

Interviewer: How did your activism evolve?

MS: I think it became much more political, or if not political, much more active openly as I started thinking about myself as an activist at the same time as this transformation creatively happened, which was in the years of *The Mahabharata*. Those were very lonely years. I was left without any support system for the first time in my life and had to fall back on my own resources constantly. I realized for the first time that I did have those resources. That yes, my support system had made me that strong and that I did have the possibility of standing my ground.

The year 1992 and the demolition of Babri Masjid changed me, I saw the whole event on television and what I saw just appalled me, and I remember creating my first political piece the next morning. Somebody had sent me a beautiful piece of music called *Anjali*, which means devotion, and the Perth Festival had commissioned me to work with this extraordinary musician called Mani in Bangalore. And I had this piece of music, which is soft and devotional, and I created a piece called *Mean Streets on Earth* the next morning, which was a reflection of what I had seen on television the previous day, which was religious chants being chanted while mayhem happened. While violence of the most frightening kind was unleashed and people went crazy, there was jubilation at the violence. I think that is when I became political.

Twelve years earlier I had already started Darpana for Development, but I didn't realize that development and political issues were so merged. Today I think what I wear is a political statement, what I eat is a political statement, if I eat organic food and not Monsanto products, that is a political statement. If I wear handloom and not nylon, that is a political statement and if I don't wear blood diamonds, I don't wear diamonds at all, that is a political statement, which newspaper I read or which Internet paper I read are all political statements. I wasn't like that, but I did start getting very involved in actively talking of feminism, talking of human rights, talking of Dalit abuse, talking of violence, etc.

Interviewer: Can you tell us more about the activities of Darpana in the early 1990s?

MS: We started in 1992, immediately after the Babri Masjid incident, the first centre for non-violence through the arts, which is still active. We wanted to try and engender artists to look at issues of violence and non-violence, to create more works, to bring the topic back into the mainstream, because nobody was talking about non-violence by then. I mean Gandhi was dead and gone, and so was non-violence. So we engaged in campaigning against violence, whether it was violence against animals, or violence against the environment, or violence against women or violence against other communities. I started writing. I also started doing much more television work in which I would try and bring up this issue. Television had opened up in the 1990s, but I would raise the issue in many insidious ways. So, for instance, for StarPlus I created a fifty-two-part series on Indian folk tales using puppetry. We had a very clear idea to promote the understanding that there are Indians of many different appearances, and their beliefs and their customs are as valid as ours are. This was important because already this feeling had started that you have to be like this to be a true Indian and you can't have a flat nose, you can't believe in this god, or you can't believe in this and that.

And so through these folk stories and through great detailing of things like costume and food habits in the folk stories, we were trying to get through to children subliminally that this is also India or people live like this, they wear clothing like this, their house is on stilts, or they live in houses like this, or this is the kind of hut they have, these are the kind of wraps they wear, and so on. So it was very much that kind of usage of art. By that time my first piece, *Shakti—The Power of Women*, had already been created and had created quite a stir all across India and everywhere, and I was already beginning to work on my second piece . . . *Sita's Daughters*, which has done over 600 performances in three languages, and which I have just been forced to revive because this generation of women and young men now who have the same problems haven't seen it. So after ten years I have just revived it.

Interviewer: Over time, your social activism has combined with political activism. How did this transition happen?

MS: Taking a political stand or getting involved with mainstream politics was not on my agenda for a long time. It was really only when the Gujarat riots in 2002 happened and I saw the complete lack of will to question what was happening that I jumped into the fray. It was not a planned decision, it was not meant to be the way it was, I just thought somebody had to speak. And that somebody had to question . . . It wasn't premeditated at all, but I just wrote a piece a few days after the massacres based on Alfred Dreyfus' 'J'accuse'. It was printed on the first page of the *Times of India*'s editions across the country, where I tried to talk to the rest of the country to state, 'This is not a riot'. And it really came from my deep anguish at what was happening to fellow citizens, it wasn't political in that sense, it wasn't against a particular ideology, it was against what was happening. I had seen it build from 1992, I had seen textbooks change, I had seen language in newspapers change and it appalled me. The way people talked appalled me. I think it all just came out and I suddenly found myself in the firing line and I suddenly found myself in the midst of a tsunami that I had no idea was waiting for me.

Interviewer: Tell us about your run for a seat in Parliament in the 2009 general election. What prompted this?

MS: My standing for election in 2009 as an Independent, and not accepting the ticket of the Congress Party, was really something that came out of the belief, naïve as it seems today, that I could get together a band of 200 people—and 200 is an arbitrary number across the country—who would go in to committing political hara-kiri, would stand with one, only one agenda and that was better governance and justice in India. Not Left, not Right, not Marxist, nothing, and why I say political hara-kiri is because I would say to them that you won't be re-elected, but if fifty of us are elected for five years, fifty is a big enough group to be able to make a huge difference and show that a different kind of governance is possible in this country. In 2009 I found that I was an army of one, so I decided to jump in and try it for myself to see what happens. It was the biggest learning curve of my life. It was also the biggest disillusionment, because I can say to you today that you cannot do it without a party, not the way it is today. You cannot do it without lots of money, and you cannot do it without muscle power, you cannot do it without goondas backing you, and you cannot do it as an Independent. I still think we need to make it possible, I think it becomes more evident that unless you put that weakest person at the centre of policy and find innovative ways of bringing justice and development and health and education, we will remain where we are: where the proverbial rich get richer and the proverbial poor get weaker.

Learnings from Mallika Sarabhai: Cultural industries can and should serve as vehicles to emphasize the importance of human rights and social justice.

2(e)

Seema Aziz

Seema Aziz is the founder and managing director of Sefam, a major fashion retail brand in Pakistan, and the chairperson of CARE Foundation, Pakistan's largest educational non-profit organization, established in 1988 after a destructive flood hit the region. At the time of the interview, 716 schools were running with more than 2,30,000 children enrolled across Pakistan.

Interviewed by Tarun Khanna in Boston, Massachusetts, on 18 September 2016.

Interviewer: Am I right that when you started there was no standardization in terms of quality control of the dye process for fabrics with finer thread counts?

Seema Aziz (SA): There was little standardization at that time. Nobody was ready to create colours that didn't bleed. Of course, everybody asked, 'How do you create colours in cotton which don't bleed?' We ended up paying more for dyeing one metre of fabric than you would have to pay for buying a metre of dyed fabric. Our commitment was absolutely to quality. Then of course, the question was: how are we going to sell it? So we looked around, got ourselves a very small shop in the basement of the biggest smuggled fabric market in Lahore. It was all we could afford . . .

Interviewer: Because that's where quality was being sold?

SA: That's where all the women came to buy expensive fabric. As far as the embroidery machines went, we got the fabric, got the dyeing done, tweaked the embroidery machines to get the quality of embroidery that we wanted, put together a small range and opened shop. I remember all the shopkeepers in the area came by to see what we were doing because the shop was being built differently. It was designed for people to stand and serve customers. They just said, 'You think you can sell this fabric here? You'll never be able to sell it.' We had some solid offers from people saying, 'We'll buy the whole lot and we'll stamp it with made in Japan or made in France.' I still remember saying,

'We'll stamp each metre with "Made in Pakistan". If it doesn't sell, then we'll just put it in the centre of the market and burn it. But we're not going to sell it to you.'

The first lots were actually stamped with 'Made in Pakistan'—every metre. Luckily or unluckily, some of the stamps were crooked. There were also instances where the colour bled. We never stamped fabric after that. Experience taught us that people could copy a stamp or anything written on fabric. As a result, our quality became our hallmark. Our quality was our stamp. People could determine the quality of our fabric by just looking at it.

Interviewer: You and your brother, Hamid, share a deep commitment to quality and passion for saying, 'We should be Pakistan's first brand'.

SA: Well, we wanted to create a product that was made in Pakistan and equal in quality to the best in the world. It was as crazy an idea as possible, but we just wanted to do it. Somehow, we knew we could do it.

Interviewer: Can you talk more about sourcing the fabric, getting the right entity to do the dyeing for you in a particular way, going to the factories, going to the distributors, etc. Presumably your ethic of quality had to permeate the entire system.

SA: There was no distributor. That was the biggest thing. When everybody said to us, 'How will you ever sell it?', we understood what they meant. No wholesaler or existing store would pay a premium for quality—nobody would want to buy. That's why we opened our own store. We have never distributed. After that first store, we made another one and another one. Today, we sell through 610 points of sale nationwide and some abroad.

It's always our own stores, because when you create something so different from the norm, you have to market it a different way. I also feel that we were able to sell our fabric because of the way it was marketed. The shops were different. The ethos was different.

Interviewer: Can you say more about the ethos and the shop and the critical setting and the ambiance?

SA: Traditionally, people would sit on low stools and the fabric would be opened and thrown in front of them. That was a whole other culture, whereas our fabrics weren't presented in that manner. We made higher counters on which fabric was sold. Nobody sat anywhere. In the beginning, either our salesperson or one of us pulled out rolls of fabric, unlike other fabric shops. Then quality was critical for us.

Interviewer: How did you stand behind this quality commitment to make it credible?

SA: We were the first company to stand behind our product. Since we were making it and selling it, we, from day one, said, 'If something's wrong with it, you bring it back.' In the beginning, we made many mistakes. If anything was wrong—if there was a fault in the embroidery or the colour bled or there was some other defect, people could bring it back. In the early years, a fair amount would come back, and we'd replace it. Then, after a few years, we realized that some people were bringing back what they had bought in the summer. At the beginning of winter, they'd start bringing back their fabric, which was clearly clever of them. Then we put time limits, saying that people could return their fabric within a month or two of buying. That was absolute commitment of integrity to the product, integrity to the customer, and integrity to our teams.

Interviewer: Tell me about the people who work in these stores. Because obviously, you can't stand on your own behind 610 stores. So, you obviously cultivated a whole collection of people?

SA: Right. Quality is definitely something we talk about. Everybody throughout the network is aware of that. Right from our production units—we still produce all the fabric. The embroideries are all done in companies that we own. Many years ago, we set up a dyeing–finishing plant too, because it was very difficult to get the right quality of dyeing and finishing from outside vendors. It worked—we had much more control over the quality and finishing since we set up our own plant. We now do our own weaving too.

Interviewer: Let's talk about the training of these people. I realize you said several times that you emphasized the quality and that it's not something you compromise on and so on. What are the mechanics through which that's done? Is there a training institute of sorts inside the company?

SA: I think it's by example. It's what you believe in. I think that permeates through the company when people hear it all the time. We didn't grow in a day. We first had the one store, then the second, and so on. We have people who have been working with us since the day we started. Many others have been with us for more than twenty-five or twenty-six years. I feel that a culture is formulated over time. It becomes a way of life.

The new people who join us enter a culture that believes in absolute quality and integrity, nothing wrong or substandard will ever be sold to a customer. It's a policy we made right from the beginning. If something's wrong with the embroidery, we put a sticker on it so that every salesman knows they have to tell the customer that there is a slight flaw in the fabric. Customers often can't see the difference or can't tell on their own. This way, customers make the decision to buy the fabric knowing that it has a flaw. I think it's something, which through practise, has become instilled in our culture. Everyone knows that this is the way we want to work.

Interviewer: What about in selecting the franchisees? How do you do that? In most developing countries that I've spent any time in, it's a complete nightmare to find the kinds of people who would subscribe to high ethics and high quality. What is your experience?

SA: You're absolutely right. It's a dilemma when you allow franchisees to run stores. We have a whole system of management in which the stores get divided into clusters, and then into areas, and then into zones. We have our own managers and management who check all the shops with the same level of care, whether they are franchised shops or our own. There are a lot of ways to ensure they do the right thing, but it is still very difficult. Even at this time, we are actually deliberating on whether we should franchise any more stores in the future or run them all ourselves.

Interviewer: In a sense, you are controlling a lot of the process. You're controlling the way that it's presented to the end customer, you're controlling the dyeing, you're controlling the weaving?

SA: That's right.

Interviewer: As the industry has perhaps matured and maybe other people have—I hope—aspired to your quality levels in different entities, have you found that you're able to move away from this fully integrated system or do you still adopt that fully integrated control system?

SA: We're the design house too, actually. We design everything. Over the years, we've launched many more brands. The fabric was the first brand. About seven, eight, maybe ten years later, we thought, 'How long is the fabric going to last?' The whole world's going into ready-to-wear. Around 1995, we launched our first ready-to-wear brand of clothes for children and young adults from ages five years to sixteen years. Then later on, we went on to create a brand for newborns from ages newborn to five called Minnie Minors. Various other brands followed. All our brands across the board have the same concept of quality, in the sense that it must be equal to the best in the world. That concept drives all our work and our products. When it comes to fabric, we definitely still need to control the entire process.

Learnings from Seema Aziz: A high-quality final product or service demands managerial attention across the whole value chain, including franchisees, and rigorous training of employees.

2(f)

Shinta Kamdani

Sintesa Group

Shinta Kamdani is the CEO of Sintesa Group in Indonesia. Sintesa is a family business that was founded in 1919 as a rubber plantation called N.V. Handelsbouw en cultuur Maatschappij. In 1959, the company was renamed Tigaraksa, and trading became the focus of business. In 1999, under Kamdani, the company was renamed Sintesa Group. Sintesa is now a major consolidated holding company in consumer and industrial products, property development and energy. Kamdani is also the founder of the Global Entrepreneurship Program Indonesia, which seeks to promote and support entrepreneurs by providing training, financing and mentorship. She also started the first Angel Investment Network in Indonesia, which now has forty angels who invest in different start-ups. She was named in *Forbes Asia*'s fifty powerful businesswomen list in 2012, 2013 and 2016.

Interviewed by Meg Rithmire in Jakarta, Indonesia, on 28 November 2016.

Interviewer*: In 1999, you took over the family company. You changed the nature of the management of the group, as well as undertaking a sort of structural change in the diversification of the holding group—what industries you were in, and that kind of thing. So, let's talk about the management practices first. In 1999, you came to your father and said now is the time for me. And you had this vision for transitioning from a family business to a professionally managed organization. So how did you do it? What was the transformation?*

Shinta Kamdani (SK): Well, first of all, I started with the people, because to me the people are the foundation of it all. If you don't have the right team in place, it's very difficult to move forward, right? So what was the right team? When we want to transform, we have to also understand that it may not be business as usual. So we had to recruit a new team, and I called it my A-team—because if I am being given the opportunity to lead this organization, I want to have my own A-team, my own leadership team.

So the management team that I created was actually the first time we had what we call an executive committee [within the group], because my father managed in the past basically in an authoritarian style. He was the owner, he was the CEO. So basically, whatever his decision was, everybody would just follow. So there was no such thing as a democratic leader. There was no such thing as making decisions together. So I changed the whole management through a consolidated holding. Before, each of the businesses operated on their own. I introduced the executive committee, which consisted of some people that were already in the group and some people that I recruited.

I needed to have a mixture. If I wanted to have a professional management team, then I needed to have people coming from different backgrounds—from the outside, from multinationals—because I wanted to bring that culture in. So while there were people who had been in the business for quite some time, I mixed them with people who were coming from more multinational cultures, and put them in this executive committee. And that was actually the toughest part: trying to introduce this kind of this culture and create our own culture moving ahead, while maintaining the corporate values that basically bring us together.

Interviewer: How would you describe those corporate values? I mean, because, if it was really your father who kind of ran everything, and then you made this transition, then that was part of what you did as well.

SK: Well, it's interesting, because we have four E's as our corporate values. And these four E's of corporate value I actually brought from the family values that I learnt in the past. So our code of values begins with empowerment. We would like to empower people within our organization. This is a big part of the group. And the second is—we call it entrepreneurship. Why entrepreneurship? Because we want to encourage people with entrepreneurial mindsets. Even though they work for an organization, they can have that entrepreneurial spirit within them. The sense of belonging—that this is my company, my organization—has to be part of each employee. It's not just me because I'm the owner, but the employee has to have that feeling that I am an entrepreneur within this organization. So we created ways—even with the remuneration system—related to being an entrepreneur within that organization.

And then the third is excellence, because of course everybody needs to give the best they can—good services—so excellence is the third E.

And the fourth is empathy, because I learnt that, at the end of the day, we have to give back to our community. So it is part of our corporate social responsibility—empathy is the fourth E.

So the four E's are the first things that everybody needs to understand—that everybody needs to learn. And actually, I put the four E's within our key performance indicators [KPIs] as well. So when I set up the KPIs in evaluation and assessment, we also put our corporate culture as a KPI. It's not just about performance evaluation, or how well the company is doing financially, but we also need to have an indication of how well we are actually doing in each of these corporate values. So we kind of embedded what we believe is important in the four corporate values.

Interviewer: And that's across all of the sectors—consumer, industrial, property, etc.?

SK: Yes. So for the first time, we brought everybody together and said, hey, we have set up and consolidated the holding.

Tigaraksa was still there, focusing on consumers, but then we had a holding company. We branded it Sintesa Group—Sintesa means synergy. So it's synergizing all the different operations and people, when before that everybody just stood on their own. So now they are part of this big family, and we have the same values. This is important—having the same vision, the same common mission and the same common corporate values.

Learnings from Shinta Kamdani: Family values can become powerful tools of corporate renewal.

2(g)

Robert Brozin

Robert Brozin

Robert Brozin is the co-founder of Nando's, a South Africa-based restaurant chain specializing in Portuguese food, especially peri-peri chicken, which now operates over 1000 restaurants in thirty-five countries. Nando's was founded after Brozin and his business partner purchased a 67 per cent stake in a Portuguese takeout restaurant business called Chickenland, which was where they frequently had lunch. In 1990, they bought Chickenland entirely and rebranded it as Nando's. Brozin stepped away from Nando's in 2010 and became involved in social impact projects in Africa, including campaigns for promoting youth employment and against malaria.

Interviewed by Nien-hê Hsieh in Johannesburg, South Africa, on 23 September 2019.

Interviewer: If I am a customer, I come in and I eat at Nando's. What are the ways in which you concretely inspire people?

Robert Brozin (RB): The first way to do it—the first way we look at it is we say great brands are built from the inside out. So we look at our people, and we say that for us to inspire you as a customer, we need inspired people. Because if our people aren't inspired, there's no way they're going to inspire you. So we need to really work with our people, and the golden law—if you ever say to me, what's the golden law of Nando's—it's treat people the way you would want to be treated. That, to me, is the essence of Nando's.

We're hiring diverse people. We're hiring people that . . . we come from humble beginnings, so we don't mind that you come from humble beginnings. We take people from the humblest of beginnings or the roughest of neighbourhoods, whose journeys . . . haven't been as easy as that of a lot of other people. I love when those people come into the business because we give them dignity. We give people a chance to actually prove themselves as an individual. We love individuals. We love people coming and providing their individual magic.

Because . . . ultimately, it's individuals that have created Nando's. It's not through a business plan. It's not through some clever kind of business school. It's really been created by individuals that have come in and added their touch to what we've done. So it's an individual brand, and we say we're only as good as all of us together. That's the starting point.

So you start respecting people. And if you can build a culture of diversity, a culture of respect, a culture of treating people right, treating people with dignity, with a sense of understanding— that if you're religious, you can come in with that headgear. If you need to take certain holidays, you take those holidays. We understand those holidays. It's not something that we say if you're Muslim or you're a Jew, we understand that . . . if you're going to a dinner party with Nando's and you don't want to eat, that's fine. You don't have to. We understand the sensitivities of different religions, and we actually respect it. As shareholders, big time, we respect it, and we expect our business to do that.

So that then manifests itself in the way that you as a customer coming into Nando's are going to be served, so that if you come into a Nando's restaurant where the people are happy, people are inspired, they're motivated, and they've come from diverse backgrounds, you're going to come to Nando's, and your experience at Nando's is going to be magical . . . we've got a thing on at the moment . . . It's called the Master Grillers Championships. And we take grillers, the guy that cooks the chicken . . . we take them from around the world. We run regional competitions, then country competitions, and we have a world champion grilling competition in different locations. Last year was Australia. This year is Ireland. Next year is Mauritius. And you take guys who have never had passports before, from all around the world, they come and they enter this competition.

I think there are like forty-five grillers, the country winners, that compete globally. But the kind of respect that this competition gets is enormous—because you can come from Khayelitsha in Cape Town and end up in Ireland, or from the South Side of Chicago and you're in Ireland. You have to get your passport and go off to Ireland, Malaysia, or Singapore. Guys come from—the country winners come, and they compete.

That's one element of so much that we do within the organization. It's the way we look at our art. It's the way we look at the design of our furniture. It's the way we look at just so many different little programmes that when you join Nando's and you understand the essence, it's not one thing. It's a combination of a whole lot of things.

There's a safety that you come in here and if you're slightly different, you're okay. If you're a refugee, we welcome you in. But you have to work. It's not like you're coming in and you can freestyle and end up doing nothing. You'll be caught very quickly, and you'll go. There is accountability. There are key performance indicators [KPIs]. You have to deliver, certainly at restaurant levels, very strong KPIs. But there's a strong fun element to everything as well—conferences and Christmas parties and family events. And there's so many different— the managers of each of the restaurants . . . are encouraged to understand lots of issues around mental health, understand issues around family wellness. There's got to be sensitivity. It's not one thing. There's a whole lot of things. It's like a philosophy of how we're doing it. And we're getting better and better and better at it. It's also a journey. We're learning.

In South Africa, for example, a big factor is financial literacy and financial understanding. When you're earning, say, above minimum wage, but really it's not like you've got a lot of free cash at the end of the month, your financial discipline . . .

as an individual can be very testing. Unfortunately, there are a lot of products in the South African market that steal little percentages from the poorest of the poor on things like funeral policies and life cover.

So debt consolidation—we provide debt consolidation for our people. There are about fifteen different programmes that the South African business provides that looks at how we can improve the lives of our Nandoca [an employee of the restaurant chain], how we can change their lives—put people through schools, through universities, through college. It's amazing, the different programmes that we've introduced throughout the world, but all done within the framework of the country.

Interviewer: Do you follow the same values everywhere that Nando's operates?

RB: There's not like one law that you say, well, we're going to do this on a global basis. Each country is looked at very differently, very uniquely, because each element is slightly different. You don't have that same element of the debt issues that we have in South Africa, where you've got guys that are charging 30 per cent on some of the loans—you might not have that in America or in the UK, whereas in South Africa, that's a massive issue. So each country's got its programmes . . . the CEOs of those countries must go deep into our people and find programmes and products that change people's lives. So it starts from looking after our own people.

Interviewer: How do you know you're succeeding?

RB: As a customer, what we want is for you to have the best experience. We want you to come into Nando's and just feel that you've been well looked after. You've had a great meal. There's been great value. And you'll come back again, and you'll recommend us to your friends and family. That's ultimately what we want. That's what keeps you coming back.

I think the big metrics for us is like-for-like sales. So it's per restaurant, how those restaurants have grown. We can't expect to impact your life more than just giving you the dignity of you coming into a restaurant and having a great experience. We're not going to change your life dramatically, other than when you come in, you must feel that you're coming into a safe space, and that you're supporting a brand that's ultimately supporting other people.

So if you came in and you bought your quarter chicken and chips, and you knew that there was a farmer in Mozambique that was well looked after, because every quarter chicken and chips you buy, a little extra chilli is being grown and his life is being impacted, or that people are being protected from malaria—but we don't talk about that much. We talk about it internally. We don't talk about it externally. We do very little branding of that to our consumer. What we do as almost a slow burn is that our own people must be our advocates, that they go and tell their friends, families about what we're doing, as opposed to me telling you how good we are at eliminating malaria. I can tell you how good I am at eliminating malaria, what I've done, etc. To me, it's boastful. When other people talk about what we've done, it's, for me, much more meaningful than me telling you what we've done.

Learnings from Robert Brozin: Hiring and motivation of a committed and diverse workforce is the starting point for building an attractive and meaningful brand.

3

Innovating for Impact

Innovation is almost tautologically the key source of firm-level and economy-wide productivity and therefore competitiveness. Some historical accounts attribute the economic lead of the Western world over South Asia, at least in part, to the latter's insufficient embrace of innovation. The World Intellectual Property Organization ranks countries' innovation ecosystems. In 2020, India ranked forty-eight out of 131 countries, having improved considerably in the past decade, and far ahead of Bangladesh, Pakistan and other South Asian countries, but still much behind China (ranked fourteen) and the US (ranked third).

Of course, innovation and entrepreneurship are linked, especially in the context of this chapter, where we focus on the innovation catalysed by iconic entrepreneurs. Contemporary entrepreneurs of the same ilk as those featured here are the reason the Indian innovation system continues to improve, even amidst other headwinds. So, perhaps a good place to start is by celebrating the German émigré and Harvard professor of economics, Joseph Schumpeter. He was the best theorist of entrepreneurship, after all.

Schumpeter accepted, like other economists of the time, that societies tended to some form of economic equilibrium, where buyers and sellers acted as per reasonably well-understood economic norms, most of the time. But every so often, there was a period of disequilibrium, when something fundamentally new happened, that caused society to lurch forward. That's the idea of 'creative destruction' that he brought into the popular imagination.

Of course, he went much further than coining this terminology. Most interesting to us in our current context is Schumpeter's repeated emphasis that it is 'not possible to explain economic change through economic factors alone', especially not the periods when innovation occurred through the disequilibrium wrought by creative destruction. One has to have a broader understanding of society at the time to have a shot at making sense of a particular episode, let alone trying to predict it. We see this reflected in the nuanced contextual understanding displayed by the iconic leaders portrayed in this chapter when it comes to the nurturing of ideas and their nursing these to fruition.

Surgeon-entrepreneur Devi Shetty is credited with developing procedures that have resulted in the lowest-priced cardiac surgery in the world, with no diminution in quality relative to the world's best hospitals. Narayana Health is able to serve its patients profitably and without turning away the indigent for between $1000 [Rs 64,000] and $2000 [Rs 1,29,000], when the same surgery would cost several tens of crores of rupees in the developed world, and maybe more.

Shetty's work over the past two decades or so has been guided by a crystal clear long-run vision. The steadfastness of purpose over profits has—in a theme that finds resonance with many featured in this volume—delivered profits handsomely, as it turns out. The vision is to ensure that everyone in the world—especially the poor—can be treated with compassion while maintaining financial viability, so that 90 per cent of the world that is denied cardiac care simply doesn't end up dying.

The same steadfastness of vision is apparent in Kiran Mazumdar-Shaw's birthing of Biocon, India's leading biotech company over the decades, now a recognizable giant not just in the Global South, but among big pharma as well. And it's also apparent in the Hamied family's desire to create an indigenous pharmaceutical powerhouse—from Khwaja Hamied to his son Yusuf Hamied—so as not to be subject to the whims of the British colonial power at the time that the elder Hamied started his work.

Where do the ideas that bring this vision to fruition come from? Shetty tells us that the dramatic improvement in efficiency he has achieved is a consequence of myriad of small experiments, each of which are guided by observation and immersion in the phenomenon. Immersion of a different sort guides the efforts of Yusuf Hamied, the chemist-turned-entrepreneur credited with providing affordable HIV medication to most of the world, taking on big pharma with gusto. Hamied's immersion is into science. He describes devouring chemistry journals to keep track of scientific progress and uncover potential process innovations through which he can find alternative ways to produce existing medications so as to dramatically undercut the prices of big pharma. Once again, the poorest of the world benefit the most.

So, ideas come from exposure to the best science in the world, even if the science isn't home-grown, as is often the case in the developing world, and even from borrowing associated technologies. Pakistani businessman and philanthropist Babar Ali describes borrowing technology from the Swiss to build his milk packaging empire in Pakistan in a similar vein.

Getting ideas through scientific and phenomenological immersion hardly suffices though. What else do our entrepreneurs need to get done to turn invention into innovation? In a word, the entrepreneur can't just create, she has to create the underlying conditions to create.

Mazumdar-Shaw wills into existence the soft and hard infrastructure needed to support the life-science cluster in Bengaluru, of which her company Biocon is a part. This includes creating a life-science industry association that lobbies for the public goods needed to support the industry. Shetty also invests heavily in the partial private provision of so-called public goods, compensating for the state's inadequacy. He has to train his own nurses and will into being medical insurance and telemedicine so as to build his heart-surgery-at-scale model, rather than wait for these services to be provided by others. Mo Ibrahim, in bringing mobile phones to Africa, has to literally invest in every infrastructural activity one can imagine in order to put up his telephone towers—electric power, security services, etc.,—as well as build a capital-intensive enterprise while being forced to eschew the use of debt, given the absence of debt markets on the continent.

Infosys co-founder Nandan Nilekani's effort, under the Government of India's auspices, is an attempt to allow others to create an ecosystem atop the biometric identities that the Aadhaar project has bequeathed to most of India's residents in less than a decade. This has been a towering technological and logistical achievement, arguably leapfrogging the rest of the world. It also illustrates that the state, even one weighed

down by regulations as in independent India, is capable of
creating salubrious conditions within which entrepreneurship
and creativity can unfold, and at scale.

If Mazumdar-Shaw, Nilekani, Shetty and Ali are conjuring
up ecosystems within national boundaries, we see an even
broader example of global ecosystem-shaping in the case of
Hamied, who skilfully mobilizes global media to take on the
immensely more powerful big pharma and to shame them into
recognizing that his HIV medication is as good and much
cheaper than theirs. His case makes it clear that the global
societal context can be mobilized to support innovation in a
developing country.

South Asia and societies of its ilk are characterized by
institutional inadequacies that bedevil innovation, but also
make its nurturing all the more vital to development. It is
difficult for would-be buyers and sellers to come together to
consummate transactions because of a lack of infrastructure—
so called institutional voids—let alone engage in creative banter
and innovate. But if the voids bedevil creativity, they are also a
double-edged sword, in that the filling of these voids is often an
entrepreneurial activity. Ibrahim's pan-African enterprise can
be thought of as filling a gigantic communications void that in
turn triggered a groundswell of entrepreneurship across Africa.
So the Government of India's biometric identity project,
shepherded by Nilekani, can be seen as significantly correcting
a massive informational void between residents of India and the
state machinery.

3(a)

Devi Shetty

Narayana Health

Devi Shetty is a cardiac surgeon, and the founder and chairperson of Narayana Health, a chain of hospitals in India that first focused on cardiology and cardiac surgery, and now provides all forms of tertiary health. Since its founding in 2001, the cost of heart surgery at Narayana Health has fallen to being the lowest in the world without sacrificing quality. Shetty initiated the 'micro health insurance scheme' along with the government of Karnataka, which currently insures more than 40 lakh poor farmers in the state. Shetty received the Karnataka Ratna in 2001, the Padma Shri in 2004 and the Padma Bhushan in 2012.

Interviewed by Tarun Khanna in Boston, Massachusetts, on 10 October 2017.

Interviewer: How did you go from the realization that the delivery of healthcare in a country like India is a systemic operation to deciding to open the Narayana group of hospitals?

Devi Shetty (DS): After my residency in general surgery, I went to England for training in cardiac surgery—because in those days, we didn't have the opportunity to be trained as a heart surgeon in India. There were very few training positions available. I had the opportunity to work at Guy's Hospital in London, which is considered one of the best cardiac centres in Europe. Strangely, I belong to south India, but I had an offer to start a large cardiac surgical programme in Kolkata, because there weren't that many in the region—you're talking about twenty-seven or twenty-eight years ago. There weren't that many cardiac surgical programmes in India. So for me, the transition from Guy's Hospital London to Kolkata was like the difference between Heathrow and Howrah.

It's a very crowded place. I used to see a large number of patients because I was the only heart specialist. I was perhaps the second heart surgeon in that part of the world to operate on people's hearts. So I used to see a large number of patients, but no one ever turned up for treatment surgery, because they couldn't afford it. They simply couldn't afford it. I used to spend an hour convincing a patient to undergo a heart operation when I started my career. Today, if I see a patient and I tell him that he needs an operation, he nods his head and asks for the date. If I tell him that he doesn't need an operation, I need to spend an hour convincing him why he shouldn't get the operation.

Interviewer: Your most celebrated hospital is the headquarters of the Narayana Group in Bengaluru. Tell us a little bit about how you went through many interventions to make sure that it could accommodate a massive scale of operation. What are some of the key interventions within the hospital—the way surgeries were done, the way you treated patients—that come to mind as being salient?

DS: From the very beginning, we knew the data. That's very important. So when we designed the hospital, our idea was that we should be able to do sixty major heart surgeries in a day, and six days a week. We don't have the luxury of taking off on a Saturday. We all work long hours. Today, we do between twenty-seven to thirty-five heart surgeries in a day. The whole hospital is designed for heart, cardiology and cardiac surgery. In that building, we don't do anything else. So the entire system, starting from the person who receives you at the reception as a porter, they're all geared for heart care. That helps.

And over a period of time, we got recognition as a cardiac institution. We trained a large number of cardiologists, cardiac surgeons, cardiac anesthetists, so we had a huge number of people who were working long hours there. When you're an academic institution, your cost of operations goes down significantly, because at any given time we have about thirty-seven to forty young residents undergoing a training programme only in cardiac surgery and you don't pay them a salary. You pay them a stipend, and they work for you for six years. We also helped the government to run health insurance. So there are multiple things that we have done. You can't achieve this by doing one thing better. You need to do a lot of things.

Interviewer: But I think it's helpful to hear a little bit about some of these things. For instance, you've often spoken about what I would refer to as task shifting—which is where the critical care is done by the most skilled person, and then you make sure that other people are on hand to do things that are less complicated. Can you give a little bit of a flavour of how that works?

DS: Most jobs in a heart hospital or any hospital—they're repetitive jobs. You just need passionate people and you train them. Nursing education is relatively expensive, so a lot of young women—bright young women coming from poor families—are not in a position to join nursing school because of the high cost. Also, when they are getting trained for four years, they don't earn money. That is another obstacle. So, we identify such young women who couldn't get admission to nursing college, but they have all the qualifications, and we train them for a particular task—like assisting in a heart operation. So they work as nurse assistants, and over a period of time, they do amazing work.

When I operate on the heart, I put out my hand and say to the nurse, 'I want 6–0 prolene'. She knows that for the task I am doing I don't need 6–0, I need 7–0 prolene. So she gives me 7–0 prolene, but she doesn't tell me what she has given me. She gives me what I need rather than what I asked for. This is the level of maturity they attain. And they do amazing work.

Interviewer: By virtue of doing it many times, they've learnt the protocols for how to communicate and work as a team in different ways.

DS: They understand the moment—just by your body language. You don't even need to tell them. They know exactly what we want, and they're amazing. And these are the young women who train all our other nurses. Credentialling of a particular degree in a profession where you are doing a repetitive job— this is the greatest insult to human imagination.

Interviewer: Say more about that. What do you mean by that?

DS: In my office, there is a picture. It's a beautiful painting of a flowerpot, and I often ask visitors coming from various parts of the world when this discussion comes up—I ask them, 'Can you guess who the painter is? It's a beautiful painting. You can't fail to notice that.' And they start from Michelangelo to M.F. Husain, one of India's most famous painters, and all kinds of names. Then I tell them that the beautiful painting was painted by a trained elephant in Thailand. In Thailand, they have an elephant park, and they train elephants to do a particular painting. You look at a painting, and whichever painting you like, you tell them, and the elephant will pick up the brush, and the elephant will paint it in front of you, and you can buy the painting. If you can train elephants to do a beautiful painting, can't we train young women from the villages to do these simple repetitive tasks?

Interviewer: A lot of this sounds like you've taken a process that people think of as a highly skilled process—and it is a highly skilled process. But you've identified portions of it that, as you say, are repetitive and that can be farmed out to people who can be trained, so that you're not held hostage by a limited number of surgeons or highly skilled physicians.

DS: Today, we are doing it. Tomorrow, everyone will do it. The World Bank estimates that in the next twelve to thirteen years, there is going to be a shortage of 8 crore healthcare professionals. And you can't produce them overnight. It takes fourteen years to train a surgeon to operate on your hand. So unless we get into a non-traditional way of training medical specialists, unless we create a methodology of using technology to train people, this world will be in big trouble. These are very highly skilled jobs. It takes time. Irrespective of how intelligent the teacher is or how intelligent the student is, it takes time.

Interviewer: The cost of a CABG surgery—coronary artery bypass graft—is so much lower in your Bengaluru hospital than it would be in the West, maybe even two orders of magnitude lower in some ways—a few thousand dollars compared to tens of thousands of dollars, at least. What are the principal drivers that have contributed to lowering that cost?

DS: The first thing is it wasn't like that when I started my career. Twenty-six or twenty-seven years ago, when I did the first heart surgery, I clearly remember that the patient paid today's equivalent of $2000 [Rs 1,29,000] for a heart operation. Twenty-six years later, they're paying $1200 [Rs 77,000]. Nothing in this world, in service, that was $2000 [Rs 1,29,000] twenty-six years ago has come down to $1200 [Rs 77,000] today. It's only by economy of scale.

Today, we are privileged—about 12 per cent of heart surgeries in India are done by us. The companies that supply products, they look at us differently. And we have converted our hospital into an academic institution. Every hospital we build, we treat it like an academic institution to train young people. And more than anything else, we are very, very conscious of the quality. The cheapest way to produce something is to make it the best in the first attempt.

Interviewer: *Why is that?*

DS: Then you don't have to repair it. If you fix the heart properly the first time, you don't need to take back the patient for a re-exploration or give them a massive quantity of blood. Around seven years ago—I think maybe more—we wanted to get the Joint Commission International accreditation, called JCI. In the US, if you are running a hospital, you can't run a hospital without JCI accreditation. So we wanted to get our hospital accredited by the JCI. Nobody in my part of the world knows what JCI is, and it won't give any value addition in terms of getting more patients. But we wanted to do it, because we wanted to benchmark our standards—our quality—with the American or European standard.

By doing it, there are two things that we have done. One is that we have told ourselves we may be offering affordable healthcare but we are not a cheap hospital. We offer what is good compared to any of the best hospitals in the world at a price that is much, much less than what you would pay in other parts of the world. The second thing is that by insisting on quality the entire philosophy of our approach towards the care changed. You have seen how an Indian railway station is not very clean. But a good Indian airport, it's spick and span because when everything looks nice people don't mess it up. When everything looks dirty, people feel they can do a shoddy job. So quality matters.

Learnings from Devi Shetty: Dramatically innovative outcomes are the cumulation of myriads of small changes, each triggered by immersion in the problem, much experimentation and by an uncompromising attitude to quality.

3(b)

Kiran Mazumdar-Shaw

Vivan Mehra/Biocon

Kiran Mazumdar-Shaw is the chairperson and founder of Biocon Limited, India's largest biopharmaceutical company. After its founding in 1978, Biocon grew from a small operation in a rented garage in Bengaluru into a major research company with nearly 10,000 employees. Biocon is noted for many innovations, including the development of a new technology for making insulin. In 2011, Mazumdar-Shaw was named as one of *Financial Times'* top fifty women in business and in 2014, she was awarded the Othmer Gold Medal for outstanding contribution to the progress of science and chemistry. Other recognitions include being named 'EY World Entrepreneur of the Year' in 2020.

Interviewed by Tarun Khanna in Boston, Massachusetts, on 4 June 2018.

Interviewer: Can you talk about your company's transition from enzymes manufacture to pharmaceuticals?

Kiran Mazumdar-Shaw (KMS): I came to a point, about twenty years into the start of the business, where I felt I should do something else beyond enzymes, and that 'beyond enzymes' became pharmaceuticals. I felt that biopharmaceuticals was going to give me a much faster growth trajectory than enzymes would give me. Enzymes were a very different model. If I wanted to become big, I had to pursue a high-volume, low-value commoditized kind of an enzyme space, whereas what I was doing was specialty enzymes, which was high-value, low-volume and the market was limited. So because of that, I was forced to reinvent my business saying, 'What else can I do?' I didn't want to spend too much money setting up these huge capacity enzyme facilities. So I basically leveraged all the technologies that I developed for enzymes and started making pharmaceuticals instead. My first fermentation-based molecules were statins, because they were produced—lovastatin and pravastatin are produced by fermentation. So that's what I started doing.

Interviewer: And these are relatively simple molecules?

KMS: These are small molecules—but they're still fermentation-based, and they're quite complex in that sense. I became successful with the manufacturing of these products and selling the active pharmaceutical ingredients—or APIs, as they are called, bulk drugs—to global markets, especially the US and Europe. I got US Food and Drug Administration [FDA] approval for statins. So that got me off to a good start applying that technology.

And then I started making immunosuppressants, which were also produced by fermentation. My first big recombinant DNA product was insulin. India was at the epicentre of diabetes, and I thought to myself—I said, 'Why are we importing all our insulin? Why don't I try and make recombinant human insulin? I've got this DNA technology. Why don't I apply it and see if I can make insulin?' And I used a very proprietary yeast system to make insulin.

Interviewer: What's the novelty in this approach compared to [US pharma major] Eli Lilly and [Danish diabetes care giant] Novo Nordisk and others who are in the insulin business?

KMS: So Eli Lilly uses a bacterial system—E. coli—and Novo uses a saccharomyces yeast to make insulin. I used Pichia, which is a very different yeast system, which is a high-yielding yeast system—which I used then to make insulin.

Interviewer: And the intuition was yours or your scientists'—that this approach would be successful? Because of some past experience in something?

KMS: So we were using Pichia fermentation for making an enzyme. We were making a phytase enzyme using Pichia yeast. It was a very high-yielding process. It was a very elegant process. And we said, 'Hey, this process can make insulin. I think we're in business.' So we said, 'Let's try and see if we can actually insert the insulin gene into the Pichia and see whether it expresses the same way'. And we were lucky. It did. So we started making recombinant human insulin using Pichia.

Interviewer: The way you're describing it, it sounds like you were able to go from one to the other very quickly. But each of these steps requires some patience, capital and risk tolerance? Can you comment on some of that, for any of these transitions?

KMS: So let me start with enzymes. I mean, whatever's said and done, it's not as if it was easy. Even making enzymes was tough. Of course, with pharmaceuticals, it was relatively easier than making enzymes—because with enzymes, the moment you had an idea of what you wanted to do with that industrial process, you had to go back to the drawing board. You could do a lot of basic, predictable experimentation, I would say, because you knew what you were doing. You would get an enzyme, and then you basically used a lot of your time to improve the yields and improve the process and finally get a purified enzyme.

We were getting very good at it, so we could actually look at any application and say, 'Okay, now let's go and look at our repertoire of fungi and bacteria and see which one of them can produce this product'. And we would do that selection, come up with a rudimentary product, and then improve it and get a pretty good product within a very short time. So every year, for instance, we could produce maybe a couple of enzymes for various industrial applications. It was an investment, but there was more predictability in the end point.

But when we moved to pharmaceuticals, obviously it was a far more complex regulatory process. In the early days, it was okay because . . . it was still a 'copycat' kind of an approach, because I started with molecules that had already been discovered, and I was making products . . . where I was just using a different technology to get the same results.

I wanted to differentiate myself from the Lillys and the Novos, saying, 'Can I be the third insulin company making insulin with something else?' Because if you call Lilly an innovative company and if you call Novo an innovative company, then I also want to be called an innovative company—because I'm also using a different technology. So that's what I did. I didn't mimic either Lilly's technology or Novo's technology. In fact, today, we are the third largest insulin producer in the world, and we are very proprietary in our insulin technology, because nobody else uses Pichia to make insulin and insulin analogues—only we do. So I think from that point of view, you're seeing three companies with three technologies. And I think we were very reassured by the fact that we could actually develop insulin in four years.

Interviewer: So it took about four years?

KMS: It took us four years to take that technology from lab scale to plant scale. But what was good was because we were familiar with the technology—because of the enzymes that we were producing at commercial scale—I think we had that confidence to see it through quite fast. And then, of course, we had to go through a whole clinical development phase, which we had never done before. So it was a whole learning process of running clinical trials, testing your product, making sure that it works, making sure that you had all the quality systems in place to ensure that the product was safe, efficacious, and did what it had to do. So I think we went through a tremendous learning curve trying to make our first drug product. Remember, the others were drug substances.

Interviewer: I want to shift gears a little bit and go back to some of the contextual constraints in a country like India. I think one of the things that's remarkable and inspiring about this story is bucking the infrastructural odds of building a science-based enterprise in what is essentially still a very poor country. Can we talk about science and the way you think about science in a country like India, going beyond simply accessing talented Indian Institute of Technology engineers?

KMS: The way I looked at science right from the very beginning—my raison d'être for starting this company—was I said, 'I've got to create a research-led environment where I'm able to attract scientists to come and do research instead of the usual sort of exodus that we see of scientists going to other countries to do research'. So I said, 'I want to create an organization that can attract scientists.'

Today—the Biocon campus that we have in Bengaluru is home to perhaps one of the largest life-science clusters in the world. We have today, on one site, close to 7000 bioscientists working on various research programmes. Of course, almost 4000 of them can be attributed to Syngene,* because they're

---

* Syngene is a research, development and manufacturing organization that provides integrated scientific services.

offering research services to companies. But nevertheless, they are all housed in that campus doing high-end research for the global pharma industry, even non-pharma industries. And then we've got the remaining 3000—scientists, engineers, clinicians—all doing research-led work for Biocon. So it's been a very exciting journey for me because I was able to create this kind of infrastructure. And it's very high-end infrastructure.

Of course, you drive on the streets and you'll remember, oh, this is a third world country. But the moment you drive into an IT campus or a campus like ours, it's world class, because we've all invested in high-end infrastructure. Of course, these are like islands—self-supported, self-sustaining infrastructural sites. But that's what it's all about. You've got to generate your own power supply because you can't rely on the electricity supplied by the government. You've got to make sure that everything you do is going to be done to world standards, so the buildings that we make—again, we are all very focused on sustainability, and therefore the building designs are very eco-friendly, green buildings. Everything that you see anywhere in the world is also something we do there.

So I think it's a bit of a contradiction in terms, but then at the same time that's how you're able to attract the best of scientific talent. Today, our scientific talent is not just strong—from the Indian research laboratories and the Indian engineering colleges—but we're finding a lot of scientists coming back from various parts of the world because they find it's very exciting.

Interviewer: So that's a commentary on how, over several decades, you've had to compensate for problems in the Indian environment— the roads, the power, etc. But what reflections do you have on triggering change more broadly, outside of Biocon? Even if we just take Bengaluru—I mean you've been instrumental in creating or mentoring ABLE, which is the Association of Biotechnology Led Enterprises. What are your reflections on the success or lack thereof of these attempts?

KMS: I think for a long time, I felt that we used to keep talking about this missing link between academia and industry in India. And it was truly a missing link. I always felt that, unless you allow your academic faculty and professors to really pursue entrepreneurial opportunities using what they've researched and leveraging their research findings, you're not going to get this industry connect. I think after a long time, we are seeing scientist entrepreneurs. We are seeing incubators at academic institutions.

That is what is going to change things because, as a country, we have to hang our heads in shame that we spend less than 1 per cent of our gross domestic product [GDP] on research and development [R & D]. And of that, the government spends only 0.6 per cent on R & D. The rest comes from the private sector. That's very, very low for a country like India. I mean, look at Korea—it spends 4 per cent. The US spends close to 3 per cent. And if you look at even Brazil and China—they are spending 2 per cent, 2.5 per cent of their GDP.

So to be spending 0.6 per cent, and at best 1 per cent—if you add everything up, it is still woefully low. And the reason that it's woefully low is because we have the talent. If we didn't have the talent, that would be one thing. If you find other countries that don't have the talent that India has, spending 0.1 per cent or 0.2 per cent on R & D, that's excusable. But it's unconscionable that a country like India, with such a rich talent pool of scientists . . . we've been leaders in natural science and things like that in the past. We've got mathematicians, engineers, scientists—you name it. And if you don't invest in innovation and R & D, I think you're missing out on an enormous opportunity. I think this is where the governments will be blindsided—having not really focused on this particular area.

Learnings from Kiran Mazumdar-Shaw: Underlying scientific and technical capabilities can often be leveraged in entirely new directions. Innovation requires an ecosystem mindset, often having not just to create, but to also create the conditions to create.

3(c)

Yusuf Hamied

Amol Kamath

Yusuf Hamied is the chairperson of Cipla, an Indian multinational generic pharmaceuticals company founded in 1935 by his father, Khwaja Abdul Hamied. Yusuf Hamied joined the family business in 1960 and became prominent for his role in defying Western multinational pharmaceutical companies in order to provide generic AIDS treatments and other drugs to treat poor people in the developing world. In 2005, he received the Padma Bhushan from the Indian government and in 2012 was named 'CNN–IBN Indian of the Year in Business'. Interviewed by Tarun Khanna in Mumbai on 29 April 2013.

Interviewer: There are two celebrated actions taken by you that I would love for you to reflect on. One is azidothymidine [AZT] and the cocktail drugs, and the second is the antiviral in response to the avian flu and the stockpiling issue.

Yusuf Hamied (YH): First, there was this intellectual property [IP] thing in 1995,* and we did really well. In 1991, we were working very closely with the laboratories of the Council of Scientific and Industrial Research.

My friend at the National Chemical Laboratory was a gentleman called Dr Rama Rao; he assisted us with the development of many raw materials. He is still very active today, even at the age of seventy-eight, and I am still in touch with him. One day in 1991, Rama Rao came to me and said, 'Yusuf, I've developed a synthesis for AZT, zidovudine, and the government has allowed me to collect the starting material to make it, beta thymidine, which can be imported without duty in India. And this drug is for AIDS.'

---

* The Agreement on Trade-Related Aspects of Intellectual Property Rights (TRIPS Agreement), the first and most comprehensive multilateral agreement on intellectual property, became effective in 1995. Certain intellectual property rights became enforceable in all participating World Trade Organization countries.

Interviewer: Now how widely known was the AIDS epidemic?

YH: At that time, 1991, it was zero.

TK: But Rama Rao was on top of it?

YH: Rama Rao had come to me with that. So he and I went to the Indian Council of Medical Research [ICMR] to meet Dr S. P. Tripathi [the ICMR director-general from 1991 to 1994]. He said to us, 'Yes, India requires AZT, and Dr Hamied you are the only person we can look to, who has the capability of making it.'

Interviewer: What about the rest of the industry?

YH: They were all coming up.

Interviewer: But they couldn't have made that?

YH: It's not a question of making it; it's a question of who has the idea to do it? If Rama Rao wouldn't have come to me with this in 1991, I might not have taken it up. To cut a long story short, we took it up. In 1993, commercially we could make AZT. We put it on the market in the form of 100 mg capsules at the price of $2 [Rs 63] a day. The international price at that time was $12 [Rs 376] a day. Now $2 [Rs 63] a day at that time meant, I think, Rs 60 a day. So in a month, it meant Rs 1800. Nobody could afford it. So for the first six months, the sales were zero. I went back to Dr Tripathi at ICMR. I said, 'Doctor, I am sitting on 2,00,000 capsules of AZT, unsold, what should I do? Why doesn't the government buy and distribute it as they think best?' He replied, 'Dr Hamied, we have no money for treatment. We only have money to detect and prevent.' So in 1993, we shut down the manufacturing of AZT and got out of the AIDS drug business. But as a scientist or whatever you may call it, I kept abreast of what was going on in the area of AIDS, reading medical journals and various scientific publications. In 1996–97, I came across an article in one of the medical journals called HAART, and this article said that a combination of three drugs controlled HIV.

This was the cocktail. So my enthusiasm got revived and we went into it again. By the year 2000, we could get all the three ingredients for the cocktail. The timing was crucial because in the year 2000, almost 8000 people were dying per day in Africa. The treatment cost was $12,000 [Rs 5.5 lakh] per patient per year, the reason being that the three ingredients were all made by different companies. The daily dosage ran from twelve to fifteen tablets per day.

Interviewer: So compliance was poor?

YH: Yes, compliance was poor. In the year 2000, in July, the first HIV conference was held in Durban, and you will see a lot of this in the movie directed by Jamie Love, *Fire in the Blood*, the true story of HIV/AIDS, of what actually happened in the year 2000. At that conference in Durban, July 2000, our friend, Justice Edwin Cameron, he was the chief justice in South Africa; he stood up and said, 'I am alive [because he was HIV positive]. I am alive today because I can afford $400 [Rs 18,000] a month.' We had a meeting in London, some activists and myself on 12 August 2000, to discuss what can be done about HIV treatment. To cut a long story short, I was invited to speak at the European Union on 28 September 2000. I was given only three minutes to say what I had to say. At that meeting, there were 200 people. There were thirty health ministers from Africa. There were five prime ministers of various countries at this meeting. It was a closed-door meeting. The multinationals objected to an Indian being asked to speak at the European Union . . . This is the European Union . . . why should a non-European speak?

The head of the European Union turned around and told them that 'look, HIV/AIDS is not a European disease only'. Therefore, I was invited to speak. I said three things: one, we are making a cocktail of drugs, and we will give it at $800 [Rs 36,500 in 2000] per patient per year, as opposed to $12,000 [Rs 5.5 lakh] per year; two, Cipla will give technical know-how to any government of a developing country that wishes to produce its own HIV drugs; and three, we will give the drug that stops the transmission of HIV from mother to child totally free.

Interviewer: That's a different drug?

YH: One of those three, if the mother takes a dose at the time of labour, and the child takes a dose within seventy-two hours of birth, lo and behold, the child by and large is HIV free. This was on 28 September 2000. I was so disappointed, there were no takers and nobody wrote to us. It's a mystery to me. And then what happened, I was still in touch with some of the people who had come for my original meeting in August 2000, and one of them was a gentleman called Jamie Love. Jamie Love still runs an NGO in Washington, and he wrote to us in February 2001, the exact date I know, 6 February 2001, 'Doctor, can you somehow give the cocktail at a dollar [Rs 48]

a day?' So we did our homework in Cipla on 6 February 2001.
I remember the date distinctly and it was very difficult to do at
that time.

*Interviewer: Now at $800 [Rs 38,000 in 2001] a year you were
breaking even?*

YH: Yes. Fine. But not at $300 [Rs 14,000]. So we said we are
making so many drugs if we lose on one or two drugs, what
difference does it make? It's a cause; it was a humanitarian
approach. But we said that instead of giving it freely, we will
give it selectively. Therefore, we then approached Médecins Sans
Frontières [MSF or Doctors Without Borders]. At that time, in
2001, they were the biggest and the best NGO for HIV/AIDS;
they would receive the Nobel Prize a few years later.

On 6 February 2001, we wrote a fax or a telex or whatever,
there was no email at that time. We wrote to MSF and offered
them the cocktail drugs, two tablets a day, morning and night,
at $350 [Rs 17,000]. On 6 February, that night, I was at a
dinner party in Bombay. We had sent them a fax but there was
no response to it. Then at 12 o'clock in the night my mobile
phone rings:

'Donald McNeil here.'
'Yes, Donald. What can I do for you?'
Now Donald McNeil, a reporter from the *New York Times*,
had been to India in December 2000. And then he had written
a feature article in December 2000; he had interviewed me,
so I knew him.
'Doctor, can I speak to you?'
'Yes, Donald what can I do for you?'

It was late at night.

'Have you offered the AIDS cocktail to MSF at $350?'

I said, 'Yes, I have.'

'Can I ask you a few questions?'

I said, 'Donald, I know you so well, go ahead.'

So he asked me a few questions. And then he said, 'Dr Hamied, your life will not be the same after tomorrow.'

I laughed and I put the phone down, and subsequently I met him quite often. I meet him every time I am in New York, and I remind him of that. I say, 'Donald, you've changed my life and I don't know whether it's been for the good or the bad.'

So on the front page of the *New York Times*, 7 February 2001, was this: 'Indian Company Offers AIDS Cocktail at a Dollar a Day'. And lo and behold, my life has not been the same since then. That's all I can say.

That offer was taken up. Subsequently, today [2013] the drug costs below $100 [Rs 6000] a year. The drug that we gave at $350 [Rs 17,000] is not used any more but similar types of cocktails are being sold today at $60 [Rs 3600] per patient per year.

Interviewer: That's because the science has developed?

YH: Science has developed. New combinations have come up, etc.

Interviewer: And the processes have improved?

YH: The processes have improved. India today produces, in finished form, 92 per cent, in volume, of all the HIV drugs in

the world. In value, this is equal to $1 billion [Rs 6000 crore].
The remaining 8 per cent is equal to $16 billion [Rs 96,000
crore] in value. So that's been a big change. In fact, the world's
number one AIDS drug today, by an American company, is
called Atripla. In America, the price is $24,000 [Rs 14.5 lakh]
per patient per year. You know at what price I am giving it to
Africa? At $96 [Rs 5800] per patient per year. Now where is
$96 [Rs 5800], my dear friend, and where is $24,000 [Rs 14.5
lakh]?

*Interviewer: Now just to go back to your position on intellectual
property which is a foundation of much of this. Our position is
that even $96 [Rs 5800] is a fair thing to do because it more than
compensates the makers of this wonder drug for whatever effort they
or the society has put into making it? Is that what you are saying?*

YH: If you look at the cocktail by Gilead, it has been sold today
for $24,000 [Rs 14.5 lakh], and I am not discrediting them. It
contains three components. The first is tenofovir. Tenofovir
was originally invented in 1992. They got it patented post-
1995. We took them to court in India, and we won our case.
The tenofovir patent was not granted in India. The second
ingredient, emtricitabine, pre-1995*, and the third ingredient
efavirenz, pre-1995, was also not patented in India. So the
three ingredients were not patented in India. Hence, whatever
I am doing in India is totally legal.

In spite of the fact that I mentioned the ten-year transition
period, all the three ingredients are pre-1995. Now what is

---

* After the TRIPS Agreement was ratified, the patents for these ingredients
became enforced in all participating World Trade Countries, including India.

likely to happen is that, as resistance to drugs goes on, some of the newer anti-AIDS drugs, the major ones that are being developed and may revolutionize the HIV treatment in 2014–15, I won't be able to market them.

Interviewer: Because they are now under patent in India?

YH: Because they are under patent in India. Before 2005, under the rules of the 1970 patent Act, I could have marketed these products cheaply. However, after 2005 India committed to following global IP rules. So essentially for the newer products, we have to go with a begging bowl to the multinationals. In India's interest, where I feel that they have a very good case, I go to them with a begging bowl. Where I feel that we can challenge some of the patents, we have challenged them, like what you saw in the case where Cipla was fighting against Novartis [The dispute centred on whether Novartis' patents should be respected in India, with Novartis losing the case all the way to the Supreme Court]. We've challenged them where I've felt that scientifically we are on the right path.

Interviewer: So, MSF took up your offer; it has had a massive effect on the world. Can you comment on other parts of the pharmaceutical industry in the developing world?

YH: See, the countries that took an interest in HIV, which India did not by the way, were Thailand and Brazil. I think these were the two major countries that had realized the impact that HIV could have on their countries. India went very slowly. Much later on, India started the National AIDS Control

Organization [NACO] and National AIDS Research Institute [NARI] in 1992.

Even today I don't think in India it's on a proper footing, this distribution of AIDS drugs and all. I personally have a gut feeling that the figures that have been thrown about from India are totally incorrect. I would suggest you ask Ashok Alexander [director of the India office of the Bill & Melinda Gates Foundation from 2003 to 2012] as to what in his opinion are the correct figures because they've done the surveys. The figures thrown about by the Indian government are underestimated. The reason for that may be that the stigma surrounding HIV is so high in this country that people don't get tested. Particularly workers in hospitals, etc., are not getting tested.

Interviewer: So let us go to Thailand and these countries. What happened in these countries? Were the governments just more receptive?

YH: The governments were receptive. The governments have promoted local manufacturing in Brazil and Thailand. Local manufacturing means those who produce the active ingredients. That to me has been the backbone of industry, and in particular the HIV drugs have not been easy to make. And to make them economical is a big task. I must say between India and China . . . they have been able to overcome this major hurdle.

Interviewer: Has Cipla played a role in disseminating some of the know-how?

YH: I think indirectly we have done it all. When people leave you and join other companies, they are likely to take up the same product.

Interviewer: So can we talk about the incident of stockpiling the antiviral?

YH: I will talk to you about that, but this is what has happened in the area of HIV. After 9/11 the next incident that took place was the anthrax scare. Just to give you the story of what happened with anthrax, we were approached again I think by Donald McNeil, on ciprofloxacin. We make cipro, which was approved in America; he asked me, if the American government wanted to, in an emergency, could we supply them ciprofloxacin? I said Cipla will be happy to supply it, and we will give you a 500 mg tablet for ten cents a tablet. At that time do you know the price of the drug supplied by Bayer [the pharma giant] in America? The wholesale price was $5 [Rs 303] a tablet.

Interviewer: $5 [Rs 303] versus 10 cents [Rs 6]?

YH: $5 [Rs 303] versus 10 cents [Rs 6] . . . the American government . . . they could have announced a compulsory licence, they could have if they wanted to. But what they did, they took our quote and bargained with Bayer, and they brought down the Bayer price to 75 cents [Rs 45] a tablet.

Guess how many tablets they bought. Would you like to know? 1.5 billion [150 crore] tablets. I would like to know from your friends in the government, as to what happened to those tablets? Where are they lying? They've all expired now. So where are those tablets? Probably at the bottom of the Pacific! But they did buy 1.5 billion [150 crore] tablets and paid $1 billion [Rs 100 crore] to Bayer. So that was with anthrax.

Then I will tell you a very interesting story of what happened with bird flu and swine flu. . . . I forget the date of the bird flu or swine flu. In 2005, I remember sitting in my office with a good friend of mine, who later became the head of the equivalent of the FDA in India [the Central Drugs Standard Control Organisation or CDSCO]. His name was Dr Mamidanna Venkateswarlu.

I asked him, 'Dr Venkateswarlu, tell me, if bird flu breaks out in India, what will the Indian government do?' He smiled at me and said to my face, 'We would surrender.' So I looked at him and said, 'Dr Venkateswarlu, from this moment you surrender and I will take up the challenge.' In front of him I picked up the phone, rang up my R & D boys. It was 11 o'clock in the morning, 'Get whatever literature you can on the drug oseltamivir and come and see me in the afternoon.'

At that time in the press, and scientifically, Roche had announced that making oseltamivir was a twenty-step process. Two of those steps were extremely hazardous. And the cycle to make those twenty steps took two years.

Interviewer: So the idea was that nobody would look into it since it was so complicated?

YH: Yes. That afternoon, we looked into the synthesis of oseltamivir, and it was, and still is, extremely difficult. The starting material is a plant product, which is the star aniseed. It is called star anise. And it contains a chemical called shikimic acid. Shikimic acid is then transformed into oseltamivir phosphate in twenty steps.

We couldn't do it on our own. So we involved our partners in China because shikimic acid is native to China. Roche had cornered all the shikimic acid that was available in China. But to cut a long story short, what we have achieved today was with our Chinese partners. We couldn't have done it on our own. They shrunk the shikimic acid process to eight or nine steps, and we cut it down to twelve steps with no hazardous steps.

Interviewer: So there is some original science in this?

YH: A little. What I call incremental innovation.

Interviewer: But twenty steps to twelve steps?

YH: Yes, incremental innovation. We Indians are very good at incremental innovation. Anyway, to cut a long story short, in October 2005, we were ready with it. That's when Donald McNeil wrote an article on us, on oseltamivir.

What was the impact in India? The day we got permission to market oseltamivir in India, the Indian government passed a law that we could not sell it in chemist shops. They said it will be misused. People will stockpile. It is meant for bird flu. I said it is not meant for bird flu. Here is an antiviral which is for seasonal flu. Winter comes and you get seasonal flu. Hospitals need it for seasonal flu.

Sorry, only the government will buy it if they want. I said the government doesn't buy. You know as of today, and this gospel truth, they blocked us in 2005 from selling oseltamivir in India. As of today, in 2013, and I was in the factory two days ago in Pune where it was made, we have Rs 67 crore [Rs 1 crore equals Rs 10 million] worth of raw materials, at various stages, in stock. No customers, totally dead situation. They blocked us from marketing this drug from 2005.

Interviewer: So why do you have these stockpiles?

YH: It has been stockpiled for the last five to seven years. If there is an emergency tomorrow and the government wants it, what are they going to do? From where are they going to get it? At least, when all is said and done, with my stockpile, within a month or two, I could give them huge quantities.

Interviewer: Are you doing this consciously?

YH: No, this is the result of the government bringing in this law, and in spite of all efforts, believe me, they are not changing it. Now is it pressure from Roche or not? I really don't want to comment on that. And I don't want to comment against the government. We have to live with them.

So it is very difficult. I do not want to comment on price control. If I tell you that story, it's a horror story of what we went through on price control. And we are now in the Supreme Court against the government.

Interviewer: So oseltamivir is available to others outside?

YH: I can export it. Our product and our formulation, by the way, are World Health Organization-approved. But which country buys it? Nobody. Who is interested in this?

Interviewer: Well, the next time there is bird flu?

YH: Yes, but in the meantime what do you do? What I mean to say, it is an antiviral drug; we introduced a second antiviral drug, which is not oseltamivir, which was zanamivir. Now zanamivir is given in a capsule to inhale. It's an inhaled product. GlaxoSmithKline [GSK] also has a product and their product is called Relenza. Our product is marketed under the brand name Virenza. And suddenly one fine day the government put zanamivir in the same category as oseltamivir. Both the drugs cannot be sold in chemist shops in India.

Interviewer: But the GSK drug is sold?

YH: Even Roche's Tamiflu is not allowed to be sold. But if you go to hospitals, you will find it there. God knows what is happening. This ban should be removed, and if not, it is very sad.

This is where I . . . see other governments of the world supporting their indigenous industry. I see how they are trying to promote their own industry in their country. And here, unfortunately, I find that the indigenous industry is not being supported.

Interviewer: My understanding is, and I could be wrong, some of the other Indian companies have at least made public statements saying that they intend to do more than the usual incremental innovation; they will try to develop the capability to do original molecule research. Is that different?

YH: In the pharmaceutical industry there are two types of R & D. There is concept R & D, and there is 'me-too' R & D. By concept R & D what do I mean? The first beta blocker, propranolol; the first tranquillizer, diazepam, the first fluoroquinolone, these are concept R & D. Towards concept research in America, the American government put in $31 billion last year [Rs 1,65,000 crore in 2012], $31 billion towards concept R & D—which is substantial. A company like Pfizer spends $8 billion [Rs 42,600 crore] a year on the so-called R & D, less than 10 per cent is on concept by the way. The rest is 'me-too'.

Interviewer: So they are, in effect, free riding on the American government's R & D?

YH: Absolutely. For example, the first betablocker, propranolol, was invented under concept R & D, whereas the subsequent betablockers belonging to the same family are essentially 'me-too' drugs.

Similarly, norfloxacin and levofloxacin are similar molecules under the same class of antibiotics. To me, that is all 'me-too' research. Dr Reddy's Laboratories claimed that they were doing new work on glitazones, but that again belongs to a family class of drugs. They call it concept, but to me it is only 'me-too' R & D.

Learnings from Yusuf Hamied: Innovation, even proceeding from the deepest understanding of science, typically requires deep understanding of the sociopolitical milieu within which its effects will ensue, so as to nudge the context in a way that predisposes itself to a salubrious outcome.

3(d)

Nandan Nilekani

Namas Bhojani/Nandan Nilekani

Nandan Nilekani is the co-founder of Infosys, a leading IT services company. He was also chairperson of the Unique Identification Authority of India (UIDAI), where he worked on Aadhaar, the twelve-digit unique identity number issued to all residents of India. Launched in 2009, Aadhaar is currently the largest biometric ID system in the world. Following his time at UIDAI, he co-founded and became the chairperson of EkStep, a non-profit literacy and numeracy programme. In 2017, he returned to Infosys as its non-executive chairperson. Among many recognitions, in 2006 he received the Padma Bhushan and was named 'Businessman of the Year' by *Forbes Asia*. In 2009, he was listed as one of 100 most influential people in the world by *Time* magazine.

Interviewed by Tarun Khanna in Cambridge, Massachusetts, on 25 September 2017.

Interviewer: *Can you tell us about the programming interface—or ecosystem—the government established for Aadhaar?*

Nandan Nilekani (NN): Everything in this system is built as application programming interfaces [APIs], which means people can build applications on top of this. Initially, the applications have been in the government sector like direct cash transfers and so on or right now there is an attendance system that has been implemented. It's a hybrid model because if you look at digital ecosystems, there are a class of digital ecosystems that come from the government and there are a class of digital ecosystems built by companies and they have different attributes. If you think of the two most common or most powerful government-built ecosystems—one is the Internet and the other is GPS. Now in both these cases, what they have become today is very far from what they were conceived as. The Internet was essentially a defence-funded project in the US.

The first technology of the Internet, the Transmission Control Protocol/Internet Protocol [TCP/IP] protocol, was built forty years ago and funded by the Defense Advanced Research Projects Agency [DARPA], the defence agency of the US, essentially for dissimilar computers to communicate with each other and that was the original goal, to develop communication, and that is how it was developed forty years ago. The next big thing in the government ecosystem was funded by European governments in CERN [European Organization for Nuclear Research], where Tim Berners-Lee came up with the idea of the World Wide Web and the http protocol . . . he wanted an easy way for researchers to go from one website to another site. The third big development of the Internet was once again government-funded at the University of Illinois, where the first browser was built, Mosaic. The idea again was to have a simple graphic user interface for the web and then private sector usage. So all your Googles and Facebooks started after all these fundamental investments happened. But it took forty years for the Internet to go from the first message sent to what we have today. So when you have a government ecosystem, it was not planned from day one to be that ecosystem. It was not decided forty years back that we will have some app here. So I think a government-funded system takes time to evolve because different people at different points of time in history make decisions that ultimately lead to an ecosystem flourishing.

Interviewer: What is the difference between an ecosystem developed by government versus a private company? Do the time frames differ?

NN: When you think of private ecosystems done by companies, they happen much faster. Because private companies with especially a stable management can have a clear idea of what they are doing. And do that very quickly. If you look at Apple, it was barely 2001 when Steve Jobs talked about the digital lifestyle, and if you go back to his speech which he gave at MacWorld in January 2001, he talked about a future where it was going to be a digital lifestyle where you used a camera on your personal computer [PC] and so forth, and in some sense in that speech you had elements of the iPod, which came two years later, you had the iPhone, which came in 2007, you had the iPad—so he had a vision of what that digital lifestyle would look like and he had ten to twelve years to roll that out. So similarly if you look at Facebook and the goal to connect everybody, they were about to connect 100 crore users in ten years. So private companies can focus on something and they can come out with a vision. They can actually stick to the vision very well. So you have a government ecosystem that takes a long time because you know . . . several events happen, and you can have private systems that build quickly.

What we were trying to do was build a hybrid of this— build a government ecosystem but build it in such a way that was premeditated so that in a very short time we were able to actually create scale in the operation, so that makes it a little more complex to do and there were a few principles that we had. The first was that it should be too big to reverse. So, the basic principle is that when you are operating in a political system, the window that you have for driving change is at best five years. Could be more if the same government continues, but you have to assume that things will change. So you have a window of five years to accomplish something and therefore you have to be quick and scale up so quickly that it reaches a size which makes it essentially sustainable. That is why from day one our goal was to have 60 crore people on a system, you know 60 crore is a lot of people on the system so you cannot change that.

The second principle in this whole thing is make sure it's embedded in as many applications as possible. So the moment you embed it in applications like cash transfers or subsidiary reform or whatever, it automatically gets more in the system. These were some of the principles that we had, which were to create a scale that was essentially irrefutable. We were very fortunate that even though we had a change of government, the new government really adopted Aadhaar in a big way and they are accelerating the usage for cash transfers, for subsidy reform, for attendance systems—they are going to go to a billion users by next year.

I think it goes to show that when you try to build a digital ecosystem in the public world, if you can bring the speed of what is possible in the private world and do it in the public world, the effect you get is a lot of strategic value. And I am very confident that this is actually the basis for a large number of reforms that will happen in India.

Learnings from Nandan Nilekani: Public scientific goods created for one ostensible purpose often have far-reaching applications in unanticipated arenas. Further, innovative methods originating in the private sector can be applied to public sector organizations as well, and often at dramatically greater scale.

3(e)

Syed Babar Ali

Syed Babar Ali is a Pakistani businessman and philanthropist. During the 1950s, he created Packages Limited with the assistance of Swedish industrialist Hans Rausing of the Tetra Pak company. In 1976, Ali and Rausing diversified into milk processing and created Milk Pak. Nestlé, which had entered Pakistan in 1988 in a joint venture with Milk Pak, took over its management in 1992 and it became a publicly quoted company in Pakistan. In 1984, Ali founded the Lahore University of Management Sciences (LUMS), one of Pakistan's leading educational institutions.

Interviewed by Tarun Khanna in Cambridge, Massachusetts, on 4 May 2016.

Interviewer: You have emphasized the role of multinationals as a source both of professionalism, the idea of meritocracy, and of course technology and so on. Can you reflect on your relationship with the Rausing family and the push to introduce Tetra Pak in Pakistan?

Syed Babar Ali (SBA): Our relationship with the Rausing family, the owners of Tetra Pak, was good, and they were very keen that Tetra Pak should be introduced in Pakistan. And I sort of kept arguing with them that milk was the kind of business that no industrialist in Pakistan would be interested in. I knew the merit of milk and its packaging. But Hans Rausing said, 'Why don't you sell this idea to the other industrialists.' And I went around, and they even sent one of their marketing managers who was stationed in our office for two years, and he went around knocking on people's doors and telling them about the opportunity there was for processing milk and putting it in containers, and the UHT process—the ultra-heat treatment process where you could stretch the life of milk in a Tetra Pak container for many weeks. Nobody was interested in it.

Interviewer: And this is important because there was no cold supply chain at the time.

SBA: Even today, the cold supply chain is non-existent in Pakistan. So I kept arguing with Hans Rausing. He at that time was the president of the company. And he said, 'For ten years, you're not doing anything for Tetra Pak.' And I said, 'The only way is to put up a plant ourselves and to demonstrate to people that it can be done.' So he finally agreed, and he said, 'I can't do a thing that will compete with my customers.' And I said, 'You'll have to open the first plant yourself. I can't do it on my own. You'll have to provide me with the know-how and the resources.' So we put up the first plant. And because Packages Limited had a good track record, it was a success.

Interviewer: So this is a plant to process milk?

SBA: Yes, it is a plant to process milk. First, to collect milk, process it, and sell it. So it had its own teething troubles, which you had to learn about, regarding the collection of milk, because I didn't realize that milk was a very fragile commodity. As soon as it leaves the udder, it starts deteriorating. So you've got to put it in a cold chiller right from the beginning and bring it to the plant in insulated tankers to process it. Then of course, the challenge was to sell it to people who wouldn't believe that without chemicals you could maintain the quality. So it took me ten years, really, to learn about this business and to make it a success. Nestlé was looking at Pakistan, and they had no industrial experience there. They were exporting goods out of their factories to Pakistan. And they carried out a survey. And they came to me and they said, 'We want to put up a plant in Pakistan, the kind of work that you are doing. And we have two choices, either to put up a greenfield plant, or would you consider taking us as a partner.' And in ten years I had found out that there was no money in just processing milk. You had to have value-added products, you had to have a brand. So I said, 'I'm looking for a partner.' And so they came on board.

Interviewer: What happened to Hans Rausing?

SBA: Hans Rausing was very happy to sell his shares to Nestlé. And so he went and I got those shares transferred to them. So Nestlé and I became partners.

Interviewer: It's a wonderful story. It's a wonderful catalytic role, where your relationship with the Rausing family induced them to seed the market, in effect, and then, when the time was right, you asset-swapped with the different technology, which is the Nestlé know-how.

SBA: And Nestlé came in, and this was a wonderful opportunity for Nestlé and for us, and I didn't bargain with them at all, because I wanted them. It was a publicly quoted company, and they said, 'What is the price of the share?' I said, 'What is on the stock exchange today?' It was [PKR] Rs 27 [Rs 33 in 1992]. And the share, last year [in 2015], was [PKR] Rs 10,000 [Rs 6372]. So we didn't do too badly.

What Nestlé did was to bring in their total know-how and invest a lot of money in the company, but more so technology and their skill and know-how in collecting milk from the farmers. Today, they collect almost 20 lakh litres of milk from 2,00,000 farmers every day, over an area as large as Switzerland. So they brought in the cold supply chain for collection of milk, and then, of course, the processing of value-added products, baby food and other things.

Learnings from Syed Babar Ali: To innovate based on relevant technology produced in the developed world, judicious selection of partners is needed, each suited to particular lifestyle stages of an enterprise. That, in turn, is predicated on foundational relationships that take the very long view.

3(f)

Mo Ibrahim

Mo Ibrahim is a Sudanese-born businessman and corporate philanthropist. In 1998, he founded Celtel, a pan-African telecommunications company, which was acquired by and became a subsidiary of Zain Group (formerly the Mobile Telecommunications Company) in 2005. After selling Celtel, Ibrahim established the Mo Ibrahim Foundation to encourage better governance on the African continent. The foundation is famous for the Ibrahim Index of African Governance, a governance index that measures, through ninety indicators in over fourteen subcategories, the overall governance performance of African countries.

Interviewed by Tarun Khanna in London, Britain, on 15 September 2017.

Interviewer: How difficult was it to build a mobile network in Africa?

Mo Ibrahim (MI): Building a mobile network in Africa was really tough. By that time, we had built so many mobile networks almost everywhere. Typically, all you needed to do was to overlay the mobility part of the network over the fixed network, because the incumbent—the telephone company operator—would have already brought all the wires, the microwaves, the cables—it would usually be theirs. Typically, you would just put some switches and some radio stations, and you would connect using the infrastructure of the incumbent, the telephone company operating.

In Africa, there was nothing like that. There was no infrastructure. Telephone companies in Africa have had a difficult time. They existed for so many years, but they could not really invest for the simple reason that their main customers were government departments, and those guys never paid their bills.

There was a telecom department that reported to the minister of transport, telecom, postal, and roads, and whatever. So it was a small department. The director of that department did not dare cut off the minister of defence or the foreign ministry. You would not just cut off your customers if they didn't pay. So this telecom company was really bankrupt. They appeared to have great leverage, but they all had bad debts—bad debts that could not be settled, actually. So there was no money to invest. If you made a profit, you had to hand your profit over to the treasury. And then, the finance minister would decide whether to give you some money or not. So there was no investment, really. The total number of fixed lines in a continent of 100 crore people was no more than 30 lakh. Most of them were in South Africa, Egypt and Morocco. Sub-Saharan Africa? Nothing. The Democratic Republic of the Congo [DRC], with 6 crore people, had 3000 lines—most of them not working, actually. So that was the situation. The continent was hungry for connection.

When you look at the equity in a mobile call, you always look at the value of a mobile call—a mobile phone. If I'm here in London right now, what is the value of a mobile call? I have so many alternatives if I want to communicate. Let's not even talk about the Internet, because at that time we did not have Internet. But we had fixed lines. We had quite a high penetration of fixed lines, so that was one option. We have the tube, we have the underground, we have taxis we can take. We have a postal service that guarantees you delivery in twenty-four hours. We have all these sort of things. You don't have that in Africa. You don't have that. If you want to call or communicate with somebody who is just 32 km away from you, that can take a whole day—a physical trip. So the equity in a phone call in a place so wide—Africa's a huge space—is really immense. So that was the situation when we went to Africa.

Interviewer: When you talk about the equity value of a call, it's probably determined by two things: one is, what's the value to the person initiating the call and receiving it—which is very high because they have no alternatives—and the second is, how much can they pay for it? The paying capacity is low on average, I assume.

MI: That was, of course, one of the issues we were looking into. To our surprise, we discovered that the equity of the call was so overwhelming that people had to make a decision at the end of the day—shall I buy a beer or shall I buy a scratch card?

What shall I buy? We ended up winning most of these deliberations, but our friends in the beverage industry would say, 'You guys are hurting us'. So that was a challenge. Then, from the outset, I thought the main challenge would be putting in place the infrastructure, because we had to put in the infrastructure. That's why the job was harder—I had to lay cable, I had to use microwave, I had to produce the backbone of connectivity in order to do it. But added to that were some other problems—take power, for example. We take power for granted, because in our experience, power comes from a small socket somewhere in the room and we just plug into it. It's everywhere. Power is around us. Unfortunately, in Africa, we don't have that. Power is not there in most of the geographical areas we work in and when it is there, it is not reliable. So this means you have to use generators everywhere, and, of course, backup batteries. Now, if you provide the country's coverage, this means you have to have an army of people who are visiting all these remote locations every day to bring diesel for the generators and to check the batteries. Doing this is a massive operation, but you have to do it. It is something we didn't have to do in Europe. So that was a real challenge, especially because of the difficulties with roads. When you have to go to a mountain, sometimes you have to use helicopters to lift the equipment, or you have to use mules to carry things. So it was hard work to put the infrastructure in place and keep it operational. The main challenge, and it was a most difficult one, was the financing. Banks at that time did not want to do anything in Africa, all these great banks. It was such an unbelievable situation. I don't know of any other telephone company in the world that had to be funded completely by equity. Typically, with most of these companies, you have 50 per cent debt of your capital. We had to fund it by raising capital. In seven years [the lifespan of the company], we had nine rounds of financing. We had to fund it by equity. There was no other way, no debt. Banks didn't want to touch us.

Interviewer: And even the governments wouldn't step in over time, as the networks became viable?

MI: No. The government was looking for more revenue, so actually they tapped us for more taxes. We were happy to pay taxes. Actually, we loved being the largest taxpayer in about ten countries. If I'm paying tax, it means I'm making a profit. So I'm happy, there's no issue there. But whenever there's a problem, they come and say, 'oh, let us invent a new tax'. In one country they use something—they call it an air tax. It's using the air. I said, 'I use air, you use air, you breathe, as well. Why are you charging me for the air?' But we understood. The business was so profitable anyway; it was not a major issue for us.

I'll tell you the story. The company, at that stage of development, I think our revenue was about $1 billion [Rs 4,200 crore]. We were making a profit of around $300 million [Rs 1,260 crore] a year—profit—after tax. So we were in a really good position. The problem for us was we, at that stage, were growing around 50–60 per cent per year. This requires a huge investment, and this job of financing is really tough—very distracting for the management. My chief financial officer [CFO] had no other job other than to raise money. He had no time to do any other thing. Really. So we started to talk about our next phase. At that time, we had fourteen operations. All of these operations, of course, were independent companies that we owned—if not 100 per cent, at least 80–90 per cent of the operations. We had the diversity—the diverse operations—so it was very secure. I just couldn't understand how the banks were looking at it. It wasn't like there was civil disorder in this country, and then, if something were to go wrong here, I had fourteen operations . . .

Interviewer: It was a safe bet.

MI: A very safe bet. Operations were all profitable. Our only problem was cash flow, because we were growing, growing so fast. I thought growth was a wonderful thing, and I needed really to keep building. But banks would not deal with us. The same banks, which were piling on real estate in the US and doing all kinds of stupid stuff elsewhere, they would not invest in an African company with such amazing financials. We just couldn't understand. Then we decided to list the company. We said, 'By listing the company in UK, we can move quickly to join the Fortune 100, where we can easily access funds.'

Interviewer: There was no real option for an African listing in Johannesburg or elsewhere?

MI: We thought London would be a better listing. I also wanted to bring the story of investing in sub-Saharan Africa to the outside world. To say, 'Look, guys, Africa is not a basket case. Here is a company we started six–seven years ago, and we're listing it now, as one of the Fortune 100 companies.' That would have been a great story for sub-Saharan Africa. So we started the process. The board-appointed deputy chair at that time was Lord Simon Cairns, who was head of CDC Group [formerly the Commonwealth Development Corporation] before he joined our board to manage this process. We hired Goldman Sachs and Citibank to help handle it. Banks were not familiar with Africa, so it was difficult. Those guys came in and said, 'Oh, how interesting. We'll see, you know, what the company's worth, how it works, etc.' And then, in the first meeting they said, 'We think we can float it with $24 [Rs 1063] per share'—around that number was what they said. But they needed to go look at the company to see what was going on, so we said, 'Fine, you can go around'. Then they started their due diligence and when they came back from their first trip, they raised the target price to $30 [Rs 1328] per share. Another trip, the share price went up to $34 [Rs 1505] and finally $45 [Rs 1992]. Meanwhile, as we were going through this process, we started to receive unsolicited offers. We received six unsolicited offers and the board formed another committee to manage that process and the final price came out at $56 [Rs 2479 in 2005].

Interviewer: Much higher than the proposed listing price?

MI: Now here is the problem. Besides the development financial institutions, at that time we had three or four private investors come in. Suddenly, those guys found that they're making a hell of a lot of money. Our share price was $2 [Rs 84] when we started seven years earlier [1998]. It kept moving up. After six years [2004], the last round of finance, the share price was $15

[Rs 674]. Now, six months later [2005], somebody's offering us $56 [Rs 2479] for that share.

So suddenly we had this pressure from the shareholders who said, 'Wow, somebody paid $15 [Rs 674], and six months later [in 2005] is getting four times their money.' So the discussion around whether to sell or list became a little bit complicated. My personal preference really was to list. But as always, I referred to the board—I was the largest shareholder in the company by far, but I never exercised a veto in the company. I had only one seat on the board, although legally I should have seven seats or so. I had only one seat, and we had thirteen board directors, because I really needed the advice and support of the board. Some people might say, 'I can run the company myself. Why do you need a board then?' But I don't agree with this, so I tried to empower the board, to help them feel their responsibility. I got decent people anyway, so what's the problem?

So I said, 'I'm going to abstain from the whole discussion. I'm grateful for the people who funded the company and who guided the company. Well, the company's fine, you guys do what you like.' Clearly, people preferred to take the offer. Although I offered that if we list I was not going to sell any shares. So all my allocations of the secondaries, I passed on to my shareholders, just to help. But that still would not have been enough. So that's how the decision was taken to sell the company.

Interviewer: As you look back, a lot of time has passed. The company's been through Zain and now, Sunil Mittal's company bought it. What is your reflection on how mobile telephony has shaped up?

MI: Of course, I always feel that we sold a bit too early. The same company was sold three or four years later for nine billion. Anyway, so what? C'est la vie. It's a good story. Our people also did very well, which was great. We created over 150 millionaires in the company, which was nice. For me, it is a slightly different picture now. Mobile phones became very popular, and investment in companies in Africa started to flow, because before everybody thought they had lied about the amount of money you made there. So banks are all over themselves, now, to fund things like this.

Learnings from Mo Ibrahim: The value of an innovation is often dramatically a function of the context. The latter should be thought of in an encompassing and holistic sense, including the physical ambience but also considering its social and cultural dimensions. The same contextual understanding can clarify what other soft and hard infrastructural investments are needed for an enterprise to come to fruition.

4

Contesting Corruption

When we teach courses on emerging markets, a common way to start a class is to ask students— those in our Harvard MBA or various executive education programmes—what images can they conjure up about a particular developing country in question? Invariably, corruption is right up there on the list of realities to deal with, as a constraint to development. Transparency International's Corruption Perception Index ranked India in 2020 at a dismal eighty-six out of 180 countries. While it's true that, by this reckoning, India is a lot less corrupt than its neighbours Bangladesh and Pakistan, it's hardly anything to celebrate. There has also been only marginal aggregate improvement in the past decade, the efforts of the stalwarts profiled here notwithstanding.

So, let's start with a workmanlike definition of corruption. To be corrupt is generally to take actions for private gain that are against public interest. Of course, public interest is determined by rules, regulations and laws, codified over time as societies coalesce on ways in which constituents agree to manage their affairs. That's why our conversation with Jaithirth 'Jerry' Rao, entrepreneur, and a sometime poet and member of the literati, is a great place to start this chapter.

Rao tells us that the origins of corruption in India lie in the palimpsest of rules and regulations. For decades, indeed for over a century, many modifications of rules have left prior rules untouched. This means that one is always in danger of violating multiple laws. What he does not quite say, but is useful as background, is that it's often difficult to even know these various rules, not just as an outsider, but even as a resident of India. That in turn leads to unscrupulous agents effectively holding one to ransom or suggesting facilitating payments to find ways through this regulatory morass.

We are reminded of Nobel Prize-winning author Sir V.S. Naipaul's evocative book published in 1990, which suggested that India is a land of a million mutinies. Paraphrasing that writer, perhaps entrepreneurs seeking to stick to the straight and narrow are subject to a million vetoes.

Further, unilateral action can't resolve this problem, says Rao, since there are so many others in the ecosystem who are then targeted. You might avoid it by a holier-than-thou attitude, but the effects of others acquiescing to the corruption will ultimately get passed through to you in the form of higher costs, or in altered terms of transaction, if you will, so that it's not much different than if you yourself acquiesced to the corruption. Anu Aga agrees that deflecting corrupt behaviour towards arms-length agents is not much better than engaging in such corruption oneself. Narayanan Vaghul, one of India's pre-eminent bankers, alludes to the history of how banking in India became corrupted, reminding us also that some of the rules, and indeed the brazen departures from other rules, originate from political opportunism.

With this clear-eyed diagnosis, what is the would-be honest entrepreneur to do? Broadly, three courses of action suggest themselves in these interviews. First, where possible, avoid the thicket of rules which, in turn, are correlated with situations where one is forced to confront corrupt behaviour. Second, appeal to credible external constraints that forestall the demands from the source of the corrupt behaviour. Third, in the journey to get away from the short-run siren call of corruption, walk before you can run.

The first is apparent in the interview with industrialist Suresh Krishna. He is clear that he has avoided entanglements with the government, especially during the licence raj, for this reason. This is not to say that the government is synonymous with corruption, and that the private sector is pristine—far from it—but staying away from the 'thicket' helps. In a sense, Sir Fazle Hasan Abed of the Bangladesh Rehabilitation Assistance Committee (BRAC) makes a similar point in a different way. He points out that BRAC, by far the world's largest NGO (and possibly among the world's most successful), has had precious little trouble with corruption probably because it was founded roughly contemporaneously with the new nation state in which it's headquartered, and there were no rules in place at the time to duck and dodge!

Rao alludes to one way to dodge bribes in India. He appealed to the fact that his company had to do an initial public offering (IPO) on a public stock exchange. That comes with dramatically higher scrutiny both in the US and India, so it's a plausible way to push back on demands for bribes. Elsewhere in our CEM interviews, we encounter two other similar appeals to external constraints. Mo Ibrahim uses the same logic of appealing to an external constraint, but applies it to his frontline employees, the first place where demands for bribes manifest themselves across Africa. He presents his global board—of notable heavy-hitters from the world of business, policy and the academia—as the constraint that cannot countenance bribes, in effect giving the frontline person someone to appeal to.

There are optimistic notes in the chapter as well, of entrepreneurs and professionals playing 'offence' rather than the defensive postures alluded to more often. Businesswoman and philanthropist Anu Aga tells us how Thermax has really sought to extend its anti-corruption policies to its agents and intermediaries, to avoid exactly the problem Rao identifies. Her company also attracts talent because of its clean image. But Aga is careful not to oversell this claim. She observes that it is 'almost impossible' to root out corruption in India and emphasizes that industry bodies need to walk the talk if they really want to turn anti-corruption statements into reality. Indeed, Aga stresses there are no quick fixes, as she describes the gradual emergence within her company of an ultimately zero-tolerance approach to corruption. From commitment from the top and the ethos of no-corruption spreading to others in the company's ecosystem, to the ultimate institutionalization of its reputation that serves to attract other like-minded professionals, it's a journey of multiple years, not a switch that can be turned on in an instant.

Nilekani takes on the corruption issue frontally by creating India's 'moonshot' biometric identity project, whereby his team's software prowess is harnessed so that each of India's 100-crore-plus residents can be unambiguously and uniquely identified to the state. Many forms of corruption, associated with thousands of crores of rupees of losses to the state exchequer annually, are eliminated if there is no possibility of faking identities, one's own or that of fictitious others. Vaghul steadfastly refuses to associate himself with situations where there is corruption and manages to attract the attention of like-minded 'clean' bureaucrats and politicians who enable his illustrious career.

4(a)

Jaithirth 'Jerry' Rao

VBHC Value Homes Pvt. Ltd.

Jaithirth 'Jerry' Rao founded Value and Budget Housing Corporation (now VBHC Value Homes Pvt. Ltd), a high-quality affordable housing venture in India in 2008, where he currently serves as non-executive director. He is also the former CEO of Mphasis, a Bengaluru-based IT services company.

Mphasis began in 1998 as an IT consulting company co-founded by Rao and Jeroen Tas in Santa Monica, California. It merged with India-based BFL Software in 2000, creating an Indian-based Mphasis, which quickly became one of the top ten IT and BPO companies in India. In 2004–2005, Rao was appointed chairperson of the National Association of Software and Service Companies (NASSCOM), an Indian non-governmental trade association. Among many awards, in 2001, he was named the 'EY Entrepreneur of the Year for India' and in 2004, along with Mphasis vice-chairperson, Jeroen Tas, was named the 'EY Entrepreneur of the Year' in the IT category for New York region. Texas-based Electronic Data Systems (EDS) acquired a controlling stake in 2006 for $380 million [about about Rs 1,720 crore], which passed to Hewlett-Packard two years later when it acquired EDS.

Interviewed by Geoffrey Jones in Boston, Massachusetts, on 1 June 2016.

Interviewer: Why is the problem of corruption so acute in Indian real estate?

Jaithirth 'Jerry' Rao (JR): Large chunks of land on the periphery of Bangalore or Mumbai or Delhi or Chennai are classified in government records as agricultural land. This goes back to the 1891 revenue settlement done by some British Imperial Civil Service officer. To convert that to residential land, I have to get the approval under the 1891 Act from three levels of bureaucracy.

But there is another 1921 Act, which says that if it happens to be irrigated land, then you need two more approvals. That's not enough. There's a 1956 law, which now says that if two owners prior to that land had been grantees from the state or something, then you need two more judicial approvals. Then there's a 1981 law, which says you need urban town planning approval. Then there's a 1991 law, which says you need pollution control approval. There's a 1999 law, which says you need ministry of environmental affairs' approval.

Each time the government introduced a law, it didn't get rid of the old one. So today I have to start with the British law and go all the way to the most recent law, each of which requires prior approval, there's no self-certification, which is what we did in the IT industry. Now, when you require approval, particularly from a low-level or medium-level government functionary—trust me, there is going to be corruption.

There's, for instance, a seventy-second amendment to the Constitution, which has given extraordinary powers to the village councils, the panchayats. Now, give them powers. I have no problems with that. But then take away the power from somebody else. Now that's one more approval I need. And these guys—the village councils on the peripheries of these big metropolitan cities—they suddenly realized, 'Hey, we have power now. We can afford to approve these forty apartments or say no.' So guess what? That's one more. We call them transaction costs these days. We don't call them corruption.

But anyway, the fact of the matter is that unless we do an overhaul—in a state like Karnataka, in a state like Maharashtra, we need anywhere between seventeen to twenty-five approvals before we start construction. And then we need about five or ten approvals after we complete construction. So this just goes on.

I've got right now . . . about fifty apartments ready to be handed over to customers. They're just not able to make the transfer in the register of the village. It's taking them three months. So here I am out of cash flow for three months. The customer is still paying rent in the old places, not able to move into his or her home. The government is losing taxes because I can pay the registration fees three months earlier. But the capacity, the willingness—it's just a mess. It's getting better, but it's nowhere near where it should be if we want to provide the tens of millions of homes that we have to provide if we want to give our fellow citizens a minimum level of dignity, which I think they deserve.

Interviewer: How do you respond if an official says they can make your life simpler?

JR: We've taken a pretty hard-line position on this, primarily because we want to do an IPO. I'm not saying there's any great sanctimonious stuff. You just don't want to get into a situation where, later on, it boomerangs and it becomes a problem. So they know that we, as a company, are unlikely to pay—so basically, they hit our lawyers or architects and so on and so forth, who are doing multiple projects and who probably need to keep them on their side and who can't take as holier-than-thou a position as we have chosen to take. That's the way the system works. There are intermediaries everywhere.

For instance, if I am to buy land from you and it's agricultural, and after I buy it, I have to go and get it converted to residential, and it costs x—the deal is that you will get the conversion done and then sell it to me, and I'll pay you 1.3 x. And of that 1.3 x, you've probably paid 0.15 as value add to some fixers. I don't know. But essentially the market figures it out. Residential approved land is more expensive than agricultural land right next door. And residential approved land with pollution control board approval is that much more, so each of those are factored in.

So, it's getting better. I think nowadays—there's one interesting bureaucrat outside Mumbai, who actually told our CFO, he said, 'Hey, I like your company. You people are clean. Don't worry. I'll make sure that you get your approvals without any problems.' But, you know, it's easy for him to say. The fact is that his assistant can sit on the approval for three months unless he intervenes. In any case, he'll get transferred tomorrow. Then what happens? This is so deeply embedded, and it's a result of this palimpsest of regulations, each of them well-intentioned at that time.

This culture of prior approval rather than self-certification is the real problem. You can have a panel of ten approved pollution control companies, which you can do out of a transparent tender. And then I pick one of them and I say, 'Hey, you give me a pollution control certificate that my project is okay,' like you have accounting firms, you know, and then move on. But I have to get prior approval each time. And if you've got a state pollution control board approval, why should I go to Delhi to get an environmental approval? Doesn't make any sense to keep repeating these things.

Again, I don't blame anyone. I'm just saying this has happened. But it's high time we undid some of these things. My mother used to knit sweaters when I was a young kid. I used to watch her. The ball would roll away and so on. But sometimes, if the wool got knotted up, you had no choice but to cut it. You couldn't unknot it. We are like that. We have to do some major surgeries. And it has to be done at the state and city and village level, not just in Delhi, if we want to get moving.

Interviewer Can business leaders do more in this respect, or does the problem have to be solved at the political level?

JR: No. Look, as far as I am concerned, I speak my mind. I write about this all the time in newspapers and magazines. And there are several others, and I think we've had some impact. Has it been as much as we would like? No way—not even a fraction of what we would like. But is it directionally correct? The answer is yes.

That's the story with India. I think it's always a country which is falling short of its potential and promise, because we are a little more casual about time than others. And that casual thing—the big price is paid by our poor, because we are postponing their exit from poverty by taking time so casually. So one more generation passes. Every time you take time casually and say it's okay, it can happen slowly, the idea that's without a cost is a mistake. There is a social and political cost, which is frankly being paid by the poorest and the poor and the emerging middle class, not by the wealthy.

Learnings from Jaithirth 'Jerry' Rao: The roots of corruption often lie in layers of rules and regulations, typically opaque to those subjected to these. The resulting capricious subjectivity of interpretation creates a demand for the common person to seek shortcuts and worse. Appealing to a credible external constraint goes some way to shielding an enterprise from untrammelled corruption.

4(b)

Narayanan Vaghul

Narayanan Vaghul

Narayanan Vaghul is former chairperson of the Industrial Credit and Investment Corporation of India (ICICI) Bank Limited, a role he served from 1985 to 1996, and served as non-executive chairperson until 2009. Born in a remote village in south India, he began his career in the State Bank of India

(SBI), where he served for nineteen years. He went on to become the executive director of the Central Bank of India from 1978 to 1980 and the chairperson of the Bank of India from 1981 to 1984. This gave him the distinction of being the youngest chairperson of a public sector bank. Under Vaghul's leadership, ICICI went through a major transformation process in 1994, changing from a public institution to one of India's largest private banks. In 1998 Vaghul became a director of Air India Limited. He is a noted proponent of corporate philanthropy. Among many awards, he was named 'Businessman of the Year' by *Business India* in 1991, received the 'Economic Times Lifetime Achievement Award' in 2006, and received the Padma Bhushan in 2010 for his contributions to trade and industry.

Interviewed by V.G. Narayanan in Chennai on 26 October 2017.

Interviewer: What was your experience like working for a government-owned bank?

Narayanan Vaghul (NV): At Bank of India, I found for the first time that working with the government was going to be very difficult, because there was interference with everything. In one particular incident in which there was an issue, I went and discussed it with the finance minister. The finance minister agreed with my point of view—it was about a sick account—and he said, 'What you are doing is perfectly right, I agree with you.' I came back to Bombay, and his secretary called me and said the finance minister wants you to do it in a different way. I got fed up with that and so that day I decided that I would leave. Dr Manmohan Singh was the governor of the Reserve Bank of India [RBI] at that time, and I made my position known—that

I would leave. I was about forty-six at the time. He said, 'Sir, what are you going to do at the age of forty-six?' I responded, 'I haven't decided what I will do. I will go back to Chennai.' 'And in Chennai what will you do?' 'I haven't decided, but I just don't want to continue here because this is—I don't think I enjoy what is really happening, and my heart tells me that I cannot take this any longer.' Then he told me, 'I think we need people like you. You have to fight the system because the system is rotten, the system is corrupt. If people like you give up, then what happens to the system? You should stay and fight.' I said, 'No, I don't have the strength to fight because I find that this is a little too much.'

Interviewer: Can you describe how corruption crept into and embedded itself within the banking system?

NV: Well, the State Bank of India continued its high level of professionalism. Those days the saying used to be that in a crowd of bankers you could always pick the State Bank people. The State Bank believed in recruiting the best of talent. Next to the ICS examination—the civil service examination—the State Bank examination was considered to be the next best. So the people who joined the bank were people who were considered to be of very high calibre. The recruitment used to be free from nepotism or corruption. We had a recruitment board that consisted of people of high integrity. In fact, when I served as the chief of the personnel department, I had occasion to interact with the recruitment board, which was usually headed by a retired cabinet secretary, a person with ICS background. They were very strict men, with a very high level of integrity and high level of honesty. You didn't find that in private banks. The private bank employees usually came from known backgrounds and the like. So you could always differentiate between the State Bank people and private bank people. Gradually, I think in private banks—I mean the newly nationalized public sector banks—things also started changing. Bright people were still recruited, but unfortunately a new disease came into existence. The government became a very strong player in public sector banking. I remember in 1969 when banks were nationalized, I was executive assistant to Mr Talwar [Raj Kumar Talwar, the newly appointed chairperson of the State Bank of India], and I had the unique opportunity of attending the first meeting of the chairmen of nationalized banks, which the RBI governor convened. This is long before I became director of the National Institute of Bank Management—that took place in 1977, this was in 1969. Mr L.K. Jha was the governor of RBI at the time. Mr Jha said, 'Government will not interfere with the functioning of the banks. RBI will be your central authority, and we will continue to regulate banking in the way that a central bank should do, but we will not interfere with your operations. You are going to deal with the government just as you would deal with any other shareholder.' I mean, I did record that in the minutes. I was the secretary of the group of chairmen.

Unfortunately, the government never fulfilled its promise. It started interfering with banking right from the word go. Very few people know that Mr Jha, as governor of RBI, opposed the nationalization. He said that banking could be regulated differently, but the government went ahead and nationalized, and Mr Jha extracted a promise from Mrs Gandhi that the RBI would continue to be the institution which would deal with the banks. There would not be any department in the government that would deal with the banks. Within a month or so, I think, Mrs Gandhi set up the Department of Banking, and Mr Jha submitted his resignation. Not many people know this story. People only know that Jha submitted his resignation, but by then the character of banking had completely changed. It became, out and out, a banking system that was managed and run by the Government of India in a manner in which they wanted. There was a lot of political interference: a lot of political influence in the appointment of the chairman, in the appointment of executive director, in the choice of the clients and . . . the loans. I think anybody could give a call to the bank chairman and say, 'So-and-so will come and meet you; you give him a loan.' There used to be a tamasha in those days, of what you call loan melas [a 'loan festival' where banks in India offer concessions on processing fees on loans, mortgages, etc.]. You would go to the village and then assemble all the people, the local member of the Legislative Assembly would bring a lot of farmers, and the chairman would be asked to stand there and disburse loans to each and every farmer. There was no verification of the farmer—whether he had land or anything like that. So the proportion of the defaulted loans went up, skyrocketed. The government did not bother; it was around that time that I became chairman of the Central Bank of India and then the Bank of India.

I got fed up with the way in which banking was being managed. I did have the courage to say something in one meeting with the finance minister, which was not appreciated, namely, 'I am glad that government today owns the banks. I think I was the one who welcomed the move that banks should not be owned by private industrialists, they should be owned by the public. But having now nationalized the banks, can't you leave the management of the banks to professionals?

Let the professionals manage the banks. You have got a set of objectives—you want agriculture to be financed, you want rural industries to be financed, you tell us, "This is what we want". But the choice of the customers, the way in which the loans are to be given, the way in which the loans are to be recovered—why don't you leave that to us as professionals? We are trained for that; we will manage to do that. Don't try to dictate to us, that this is to be done, that has to be done.' I think the government did not agree. Somehow or the other the government got caught in that vicious cycle. They would not let the banks go.

Interviewer: Was the government able to control information at this time?

NV: Morarji Desai, within a few days of his becoming prime minister in March 1977, made a statement saying, 'My government's first job is to privatize the banks, I don't want the government to own the banks. And I will be putting it before the cabinet and taking the decision.' Mr H.M. Patel was the finance minister. There was quite a stir in the audience of the public sector banks; there were press people also present. But this was not a cabinet decision. The prime minister could not just announce that, and the next day I knew there would be a banner headline in all the newspapers saying that the government had decided to privatize the banks, and that it would be a serious embarrassment to the government. After the prime minister finished his speech, and I escorted him out to the car, the finance minister turned to me and he said, 'You kill the story.' I said, 'How do you kill a story?' I was not aware that this could be done. He saw the confusion on my face and said, 'No, I know that you will not be able to do that, you talk to the Press Information Bureau [PIB],' and he mentioned a person's name. He said, 'He is in PIB. You go and tell him; this story should not appear in the press tomorrow.' So that's the first time I knew that the government had hands that could reach everywhere. The next day, newspapers never carried that news item. I don't know how PIB could kill the story—there were at least twenty media people present in that meeting—but not one of them carried the news of the privatization of the public sector banks.

Interviewer: How would you characterize the banking system in India today?

NV: As far as the banking situation is concerned, today, I have no hesitation in saying that banking is a mess, and this mess is not something that is new; it has been happening since 1969. This is the cumulative effect of bad selection of managers, bad selection of projects, and growing interference from the government. These are all things that contributed to what is happening today—an inevitable by-product of the decision that was taken in 1969.

Interviewer: Are there regulations to protect against corruption?

NV: Some of our regulations go back to the 1850s, and they continue to remain in the statute book, but they are no longer relevant, they have ceased to have any meaning at all. But still, we continue with them. This government came to office with a very clear principle that we have to re-examine the regulations and make it easier for businesses to run their enterprises. This is the promise that was made that has not happened at all. They have not touched one single piece of regulation. They enacted a Companies Act, which has made it more complicated than ever, and which is making the functioning of the board less efficient.

Interviewer: *How far does the government's grasp on industries reach? Does it go beyond the public sector?*

NV: It is not only banks that we are talking about, it is the public sector. They don't want to let the public sector go. I used to be a director on the Air India board. Ten years ago, we came to the conclusion that Air India could not run on profitable lines, but the government was not willing to let Air India go. In fact, I asked this question several times as a member of the Air India board, 'Why are we not letting this happen?' Because Air India is a government body, it provides perquisites, you can upgrade seats from business class to first class for bureaucrats and ministers. These are all very small issues, and Air India today is sitting on a huge debt burden. And even if it is being put on a divestment now, I don't know how many buyers there will be. And if there are buyers, it is going to cost the government more, rather than bring any money to the exchequer, because most of the loans in Air India are being guaranteed by the government, and there is going to be a huge haircut.

You can talk in terms of hundreds of public sector enterprises that are languishing, for which there is no solution. This is despite the promise of the government functionaries saying that it is not our business to run these enterprises. So why are they not doing it? Somehow or other, the system as a whole in which we are functioning—not only the banking system, but the system of administration, as well—is getting used to the status quo.

Learnings from Narayanan Vaghul: Corruption in financial services has increased over time as the extent of government intervention has grown. Yet, there is space for honest individuals with technocratic skill sets to continue to contribute while remaining untainted by unsavoury practices.

4(c)

Sir Fazle Hasan Abed

Sir Fazle Hasan Abed founded BRAC in 1972, shortly after Bangladesh became an independent country. BRAC went international in 2002 and is currently the world's largest NGO, functioning in twelve countries in multiple development spheres, including microfinance, education, healthcare and human rights, among many others. In 2010, he was appointed Knight Commander of the Order of St Michael and St

George in Britain for his contribution to addressing poverty in Bangladesh and globally. In 2014 and 2017, Abed was named in *Fortune*'s list of the World's 50 Greatest Leaders. He passed away in 2019.

Interviewed by Tarun Khanna in Cambridge, Massachusetts, on 24 April 2014.

Interviewer: Can I ask you a difficult question about the relations with the state and the government? As an outsider and observer, it seems an incredibly convoluted political process, and you, as an entrepreneur and builder of an organization, have had to navigate that, presumably. What can you share about that experience?

Sir Fazle Hasan Abed: One thing about Bangladesh is that the Bangladesh government was not very strong when we inherited a government in East Pakistan. The power elite were the West Pakistanis. So we had a very weak government. And that meant the government didn't have the resources to provide services to all, and so they said, 'all right, you people do whatever you can'. So the space was given to us to do the things that we wanted to do. During the first eight years of BRAC's work, there was no permission needed from anybody to go anywhere and do work. In 1978, the first legislation came, and it was called the foreign donations ordinance. And immediately I went to see the president of Bangladesh, who was Ziaur Rahman. I said, 'Why are you trying to stop us from getting money from foreign countries?' He said, 'This is not for you; this is for Libya's President Gaddafi trying to create madrasas in Bangladesh, which I'm trying to stop.' But then he couldn't stop President Gaddafi sending money to create madrasas in Bangladesh. He stopped us from getting money without government permission.

What was intended and what actually happened was quite different. We became a little more restricted—every time we received money from abroad, we had to go to the government saying that this money was for this. A bureaucracy was added to our operations. We had to spend a little more to have one officer who would just go from one government office to another government office and wait to get permissions, and that wouldn't have been required if the president hadn't brought in this ordinance.

So this was one. And then, of course, as we became larger and larger, some politicians became very jealous as to why we people were becoming so powerful and even controlled some of the votes. They thought that if I told our group members to vote for someone, he would get all the votes. So every time an election started approaching, I started getting phone calls: 'Please ask your people to vote for me.' I said, 'I can't do that.' I'm neither for the Bangladesh Nationalist Party [BNP], nor for the Communist Party, nor for any of these parties, and our group members are not selected on the basis of which party they support. We had a staff of 30,000 at the time. I never asked them which party they belonged to. It could be BNP; it could be anybody. How could I ask people to vote for a particular person or party? It was very difficult.

Learnings from Sir Fazle Hasan Abed: Whenever there have been fewer regulations, there has been far less opportunity for corruption to flourish.

4(d)

Suresh Krishna

Suresh Krishna

Suresh Krishna is the founder and chair of Sundram Fasteners, the largest manufacturer of industrial fasteners for India's auto industry and a prominent Indian-owned global firm. Sundram Fasteners was established in 1962 after it grew out of the TVS Group, established in 1911 by his grandfather, T.V. Sundram

Iyengar. Sundram Fasteners has secured contracts with companies including Tata Motors and General Motors. Among many recognitions, *Business India* named him Businessman of the Year in 1995 and the Indian government awarded him the Padma Shri in 2006 for his contribution to industry.

Interviewed by Tarun Khanna in Chennai on 19 December 2012.

Interviewer: There is always much discussion about corruption, but a few groups, including the TVS Group, have retained stellar reputations. But in your different vantage points, including as a representative of Indian industry, how do you see that transition? And how do you see where we are today?

Suresh Krishna: When we were totally controlled by the government, there was no question of trying to do anything that was not accepted as a norm, but the minute we got liberalized there were two distinct sectors of society—one which was government controlled, like, say, cement, coal, iron and steel, ore mining, gas, telecommunication. These were still held by the government, to a large extent. Then there were people like us, like automotive component manufacturers, or consumer durables, like washing machines.

So people like us got out of the government's clutches completely; the government only concentrated on big commodity products. Not even the big commodity products, like iron and steel, but on iron ore mining, gas exploration, telecommunication, subcontracting for nuclear energy. So the big boys played in it, and we had a lot of problems early on. How do you get a certain privileged position inside that kind of niche?

We, in our group, have never been comfortable with dealing with the government in this manner. So one of the policies of the group has been, regardless of however attractive it is, to stay away from any industry which is under the control of the government. We have not gone into telecommunications, we have not gone into cement, we have not gone into paper, we have not gone into iron ore mining, and we have not gone into any of those things which are controlled by the government. We only choose areas over which government has no control.

It makes life much easier for us if we don't have to spend time with the government. We don't have to compete to be the highest bidder, and what the basis is for our bid, and get into controversies, and get our name published on the front page of newspapers. We quietly make our money. And we have a certain clientele, which appreciates us. Now people can say that, given your strength, you could have grown much more, and that you are not ambitious enough, and you could have done this, you could have done that, but it's a moot point. I have known people who wanted to grow big, and they went ahead and grew big, and then suddenly fell on their face, because they couldn't manage it, for many reasons.

TVS company, by and large, because of a certain amount of conservative thinking of a southern-based company, has grown on a step-by-step basis, over a period of time. We have never gone in for huge acquisitions and huge expansions. We have expanded, we have made acquisitions, but it has never been done at a high magnitude.

Learnings from Suresh Krishna: Most corruption is concentrated in sectors that have pervasive public sector involvement. Eschewing these amounts to at least not inadvertently exacerbating corruption in those theatres.

4(e)

Anu Aga

Thermax Ltd

Anu Aga is former head of Thermax, an equipment manufacturer. The company that eventually became Thermax Global was founded in 1966 by A.S. Bhathena, Aga's father, as a hospital equipment company in partnership with a Belgian company called Wanson (Babcock Wanson since 1990). Aga inherited the leadership of the family-owned company in 1996 after the sudden passing away of her husband, Rohinton Aga. In 2004, Aga stepped down as chairperson and was succeeded by her daughter, Meher Pudumjee. Since then, Aga has served as the chairperson of the Thermax Foundation and supports other philanthropic activities, including non-government organizations Akanksha and Teach for India.

Interviewed by Geoffrey Jones in Mumbai on 14 February 2017, and by Anjali Raina and Kairavi Dey in Mumbai on 2 August 2021.

Interviewer: So many of the interviews with Indian business leaders that we have conducted deal with the problem of corruption in the country. How did you deal with that issue inside your own firm?

Anu Aga (AA): I think during my husband's time and when I first took over, we said we will not succumb to paying bribes except as a last resort. So it wasn't 100 per cent definite no. In India, to be 100 per cent honest is next to impossible, so we put up with it as long as the family didn't extract anything for personal gain. I know many family-owned businesses in India take a lot from the company for themselves. We might have to do it occasionally to secure business through a third party. But some years ago, I kept telling the executives that I am very uncomfortable, I have no moral right to talk about corruption if we are not 100 per cent honest, and they felt I was being an idealist and a stupid woman. But some years ago, we were raided because of business issues and our executives learnt their lesson. The family was pleading, 'Let's be 100 per cent honest,' and finally the executives said, 'We have learnt our lesson, we will never do it.' I am delighted, and it gives me the moral right to speak against corruption. Otherwise in India we all grumble about corruption but keep adding to it.

Interviewer: I wonder how you enforce that policy much lower down your hierarchy?

AA: We make every employee sign a declaration that we do not want any corrupt practices, and if they want to work for the company, they sign it. There are a couple of cases where we found that people were not following it. We asked them to leave; the message gets out very fast. I think if the top people are serious, then the message is very clear, and I think everyone as far as I know is adhering to it.

Interviewer: What is your policy towards your agents regarding corruption?

AA: Many companies say they're honest, but they feel that giving through the agent is not their responsibility, that they're honest. We took it a step further and said not even through an agent. My people were a little afraid that we might lose business and yes, we may, if there was no price why would people be corrupt? So, we knew there was a price. But I also felt if we improved our quality, our delivery and customer service, many orders which our competitor gets, we could get . . . by giving better quality and service delivery. And we can't say that because of not bribing we lost the order; very often we lose an order because of the service quality or the product quality and blame it on corruption. So, it helped us look at our quality also. And I think, over time, I can say that we do not take any orders with any corruption. Buy-in by the senior people and meticulously following what you have said, these are the two ways senior management can help ensure there is no corruption within the company—now if there is one person doing something which doesn't come to my knowledge, I can't swear by it. But no, I would say substantially we are not corrupt.

Interviewer: You left an active role in the company some time ago. How did you manage to root the avoidance of corruption into the company? Why did the problem not reappear when you left?

AA: Well, Meher and [Aga's son-in-law] Pheroz have bought into it, and my current MD who took over after M.S. Unnikrishnan retired, Ashish Bhandari, strongly believes in it. By then the divisional heads had also bought into it. So I think it was a very strong culture. And people, even our employees feel proud that they are working for a company that is not indulging in corrupt practices. Let me tell you that there is certain administrative corruption, like the boiler inspector or the factory inspector, if you do not give him something he wants, it could be the guest house or anything he wants, he could close down your factory or harass you for months and years. So I'm not so sure if we can root out corruption against these, I mean, it's almost impossible in India. But I'm talking about 95 per cent of corruption, which takes place in getting orders or bribing the government to get something for yourself, we would never do that, to change a policy or to put pressure, none of that.

I feel good because I know some companies who say they are not corrupt, do it through agents, and I think that's not right. And earlier, I used to think that in dealing with government, there is corruption, but I found out that even in the private sector, there is a lot of corruption. So it's both that we have to deal with. And you will be surprised, many business houses have realized that it's no use doing this with Thermax, they will not . . . So they come to us if they also want a clean order and want good quality.

Interviewer: Can you provide your perspective on the role of industry bodies in mobilizing clean companies against corrupt practices? I know that in your role in these industry bodies, you played a very active role in making this happen.

AA: I've been closely associated with CII only, but I'm sure the same goes for all the bodies—FICCI and ASSOCHAM—all the other bodies. You know, industrial bodies are made of hundreds of different types of industries. So to get everyone to agree and keep to the promise is a very difficult task. During the Congress rule when there was a lot of corruption, which . . . came out in the papers, CII called the industries and said let's make a promise, let's sign a code saying we will not be dishonest. And I said I will not sign that because it is so superficial unless I find out from my company why we are corrupt. And if you want to root out corruption, how can we sit with government people like a factory inspector and talk about what we are forced to do. It's a Boy Scout promise which doesn't have meaning. So I was one of the few who refused to sign.

And I don't think . . . I can't vouch and say other companies have continued or not continued . . . I've been out of the business for fifteen to twenty years, so I don't even know the current scenario, but from what one hears, corruption hasn't been rooted out. Corruption is still very much there. So I don't think industry bodies have been able to, they talk about it, they would like to, but I don't think they've been successful in rooting out corruption. And as I said, it requires a very, very long process to find out which are the areas. See there are two types of industries—one that will be corrupt because they want to gain something for themselves at the cost of others and others that don't want to if the environment allows them to root out corruption. So those who are not willing to change, you can't do anything, but those who would like to, and I don't know what percentage that could be, that could happen if we really go into the nitty-gritty of why there is a need for corruption, sit with the external bodies also, and sort it out if that is possible. But . . . in the last fifteen to twenty years I have been out of CII also, so I don't know what's happening. So I can't talk about the current scenario. But when I was active, this hadn't taken place except as a promise signed by people.

Industry bodies may raise the issue, and everyone will agree, nobody will publicly say I want to be corrupt, and I am corrupt, so they will all agree. But will it be implemented genuinely, that's the real big question.

Interviewer: Can the industry body play a role in making an environment that is less corrupt or is that also difficult?

AA: Unless their own company members ask them to do that, why would they take that initiative? It should come from the corporate world that we want help and they will perhaps do it, I don't know.

Interviewer: Have the policies of Thermax exercised a positive impact on other companies or individuals?

AA: I don't know while recruiting if we are able to, but the word has gone around, and maybe people who want to work in a clean company, also environmentally, we go towards a clean environment. So it's both ways, you know, we are going more and more green because ours is a boiler company. So that also attracts young people, the fact that this company is making a conscious effort to go green and be honest. So I'm sure we do. I have heard many people say that we are very proud of the stand that Thermax has taken within the company. The vendors who work with us and the agents who work with us, of course had to follow the same. But the rest, I mean, the agents especially, agents can take shortcuts and give bribes, but that's not allowed by us. So we are able to influence them. But have we been able to influence the larger ecosystem, I don't think so.

Learnings from Anu Aga: A zero-tolerance policy towards corruption is hard to achieve, but it is not impossible. To be real, it must include refusal to outsource corrupt behaviour to others in the ecosystem, for example, suppliers and partners. Collective action through industry bodies would be effective if it embraced something approximating zero-tolerance, since it also gives one a moral right to speak out against corruption instead of exacerbating it through one's actions.

4(f)

Nandan Nilekani

Namas Bhojani/Nandan Nilekani

Nandan Nilekani is co-founder of Infosys, a leading IT services company. He left Infosys to become chairperson of the UIDAI, a cabinet ranking position, where he worked on Aadhaar, the twelve-digit unique identity number issued to all residents of India. He launched the brand name and logo in 2012. Aadhaar is currently the largest biometric ID system in the world. Nilekani left UIDAI in 2014, co-founded EkStep, a non-profit literacy and numeracy programme in 2015, and returned to Infosys as non-executive chairperson in 2017. Among many recognitions, in 2006 he received the Padma Bhushan and was named Businessman of the Year by *Forbes Asia*. In 2009, he was listed as one of 100 most influential people in the world by *Time* magazine. In 2017, Nilekani and his wife Rohini announced they would give away half of their wealth to philanthropy as part of the *Giving Pledge* campaign organized by Bill Gates and Warren Buffet.

Interviewed by Tarun Khanna in Cambridge, Massachusetts, on 25 September 2017.

Interviewer: Can you tell us about the Aadhaar project and the idea and reasoning behind it?

Nandan Nilekani (NN): Aadhaar is a project which was begun by the Indian government in 2009 and I joined the government to implement the project. The project was to give a unique identity number to every resident of India, which meant giving a unique identity number to a billion-odd people [about 100 crore people], and the important thing was that it should be unique, as in, everyone should be uniquely identified.

Now there were a couple of reasons for taking on this ambitious venture. The first was that there are still a large number of people in India who don't have acknowledged proof of their existence. In many states, the birth registry system doesn't work as well as it should. More than half the kids born don't have a birth certificate because they are not born in a hospital or are born in some remote village where you have to pay a bribe to get a birth certificate. As somebody recently said, in India corruption starts from womb to tomb so getting the birth certificate is part of that. Whatever the reason, a large number of people don't have birth certificates. Increasingly, that has become a bottleneck in their lives because they can't get a lot of things done because they don't have proof of existence. In some sense you can think of this as the world's largest social inclusion project because it is about giving people who are unrecorded in the system some kind of recorded identity. You can think of this as the twenty-first-century form of Ellis Island. If you remember what happened at Ellis Island in the nineteenth century, you had a lot of immigrants coming in from Ireland, Italy and eastern Europe, and whatever their name was in their home country, they were often given a new name here, and that became their name for the rest of their lives. So, think of it as people coming from the unidentified world into the identified world, so that is one reason: social inclusion.

The second reason, which is from the government's point of view, is that over the last fifteen years, the Indian government has substantially increased its expenditure on building a welfare system—entitlements, subsidies, guaranteed employment, healthcare, education, pensions, scholarships and so on. Subsidies like petroleum, food and so forth—all these entitlement subsidies really started growing, and today, are in excess of about $60 billion [Rs 3,90,000 crore] a year. All these entitlement subsidies go to individuals and when the underlying system of identifying individuals is dysfunctional, there is a very high likelihood that the money does not go to the people it is supposed to reach. The estimates vary from 20 to 40 per cent of these entitlement subsidies not reaching the intended person, which is obviously a waste of public expenditure. So the second and equally important reason for this project was to make government expenditure more efficient and more effective and make sure that benefits that are targeted to an individual actually reach that individual.

So this really came from two points of view: from the point of view of creating social inclusion for a large number of people without identity and from the point of view of creating a much more efficient way of delivering benefits to people who need them.

Interviewer: What were the uses of this ID? How is it able to protect against false benefits claims?

NN: I think the biggest and the first use that drove it was establishing uniqueness. Establishing uniqueness meant that a person had only one ID and this was very important because in government expenditure on programmes there was a fair amount of leakage because of duplicates and ghosts in the database. So, for example, if you have 100 people who have to get pension, then ask all 100 people to give their Aadhaar ID— the ID is named Aadhaar, which means foundation. Then the 100 shrinks to seventy because thirty of them don't exist or they are duplicates and therefore there is a reduction in wastage. The compression of wastage by using the uniqueness feature of the number to remove ghosts and duplicates for various entitlement programmes is capable of saving the government billions of dollars. We estimate that the Indian government spends $60 billion [Rs 3,90,000 crore] a year in entitlements and subsidies, and there is a potential to reduce that by about $10 billion [Rs 65,000 crore] a year based on what we know about the leakage happening in various programmes. So that alone makes it very attractive, to make government projects more efficient.

So the first usage of this was that it was a unique number which could eliminate ghosts and duplicates.

The second thing is that it is also the first attempt to create a digital identity. Digital identity is very important because as we are now seeing in the world, being able to confirm in a robust unequivocal manner in the digital world that you are the person you claim to be, is very, very important. As more and more services go online, as you do your transactions online—you buy online, you pay online, get all your documents online, the ability to make sure that you are the person that you claim to be becomes extremely important and we know that if that does not work well then we have a lot of fraud and people lose their credit card numbers and lose their photographs on the cloud or whatever, so having a robust way of authenticating that the person is the genuine person is very important.

Since we are already providing a digital identity system, we said let us provide a way of authenticating that the person is the person that they claim to be. So along with giving them the ID, which is a twelve-digit number, we also built an online authentication system and online verification system. We actually used the same biometric that we used for giving the number to be able to verify online. So suppose I go somewhere and I have to get some money out of my account and I say my number is 123 and they have a device on which I put my finger or they scan my eye and they confirm that I am the same person that I claim to be, then they can release the money. That was decided in 2009, and as you know, the touch ID on the Apple phone does the same thing. It basically does a biometric verification of your fingerprint. We provide that at scale in an online environment for all the 70-crore people who are in the system. So basically, apart from giving them the ID, there is also a way to use that system to give a digital biometric attribute.

Then the next issue was that what has happened in the world, especially after 9/11, is that the requirement to identify who a person is to open a bank account or to get a mobile connection has become more and more important. This is known as KYC or know your customer. Most systems that have a KYC requirement have the requirement of a government photo ID. So if you want to go to a bank and open a bank account, they will say show me your government photo ID. These things became more stringent after 9/11 when the Federally Administered Tribal Areas [FATA], the body that looks at all these things, introduced new regulations. In this process, many poor people got left out because they didn't have any ID, and therefore, they couldn't open a bank account. So the organization worked with various regulators so that if you use the Aadhaar number and the customer agrees, then the name and address that we have in the Aadhaar database can be released to the bank for the purpose of KYC. So e-KYC is also a very popular thing.

We figured out a way to link the ID to a bank account number and the government can now automatically credit money into the bank account. With a person getting a pension, you just make sure the person is unique and then you send the money to the ID and it goes to their bank account, which therefore streamlines the whole payment system. Now this is a huge issue—direct cash transfers or direct benefit transfers are a huge issue today in public policy. So what we have built is really the infrastructure for making cash transfers seamless, electronic and in real time.

Now when we designed this system, we designed it to be a platform, and it is important to understand what we mean by a platform. What happens in many countries is that identity is linked very closely to some particular usage of the identity. Identity is done for the purposes of security or financial inclusion or the election system or whatever, but here the ID is built as a pure ID, so all the ID system does is say John is John or Ashok is Ashok. But the application on top of that will decide the particular usage of the ID. So when the ID is in the banking system it will be used for banking purposes, when the ID is in the healthcare system it will be used for healthcare purposes. So the separation of the ID from the application was a very fundamental principle which allowed us to think of this as a platform. Part of the reason is that the government designed it in that way and also made sure that this project was not housed in any ministry that had a particular use for it, because then that particular use would dominate.

Learnings from Nandan Nilekani: Technology can be used to democratize access to public goods, including but not limited to information, and to create a more level playing field so that those 'without' are not left even further behind.

4(g)

Mo Ibrahim

Mo Ibrahim is a Sudanese-born British businessman and corporate philanthropist. In his early career he worked for British Telecom, where he helped design the first cellular networks in Britain. Tired of the bureaucracy of a large company, he decided to pursue an entrepreneurial career. He founded a small company called Mobile System International (MSI) in 1988. It was a consulting and software company that grew into a global undertaking with 110 operators worldwide. In 1998, Ibrahim spun off MSI-Cellular Investments, later renamed Celtel, as a mobile phone operator in Africa, where there was hardly any telecom service. This grew as a pan-African telecommunications company, which was eventually acquired by the Kuwait-based Zain Group in 2005. After selling Celtel, Ibrahim established the Mo Ibrahim Foundation to encourage better governance on the African continent. The foundation is famous for the Ibrahim Index of African Governance, a governance index that measures, through ninety indicators in over fourteen subcategories, the overall governance performance of African countries.

Interviewed by Tarun Khanna in London, Britain, on 15 September 2017.

Interviewer: Africa has a reputation for high levels of corruption. What measures did you take to counter this problem in your business?

Mo Ibrahim (MI): In our first board meeting, we said, 'Okay, how are we going to deal with that?' From the start, I had a very strong board. I always believed that as a chief executive, I had to have a very strong board, which I could recruit to work for the company for free, as well. Because in my case, at least, in what I was trying to do, I think that was important for the credibility of the company. So I had the first chief executive of Vodafone—Sir Gerry Whent, who had just retired; Sir Alan Rudge, former deputy chief executive of British Telecom; Lord Jim Prior [a prominent British Conservative politician who held ministerial positions in the 1970s and 1980s]; and Dr Salim Salim—who was head of the African Union. I had a lot of very senior people, and we said, 'We're going to institute a very high standard of governance, better than that of any listed company even in Europe. Can we do that? An African company—let us have a challenge here.'

It was very interesting, how we operated the company. So, for example, when it came to the issue of corruption, we said, 'We're sitting in our comfy rooms here, and we can talk about corruption and make wonderful statements—because somebody proposed we use the slogan "Not a Single Dollar"—but people use slogans all the time, how do we walk the talk? How do we execute?' We came up with an answer. We said, 'Okay, we know that if somebody comes under pressure, it will not be me, it will not be board members, it will be the manager on the ground, the chief executive of the company in the country where we operate, this is the guy who is vulnerable.' So the minister of interior might visit you at night and say, 'Look, we're preparing for elections, and we know you love the president, and we need something.' What are you going to say? What are you going to do? We said, 'These guys need support.' So we agreed in our regulations that any chief executive of any of our companies could not sign a cheque for more than $30,000 [Rs 4.5 lakh], we chose that number carefully. We'd just help to enable the small operation to keep ticking, and the board would be ready to really deal with any emergency and would be able to authorize funds so that we wouldn't hamper operations.

Interviewer: *How important was your board in combating corruption?*

MI: The board was amazing. For seven years of operation, I never had a problem. If there were any measures that required extra funds—some unforeseen condition where we needed to acquire some hardware or software to enhance our operation—I was able to, in twenty-four hours, communicate with the board and get their approval. This system protected our people in the field. So we said, 'Look, we don't want heroics. If anybody comes to you asking for anything, say, "Fine, what do you want? I will write to my board".' On my board, I didn't only have those great people, I also insisted on the International Finance Corporation [IFC], Centre for Disease Control and Prevention [CDC], Organization of the Petroleum Exporting Countries [OPEC], Deutsche Investitions und Entwicklungesellschafter [DEG] of Germany and the Netherlands Development Finance Company [FMO], they all came on board. I said, 'I want a senior director from each of you guys to come and sit on the board.' And the people said, 'Look, but I only have 2 per cent. Why are you offering this position?' I said, 'That's my gift to you—you come to the board.' So I had all those people on the board, people from the governments of developed countries. Nobody can look at these names and those people and say, 'Ah, you write to them, ask for a bribe.' So we never had a problem. In our experience, we found it was not an issue.

Learnings from Mo Ibrahim: Appealing to a credible external constraint protects the average employee from being forced to engage in corrupt behaviour. These external constraints can be explicitly engineered, even in the most corrupt environments, by the astute entrepreneur.

5

Challenging Gender Stereotypes

It has been said that women hold up half the sky, but all too often their opportunities and talents are held back by social constraints. Gender inequality is an almost universal phenomenon, but India is among nations that suffer the most from this problem. The 2019 Gender Inequality Index (GII) of the United Nations Development Programme (UNDP) measures inequalities in human development (such as reproductive health), empowerment (such as proportion of parliamentary seats) and economic status (such as labour market participation). None of India's BRIC peers shine in this ranking: out of 189 countries, China is ranked thirty-nine, Russia is ranked fifty, South Africa ninety-three and Brazil ninety-five. However, India is worse than all of them, with a ranking of 123. As per the 2019 GII, Indian women contribute only 18 per cent to the country's GDP—one of the lowest contributions in the world—and only a quarter of India's labour force is female. Currently, only 13.5 per cent of members of Parliament are women. The figure is 20 per cent both in neighbouring Pakistan and Bangladesh, and in Saudi Arabia, which has pursued an unusually restrictive policy on women's rights until very recently. In Norway, over 40 per cent of people elected to parliament are women.

The selections in this chapter confirm the many challenges women have faced at all levels of society in India and elsewhere and explore strategies to improve the situation. The interviewees were among the first generation of women to break through the barriers in their professions, and those barriers were considerable. Prominent lawyer Zia Mody recounts that when she worked in New York early in her career, only about a quarter of the staff in her legal practice were women, which made her feel pressured enough, but the situation was far worse in the Indian legal system, where there were even fewer women. The psychological pressures and lack of confidence that she experienced will be familiar to many women even today. We hear also from other pioneers. Banker Naina Lal Kidwai became one of the first three women to do her articles for a chartered accountant's qualification with Pricewaterhouse India, and then became the first Indian woman to enter the MBA programme at the Harvard Business School.

Our female pioneers took leadership roles to ensure that the next generation of women had more support. At the law firm of AZB & Partners, Mody cultivated future generations of female lawyers through a policy of providing mentorship and advice, especially during what she terms the 'two crisis points' of marriage and motherhood.

Deeply rooted sociocultural values and traditions drive gender inequality. It is the assumptions about gender roles in patriarchal societies that restrict access to labour markets, create glass ceilings and promote discrimination. Our selections explore the ways in which people have sought to contest such patriarchal assumptions. The movie industry has been notoriously prone to reinforce rather than contest gender stereotypes. Classic Bollywood movies presented good women as passive and demure. Shabana Azmi was one of the first prominent actors to take a leadership role contesting such stereotypes, courting societal disapproval. Azmi here recalls how she has turned down roles where women are portrayed as subservient and has been willing to take risks with her personal safety, as when she played a lesbian in the movie *Fire* (1996).

Education is an important means of contesting gender stereotypes. Much has improved since the landmark Right to Education Act in 2009, but India still has a problem educating girls. Perhaps 40 per cent of fifteen- to eighteen-year-old girls are out of school,* mostly because of the demands of housework and agricultural work. Some years back, the McKinsey Global Institute found that Indian women performed nearly ten times the unpaid care work of men. Improving the provision and quality of education for girls is key to opening more opportunities for them. A number of larger Indian business houses have a long tradition of investing in education. Keshub Mahindra of the automobile manufacturer Mahindra & Mahindra (M&M) talks of his group's commitment to education, especially for women. At the time of the interview, his group was helping educate 90,000 girls every year. Seema Aziz, who heads Pakistan's largest educational non-profit organization, emphasizes the importance of encouraging girls to study science and math. Rosario Bazán, who co-founded Danper Trujillo, one of Peru's largest agricultural companies,

---

* https://timesofindia.indiatimes.com/india/40-of-girls-aged-15-18-not-attending-school-report/articleshow/73598999.cms

started a school inside her firm to educate women workers, many of whom were heads of households.

Providing women access to capital and income is as important as access to education. This was the mission of Ela Bhatt when she founded SEWA in 1972. At that time, women in India's vast informal sector had no labour protection and no access to outside finance. Bhatt redefined work as an economic activity, not as a relationship between an employer and employee—hence the concept of self-employed. SEWA fought for the rights of such self-employed women. She went on to find a cooperative bank to help finance women in the informal sector. Social entrepreneur Shamlu Dudeja pursued another strategy to boost the incomes of rural women. Dudeja established SHE (Self-Help Enterprise) Foundation as a non-profit organization that focuses on reviving kantha—the art of traditional embroidery found in the states of West Bengal and Odisha, as well as Bangladesh—as a means to provide rural women with access to income. SHE grew from just a few women embroidering kantha in their spare time to a complex network with trained seamstresses overseeing hundreds of women workers. Dudeja explains how the revival of kantha has changed the lives of these artisans through empowerment and improved their relationships with their husbands as they raised the family income.

The provision of income for women is also a major topic for Bazán, who talks of her endeavours to provide employment to women to enable them 'to break away from the vicious cycle of poverty'. She notes the wider implications of women of having an income, including a rise in their self-esteem and the ability to speak up about issues such as domestic violence. Bazán talks of a 'social balance sheet', which can consider the many benefits from gender equality that conventional accounting statements are notoriously poor at capturing. Bazán's holistic views on measuring the impact of business raises the question whether female managers are more attuned to broader societal considerations than their male counterparts. The evidence from many of the voices heard in this chapter is that they probably are.

5(a)

Zia Mody

Zia Mody

Zia Mody is a founding and senior partner of AZB & Partners, a leading law firm in India. Inspired to go into law by her father Soli Jehangir Sorabjee, the former attorney general of India between 1989 and 1990, and again from 1998 to 2004, Mody began her career as a young lawyer in New York City at the firm of Baker McKenzie. Mody worked her way to becoming one of India's top corporate lawyers and successfully grew AZB & Partners from a small boutique firm into a major firm with more than 400 associates across India. *Fortune India* ranked her number one in the list of the most powerful women entrepreneurs in both 2018 and 2019.

Interviewed by Tarun Khanna in Mumbai on 14 February 2017.

Interviewer: *Were there a lot of women when you worked at Baker McKenzie in New York between 1980 and 1984?*

Zia Mody (ZM): About 25 per cent. Not too bad, but not what it would be today. And my senior, Norman Miller, he told me there was no pressure. But of course, there was! Here I was this foreign student, but . . . my stint in New York definitely reinforced my ability to stay the term. Coming back to India was a struggle because you were in court . . . with 100 men, maybe one woman, two women, who would actually argue rather than follow. I was very nervous and therefore this was a very defining experience for me—to give up, or not to give up. I had three children, by the way, while I was arguing, so a lot of choices, guilt 24/7, nervousness about the boys laughing at me, and worry about what the judges were thinking if I hadn't got it right and that it would somehow get back to my father. But I think all in all there has never been any great moment when I wanted to give up the law. So I would say, you can still find success and be happy, even if you lose sometimes in court. I remember the first case that I lost. I was weeping and then I was telling my father, 'But I am right, I know I am right, the judge is wrong!' And he was quiet on the other end of the line, he was in Delhi, I could see him smiling. He said, 'But someone has to lose, and you can go and appeal and you can argue first.' I think there were a lot of just natural little moments. I wouldn't say there was one big bang revelation.

Interviewer: I remember reading that someone advised you when you came back to India that to start your career as a woman lawyer you should do free cases?

ZM: Yes, so when I came back as I said there were no mergers and acquisitions, and I was a young junior and juniors never really got to argue the cases. And there were so many juniors, how do you stand out? And the only way you stand out is to get the opportunity to brief a senior, get good matters, and then slowly start arguing. So my senior basically told me that for the first year I should not charge. So if I was for free, I got more work. If I got more work I could demonstrate more capability. So that was the virtually free one year.

Interviewer: Can you speak about how you have helped cultivate women lawyers in AZB & Partners?

ZM: They are very special to me, and all the men know that. So I think the fact that I am a woman and there is leadership from a woman at the top suddenly makes it easier for our women. So what do I do actually, in real terms, rather than just the esoteric 'I love women' thing? I am a bit of a control freak when it comes to this part of life. Many women who are working with us obviously go through the lifecycles of marriage and motherhood. These are our two crisis points when we want to give up the profession or give up what we are doing. And so I have a sort of a checklist now. When someone says she is getting married, I sit her down, say here is the checklist, come back to me, tell me I am a genius, tell me I know everything, because this is exactly what's going to happen. And so I offered guidance about your infrastructure and how are you going to deal with it. We discussed questions like are you with your mother-in-law, are you not with your mother-in-law, do you have to fight with your mother-in-law, is it a sin to be friends with your mother-in-law, why don't you make people who can help you your friends and your allies. The first child is the worst time for a mother and so . . . we have our little AZB babies, and I think the best thing that you can do is to nurture the woman through that difficult period, which is not much. It is sometimes six months, it is sometimes nine months, it is sometimes a year, it's whatever they need to get their head comfortable. And then you know you don't have to judge them like every aggressive male, they bring a lot more to the table in different ways. So if the guy is doing twelve deals, if the woman at that time is doing not twelve deals but eight deals, it's okay. And if she feels she is respected, and if she feels you are not doing charity to her, she is fine. And the men get it because we have invested years in this resource and she stayed there because she is bright, she is committed, she has the DNA of the firm, she holds our letterhead high—why would we lose her? It's just stupid. So when somebody who is in a position of leadership says that I guess most people listen.

Interviewer: So how many women do you have now in the firm?

ZM: 50 per cent of partners and maybe a little more as associates.

Interviewer: We often hear about the difficulty of work–life balance. How do you think about work–life balance either by force of example

*or as you see it play out with the women who are so beloved to you
in your firm?*

ZM: So I don't stop saying that my example is a wrong example.
I personally think in hindsight, at the tender age of sixty that
I am now, that I overdid it. I think that I did not balance it
enough. I don't think there is such a thing as work-life balance,
first of all. To start with, it is how much balance. So I think
that today's women funnily enough feel the guilt more than
maybe my generation did. My generation, maybe, or your wife's
generation, had that sense of wanting to achieve because maybe
their mothers did not have that same opportunity. I think
my mother lived through me, I had to do everything that she
couldn't do. And so I get that there has to be a balance, as
always, but the balance is imperfect. If you have to be a thorough
professional, if you want to be seen as one of the best, what is
the enemy? The enemy is time, and who gets the short end of
that stick? Your family. So I guess when you are older you say
sorry more, you take more holidays, but then by that time our
children have grown up. So I think the work-life balance story,
I think in any country, probably is a difficult choice.

Learnings from Zia Mody: Mentorship is key to advancing the
professional careers of women.

5(b)

Naina Lal Kidwai

Naina Lal Kidwai

Naina Lal Kidwai is former country head of HSBC India, the first woman to head an international bank in India. She received the Padma Shri award in 2007 for her contributions to industry and trade. In 2015, she founded the India Sanitation Coalition, a multi-stakeholder platform with more than

150 organizations engaged in driving sustainable sanitation
throughout India.

Interviewed by Tarun Khanna in New Delhi on 4 April
2019.

*Interviewer: I would like you to just reflect on the broad arc of your
career. Can you tell us how your career began?*

Naina Lal Kidwai (NLK): A good starting point would be
my applying to Pricewaterhouse to start a career in chartered
accountancy right after graduating from college at Lady Shri
Ram College in 1977 here in New Delhi. The first response I
got was that they didn't hire women, and then began a process
of push and pull, trying to get them to reconsider this policy.
The good news is it took them a couple of months, but they did
come back and say that they would hire three of us women, and
that's how we started. I might add, it was exactly these turning
points that mattered. A firm like Pricewaterhouse today has
around 50 per cent of their staff as women, and sometimes they
say that they actively have to keep it that way or it may well
be more than 50 per cent women. So it just goes to show that
sometimes firms have to break with traditions early enough and
take the right decisions.

Interviewer: How long did you work at Pricewaterhouse?

NLK: I was there between 1977 and 1980. From there I went
on to Harvard Business School as the first Indian woman to
graduate from there. I think that's such a sad social comment,
but that has nothing to do with the school not taking in Indian
women, but more with the fact that Indian women just didn't

apply. I know that I had issues at home with trying to persuade my parents and others that it made sense for me to go to the US to do that MBA. So again, social change happens, and when it begins to happen, it happens quickly. If you look at what HBS is today, and the number of Indian women that went soon after I was there, it has actually grown. It goes to show how quickly things can change.

Learnings from Naina Lal Kidwai: It can be tough to open doors for aspiring professional women, but when the door opens there can be rapid progress.

5(c)

Shabana Azmi

Shabana Azmi

Shabana Azmi is a prominent Indian actor starring in groundbreaking films in both mainstream and parallel cinema, a social and women's rights activist, and was nominated as a member of Parliament in the Rajya Sabha, the upper house of India's Parliament, from 1997 to 2003. She was awarded the Padma Shri in 1988 and the Padma Bhushan in 2012.

Interviewed by Rohit Deshpande in Mumbai on 30 November 2015.

Interviewer: What challenges did you face contesting restrictive gender norms in the movie industry?

Shabana Azmi (SA): Actors within the parallel cinema were standing up against the prevailing norms of the day, particularly, I think, in their reflection and understanding of gender and women. Mainstream cinema on one side had women in traditional roles, and then you worked in parallel cinema and there were actors who were courageous enough to put themselves out and say, 'This is what we will do'. At one level it gives them a lot of respect because people respect the work that they are doing; on the other hand, when I did a film called *Fire* with Deepa Mehta, in which Nandita Das and I played lesbians, it was a calculated risk. I mean, I knew that this would raise a controversy. I was particularly concerned because I was working with women in the slums and the fact that I speak from a liberal, non-religious space already makes it difficult for women to actually join me because their husbands then say to them that 'she is not the right influence on you', etc. Now, doing a film like *Fire*, I figured . . . it would make my work even more difficult. But even so I felt it was very important that I acted in that film, because it is a film about a lesbian relationship between two sisters-in-law and before that nothing of that kind had been attempted in Hindi cinema.

Now when the film was released there was one section of the public that loved the film and said this is a really bold film to do. On the other hand, there was a group of people that

said that these are anti-national people, they are anti-Hindu
people, and they are doing this to desecrate Indian culture. A
political party, the Right-wing Shiv Sena, decided that they
will make hay while the sun shines. They pulled the film out of
the theatres, started breaking furniture and had many protests
and demonstrations, and I was personally vilified for bringing
in the wrong cultural values. That is the risk you have to take
because India's audiences are not monolithic, not everybody
reacts in the same way.

I'm very fond of saying that India is a country that lives
in several centuries simultaneously. We have people living
back-to-back from the eighteenth, nineteenth, twentieth and
twenty-first centuries, and India's people at any given time and
place encapsulate all the contradictions that come from being
a multicultural, multi-religious, multilingual society, and so it
is with audiences. This particularly impacts women, I think,
this living in several centuries, and I think *Fire* was important
because if it was a film that had been located in a Western
upper-class household it would have gotten different reactions,
but this was within a middle-class family in the heart of Delhi.
It also looked at the joint family system, and how the oppression
of that can impact this relationship.

*Interviewer: Can you talk about what you see as the role of the
film industry in empowering women, in impacting the social
mores regarding patriarchy, and can you reflect on both the role of
commercial cinema and of parallel cinema?*

SA: There is a huge section of those who are making films
who believe that the purpose of art is entertainment, nothing
more, nothing less. I don't have any problem with that, if that

is the choice that you are making, it is an informed choice, that's fine. I think that what we need to redefine is the concept of entertainment. Entertainment need not be vulgarity and crudity and really base kinds of things. You can talk about entertainment in a different way. But I grew up believing that art should be used as an instrument for social change, and I think film is a very important medium through which we can bring about changes, particularly in the characterization of women. For it to be truly impactful, it will have to be reflected in mainstream cinema because if you do it through parallel cinema then you are preaching to the already converted. So to make real impact, it has to be in the playing of the heroine, and I see that happening, and that makes me very happy. There are female actors who are choosing to lower their prices, committing to an expedited filming schedule, facilitating the making of a . . . woman-oriented film in which she is not seen within the stereotypical role. And so there has been a spate of women-oriented films that have also met with a moderate degree of commercial success. Now that is crucial because filmmakers, film producers are not here to change society. They are here to run a business. It's a speculative business, so I think audiences also have a role to play. So audiences in the choice of the films they see also impact the way that producers think.

But I do think society is ready for a change and producers . . . haven't actually realized that. And so I think today when you look at the discourse that is happening in India the need for empowerment is no longer a buzzword, it is an active thing that is being demanded by civil society. The wonderful thing about India is that there is strong resistance against all kinds of exploitation, whether it is of women or Dalits or minorities or what have you. And that I think is shaping the destiny of what

India is moving towards, in which the empowerment of women to help them become decision makers in the process is a very important thing.

Interviewer: What is your thinking on whether the film industry should lead public opinion on women's empowerment and gender issues or whether it should follow public opinion?

SA: There are different, contradictory answers to this, like everything about India. Whatever you see about India at any given point, the opposite is also true. So that is true in the film industry also because I grew up believing that art should be used as an instrument for social change and the work that I did, particularly when it came to the portrayal of women, I actively turned down roles calling for women to be subservient. I have actually not done those films even when they offered a lot of money and have done roles for which I didn't get paid at all, but I thought that it would be raising the bar for women and their rights because I think that it is important to build up contesting voices because of the multiplicity of interests that we have in a country like India. So cinema has a very important role to play in changing the mores of society, particularly when it comes to women.

Learnings from Shabana Azmi: Cinema and the arts have important roles to play in contesting gender stereotypes.

5(d)

Keshub Mahindra

Keshub Mahindra was the chairperson of the Mahindra Group, a diversified business group headquartered in India, between 1963 and 2012. The business started in 1945 in a partnership between Keshub's father and his father's friend, Ghulam Muhammad. Keshub joined the company in 1947 after graduating from Wharton with an MBA. The Group started off by selling and manufacturing utility vehicles and built market leadership in utility vehicles and tractors. However, under Keshub's leadership it also diversified into many other industries, including aerospace, agribusiness, construction equipment, defence, energy, information technology, leisure hospitality, and real estate. The group has been praised for its strong commitment to high business ethics and philanthropy, which has especially focused on promoting women's education. Interviewed by Tarun Khanna in Mumbai on 24 July 2013.

Interviewer: As you look back on building your business, were there any momentous successes that stick in your mind, which helped you understand what you would be able to become in the years to come, or any big failures that caused you to learn and reflect?

Keshub Mahindra (KM): Well, everything in life is about learning through successes and failures. Yes, we had great successes and we also had bad failures. But fundamentally I think what we believed in, and we still do, is in the dignity of the individual. We strongly feel that no matter what you do, you have to recognize that. Therefore, you set up a series of practices to really empower the people who work for you, and you look after them. It is our sacred duty and for us, I think, it has paid very high dividends. Most of our people are totally empowered. We as a family don't interfere. We give authority to people to govern within certain principles and values.

We strongly believe in a very strong value system. We will not compromise on ethics. The rewards that we get in return for being extremely strict are impossible to measure. I think our reputation speaks for itself; we strongly believe in education. I think 80 per cent of our contributions to charities go towards education, particularly women's education, because we believe that it is critical—how children are brought up in their homes. In spite of male chauvinism, we have to give credit to the mothers.

Interviewer: What would I see in the Mahindra Group pertaining to your espoused desire to promote women's education and women's empowerment that I would not see in another corporate setting in India?

KM: We are today helping educate over 90,000 girls in schools every year, which is an immense job to manage in itself, and we are soliciting help from others to increase this number. We want to go to a million. So this is one of the things we do and a lot of businesses get behind it. They have their own priorities. The Tatas do a lot of work. The Birlas [the family behind the Aditya Birla business group] also does. The Ambanis [who control Reliance Industries, India's most valuable company by market value], do also. They run a beautiful school here and they have got a beautiful hospital. But we don't have the culture you have in the United States and that is a collective doing.

Interviewer: Why don't statesmen like you do something about that?

KM: The response from business, at least over the past years, on many such issues has been disappointing. Some of them prefer to do it themselves. For instance, there are many mid-size businesses that do a lot of charitable work. Nobody has evaluated how much they do. You go to the temple and pray so that you can fight your adversary in business and seek divine blessings. It is the same culture. It will come, I think, now that the government has been taking a step towards corporate social responsibility. Many small businesses, and I have been telling Anand Mahindra [his nephew, who replaced him as group chairperson in 2012] also, I said, 'Let's offer help to the people to help them run these charities better because they don't know how to do it; they are too small to really be effective.'

Learnings from Keshub Mahindra: Education is key to advancing the progress of women in Indian society.

5(e)

Ela Bhatt

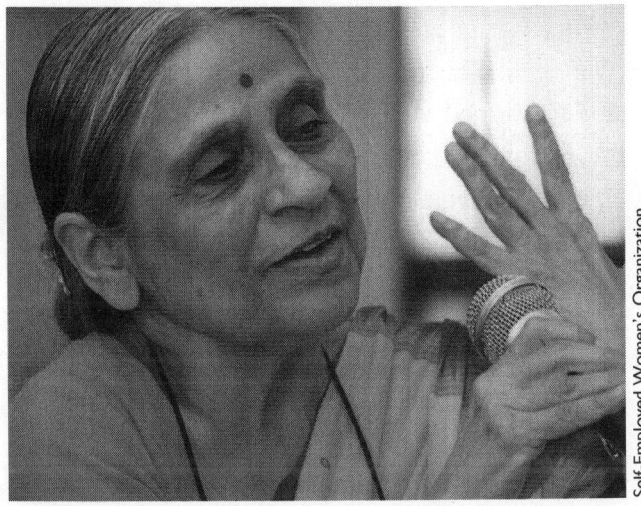

Self-Employed Women's Organization

Ela Bhatt is the founder of SEWA, established in 1972 as an organization devoted to the advancement of poor women in India. She served as president and general secretary of SEWA from 1972 to 1996. Bhatt also helped found Women's World Banking in 1979 and served as its chair between 1980 and 1998. She received the Padma Shri in 1985 and the Padma Bhushan in 1986.

Interviewed by Geoffrey Jones in Mumbai on 13 July 2017.

Interviewer: In 1955, you joined the legal department of the Textile Labour Association in Ahmedabad. The organization was founded by a woman, but I believe by the 1950s, men were the dominant concern. Can you explain what happened?

Ela Bhatt (EB): When you look at the old photographs of the third strike, which have become famous, you see that almost half of the audience in that meeting—half of the people in that general meeting—are women. You can see all the women with covered heads—they are there. There were men workers and women workers, too. It is evident that about 50 per cent of the workers were women at one time, at least in those times, when those first preliminary strikes were going on. Then, over a period of time, as it happened, as it got more and more regularized, there were fewer and fewer women. When I joined in 1955, at that time, the number of women workers had come down to almost 4 per cent. They were only in the spinning department and in the waste department. All the weaving and sizing—all those major departments—later on went to the men. Shall I tell you the story?

There was one machine called the Barber-Colman machine, which was in the spinning department. It enabled more efficient production . . . but for that machine, you needed training. When the trainees were chosen, only men were chosen—no women in the spinning department were chosen for the training. The women naturally, as they tended to do, said, 'No, no, we cannot learn how to operate the machine.' And then the leaders of the union, including men, said, 'Why should they do such labour and such slavery in a factory or in a mill? Their place is in the home and their job is to take care of the home better, and to serve better the basic needs of the family, and to raise children.' So that is how—with that attitude towards work, in general—very slowly, the number of women workers came down. When I was there, only 4 per cent remained. The only thing I could do to prevent the continued decline of women workers was to pass an ordinance from the state government saying that, now, there will be no more releasing of mill workers. Those who exist, that number must be maintained. But then, as they grew older, they one by one retired. So that is how the number of women declined. But that was still at the beginning of my career, so I didn't have the power or strength to influence my leaders. There was still the typical mentality that a women's place is in the home: women should learn better cooking and how to prepare nutritious food; why should husbands go outside to eat outside food when their wives could learn to cook those very items that are sold in the restaurants?

When I joined, there was a women's wing in the Textile Labour Association where better cooking and better household skills were being taught. So that was going on already. When I arrived, I introduced new skills for the first time, starting with stitching. But what happened was that in the 1980s . . . I was also part of the legal department of the union. I was fully active in the court, as well as the labour court, and I started taking up small cases. I was involved in negotiations with the management of the mills. Just before the 1980s, two mills closed down, and those workers from the closed mills were sitting in the union; all were busy rallying, or were busy in the court. I asked the leader of my union, 'How do these men and their involvement with the union affect their families?' Because the workers no longer had any income. I asked my leader, 'Can I go and find out how their families are impacted by all of this?' I went to the living quarters and saw women working. That opened my eyes, maybe for the first time, to the fact that women were working in so many different occupations, and they were supporting their families, since there was no income from their husbands, from their men. And then, when I tried to understand more, I realized that they had no protection of any law. They were working, they were contributing to production, to trading, to small businesses, to the service sector, and they were earning income. But if they lost their work, they had no protection of any law.

Interviewer: How did you respond when you realized the plight of these workers?

EB: After a while, I said, 'I don't want to work any more with those who are already protected. I want to work for those who are unprotected.' I realized that unprotected labourers made up roughly 90 per cent—at that time, it was 89 per cent, today it is 95.7 per cent—of the total workforce of India. At that time, women happened to make up about 50 per cent of that unprotected workforce. Later, I learnt that women also happened to be amongst the poorest in the pyramid. After seeing how women's economic participation was so crucial to the family, I said, 'I will work for those who are unprotected and unorganized.' That was how SEWA was born, as an organization that recognized women as being self-employed, rather than informal or unorganized. I did not accept those terms.

Interviewer: Why were the banks unwilling to lend to women?

EB: Who would care, who would care, first of all, for the poor? And secondly, they never saw the women's work as work: they were women, so they were supporting the family. Their work was invisible, even to the census of India. Until 1970, they were recorded as non-workers. The census inspector would go to the rural woman and stand before her while she was milking the cow, and that woman would still be recorded as a non-worker. Now, that milk is going to go to the market. It is going to bring cash income, and so it is part of the GDP of the country—part of the national income of the country. But still, that rural woman is considered a non-worker. That is how all these occupations go unaccounted for, and that's how we have 90 per cent of the workforce being unorganized and unprotected and unrecorded.

Interviewer: Was that a legacy from the British colonial period or was it a product of independent India?

EB: Well, there was a theory—an economic theory—about the definition of work. I would say that the day we registered SEWA as a labour union, after quite a long struggle, we questioned the definition of work. We questioned the definition of worker, and the definition of a labour union. Because ultimately, these definitions very much depended upon the attitude of the people, on whether they were following or building theories, or whether they were attuned to the practical features of the economic environment around them. Most people didn't see the work of these self-employed labourers as work. So in general, the problem with this self-employed sector was that their work was invisible. Because they were not organized, they were voiceless.

Their work itself was not validated, was not considered valid. I gave you the rural woman example of milking the cow, but there are thousands of such occupations, which are not considered valid work. We struggled and struggled for years to change the understanding about work and self-employed labourers, and we have succeeded.

Interviewer: Why was it so hard to make your point? Because it's sort of self-evident that it was work, and yet, you spent decades struggling. What were the obstacles?

EB: Professors like you, who teach economics! Because what is work? The definition of work pre-supposes a relationship between an employer and an employee. So that is where we derive our definitions of work, that is how we define a worker, and that relationship provides the foundation of the worker's union. But in countries like ours, and other countries as well, work is being done according to the local needs of people, and particularly, in order to satisfy the basic needs of a human being, of a human community. But since industrialization, only industrial workers are considered workers, and the rest are non-workers. It has a long history.

Interviewer: In the 1970s, India had a female leader, for example, Indira Gandhi. Was she sympathetic to the case you were trying to make, or not?

EB: No, but what she and others appreciated was that we were working to remove poverty. So most of the time, we got support because we were working for the poor and for poverty relief, and because we followed Gandhian philosophies of constructive, creative and non-violent action, which did not create any animosity. But at the conceptual level, our fight was very difficult. Even trade unions did not accept us, at the national and at the international level, and they objected to affiliation with SEWA. We were very clear that we were a union because we represented workers who were economically active. But the unions did not accept us, neither did our own union [the Textile Labour Association] nor did other European unions and unions at the international level. We went on and on, and ultimately, a point came when the International Labour Organization listened to us, and then European unions grew more favourable. Those organizations were very powerful, because they were very well organized. So over time, these organizations slowly began to understand what we were talking about. But it took sixteen years for us to get through to them. Our demand was about home work—work that is done in the home—because so many types of economic activities are being done by women in their homes without any protection, without any recognition, and without any access to social security.

Interviewer: Can we talk more about SEWA Bank, which was established in 1974. Why did you decide to lend only to women?

EB: I didn't decide. Like a good Brahmin, I knew that one should not touch another's money. And I was most ill-equipped to run a bank—really, I tell you. But we saw—I saw with my own eyes—that the first priority of these women was to come out of private debts, which were highly exploitative. So how to achieve this goal? Indira Gandhi had just announced the nationalization of Indian banks, so then we went to those nationalized banks, but it was still difficult. The kind of treatment these women received was terrible. The banks didn't believe that women could really come to the bank and be account holders, or take a loan. Then there would also be the problem of repayment from the poor, in general. So the banks, then, were not ready.

We had a big meeting of SEWA members, and in that meeting, the women poured out their difficulties with the banks and with the entire situation. Then one of them, Chanda Ben—she was a used-garment dealer in the city—said, 'Why can't we have our own bank?' I said, 'We need a lot of capital— share capital—to start a bank.' She responded, 'Yes, we are poor, but we are so many. So we can collect the necessary share capital.' And I must say, in six months' time, they did collect the necessary share capital to start a bank. Then we went for the registration.

I always believed ideologically in a cooperative. So in this case, I believed that the women should be the owners of whatever economic enterprise they established. When I went to register the bank, the registrar of cooperatives said that it sounded like a very foolish idea. First, they humoured me, and then they grew more hostile to the things that I said. They said, 'These are women, they don't know how to deal with money.' The bureaucrats at the registrar office had no idea that these were the women who were in the market every day, since their childhood—they knew how to handle money very well. Then, the registrar said, 'They are illiterate.' That was true. He continued, 'They belong to this community and that community . . . so don't trust them.' The registrar of cooperatives even said to me—like my brother said, 'One day you will have to commit suicide, because the women will not repay their loans, and you will not be able to show your face to the society.' But I had trust in the women, so far as money was concerned, because they were so highly exploited by existing institutions. I believed that, because the cooperative was their own bank, they would definitely repay in time, if it was established and run properly. So finally, we got it registered as a bank. I had always wanted, from the beginning, to be in the mainstream—that's why we made it a trade union, not an NGO. Similarly, that's why I wanted a cooperative bank—a regulated one, by the Reserve Bank of India—not a microfinance institution, which at the time was not under the stewardship of the central bank. From the second year, we have been distributing dividends of 9 to 12 per cent—without any break.

Learnings from Ela Bhatt: The very concept of work needs redefining if we are to provide proper social support for women in the informal sector.

5(f)

Shamlu Dudeja

The Hindu

Shamlu Dudeja is the founder of SHE Foundation, a non-profit organization that focuses on reviving the craft of kantha as a means to generate income for rural women. Dudeja founded SHE in 1991 by using royalties from a major maths textbook she wrote earlier in her career as a mathematics teacher. In 1995,

Dudeja also became founder and chairperson of the Calcutta Foundation, which supports Kolkata's low-income population. Interviewed by Geoffrey Jones in Kolkata on 27 April 2018.

Interviewer: You founded SHE Foundation in 1991 to further your work to revive kantha, the art of traditional embroidery found in West Bengal and Odisha. What was the motivation?

Shamlu Dudeja (SD): Recently, people have started talking about corporate social responsibility. I thought about it in 1991 and that was my motivation. I didn't want to say randomly that we were doing a welfare project for our kantha artisans. Of course, they were paid immediately, the moment the kantha textile was brought in to us. I pay the full amount due to them by cheque, so that there is never any discrepancy. But we wanted to formalize what we were doing. Say, the annual income from kantha is Rs 100, 25 per cent of that goes into SHE Foundation.

SHE, every now and again, uses that money for welfare projects, such as education for children, the wedding of a daughter in the family, the provision of woollen garments for winter months, Godrej steel cupboards to store kantha stocks and their personal possessions, expenses for surgery or any other illness, regular medical camps and eye camps. Projects for 2018 include provision of sanitary pads, prevention of excessive use of plastics and provision of a substitute for plastics bags used on a daily basis in the villages.

Now, there is a need to go back a bit. I started with three girls—now we have 800 girls. How do we manage them? If my home is the centre of a circle, then I have eight senior kantha artisans, kind of scattered around me, not deep in the rural areas, but more semi-urban. Each of these senior artisans fans out into the villages, and picks out say, two junior artisans to supervise the artisans in the interiors. They, in turn, pick up another four. These ladies fan out further into the villages. Each senior artisan now has probably about 100 girls under her, who he or she is supervising. There is one team leader from a Muslim group—their women do not like to travel to Kolkata, so they have a male team leader. The senior artisan comes to me for fabrics, for colours, for designs. If I like a sari, I tell her, 'Make two or three of these, in due course.' If I don't like it, and I feel it will not sell, I tell her, 'Don't make any more of this design for us.' The team leader takes the fabrics, the designs and the colour schemes into the villages . . . and gives them to the junior girls to work on, with full instructions. She looks at their workmanship to make sure that they [the embroideries] are tidier and more uniform. The object is also to improve the quality of workmanship. Knots and loose threads on the reverse are not appreciated. And, they are encouraged to use single thread from a skein, rather than double—most artisans do not like this; they prefer to work with double threads.

Interviewer: How do you keep consistency of the product with so many girls?

SD: This is not easy; and our team leaders deserve credit for this. The artisans travel to the homes of team leaders to get the quality of work approved. The artisans come to team leaders to get new colour combinations approved, 'My sample has only one colour, but I have used two shades of green, a shade of yellow, and a shade of brown. Does this look good? May I work with these colours?' And the team leader will give her approval, or not. After the team leader has been to me and she has chatted with my office staff or me, she knows that the green is too pale, and perhaps it does not fit in well. The team leader tells the artisans that this green is not approved; and the artisans follow the colour schemes suggested. They keep track of the quality of stitchery, the colour schemes, the time taken to complete the textile. What happens is that some of the girls may just work one hour a day, whereas some girls who have grown up children and have more time . . . they can work four, five hours a day. So, the group of girls that is prepared to work for five hours a day gets fabrics that have urgent dates of delivery. Saris that are not needed urgently will be given to the second group of artisans who take longer to complete a textile. It is not easy, but that is how we keep track of consistency of product and time taken.

Interviewer: Can you talk to us about how the revival of this craft has changed the lives of the women?

SD: You have to see it to believe it. You need to see their attitude towards their everyday life . . . that's the biggest change. I took one young woman to New York and two to Santa Fe, where we have exhibitions every year. You had to see the change in their daily behaviour—I am referring to a change for the good! They behave as if they are equal to everyone, because I treat them at an equal level. The simpler women from the villages will tend to have a more simple, shy attitude. But the kantha artisans' entire attitude to life has become better than it was before. They want education for their children; when they come to my house, they come dressed up in a good cotton sari—not a synthetic sari, which a lot of village women tend to wear.

Every year they have a birthday party for me, in my house.
This year—my eightieth birthday—they hosted a huge birthday
party for me. They brought their children; a couple of women
brought their husbands or brothers. There were fifty of us in
my garden under a kantha canopy! They had worked out a
game with a huge photograph of me. Each one of us had to tie
a hanky around our eyes, go to the photograph and put a bindi
on 'my forehead' in the photograph! Isn't that wonderful? And
there were gifts for me, to top it all! When they come to my
house, they will sit with my guests and me, at the dining table
and have a meal with us. This wouldn't have happened some
years ago—they would have waited for us to finish eating, and
then would have sat down to eat. Another point. When we go
to their homes in the villages, we are welcomed with a lot of
affection—just as they would do to a good friend. Not with
too much formality as they would have done earlier, to people
coming from the cities. They call me didi [older sister] and
truly treat me like one. I feel honoured.

*Interviewer: How does it change their relationships with their
husbands?*

SD: In a lot of cases that I know of, it has become much better.
A lot of husbands are helping their wives in expanding their
kantha activities. Some husbands shop for them, some look for
new artisans to join the group, some younger men in the family
bring stocks to us and take back the cheques in payment.

The other thing that has happened in a couple of places is
that Hindu and Muslim women sit and work together. And the
Muslim men—because their wives do not come to the city—
bring their kantha textiles to us, discuss the various aspects of

work, and take the cheque back in payment. This is being done by a Muslim group, so it is amazing that even the Muslim men have allowed their wives to go on with work, and that Hindu and Muslim families are good friends. I mean, our country needs to learn a lot from that—that there is no distinction at all among the Hindus and Muslims in the groups that we work with. If I have a Diwali party, and I invite the Muslims, they will come. My driver is a Muslim, and if I have a Diwali party, and if I invite him to come, he will come and have the prashad that is served after the puja. I am not a religious person, but what has happened is that religion is no more a partition between them. They mix together, chat together and party together. So empowerment, religious acceptance, inclusiveness, a sense of dignity and self-worth, for these rural artisans—these are all very important for us. It does not mean that if the stitchery done on the fabric is bad, that I do not tell them. Of course, I do . . . but much like I would tell a younger friend.

Learnings from Shamlu Dudeja: Providing work for rural women can do more than put cash in their pockets. It also raises their confidence and self-esteem and can even improve relationships with their husbands.

5(g)

Seema Aziz

Seema Aziz is the founder and managing director of Sefam, a major fashion retail brand in Pakistan, and the chairperson of CARE Foundation, Pakistan's largest educational non-profit organization established in 1988 after a destructive flood hit the region.

Interviewed by Tarun Khanna in Boston, Massachusetts, on 18 September 2016.

Interviewer: Can you tell me how your involvement in education began?

Seema Aziz (SA): I put together the money, got a piece of land, which was donated by somebody in the area. Then I built a school. When we opened the doors of that school, 17 January 1991, 250 children were standing outside, all barefoot, all with runny noses, matted hair, tops but no trousers or trousers but no tops. They'd all lined up for a chance to a better life, and we've never looked back. I had to create the curriculum for that school, and that's when I understood how only an equal education could equalize. My son had just joined the best school in Pakistan that year. I simply picked up that curriculum and I put it in the village school.

The medium of instruction was English. I also thought the school had to be co-educational. If I tried to segregate the school, how would I ever teach my girls science and maths? It had to be co-education. So we started by leading children to the hand pump with a towel and a comb, among other things. By the end of the first six months, they had become fabulous. In an area that had 100 per cent illiteracy, lots of disease, absolute poverty and no teachers really available, I could still find people to train so they could become teachers. By the end of the year, word had gotten around: 'There's a school where education happens.' Next year, we had 450 children. The year after that, we had 850 children. We just went on from there. We built another school and then another school.

Interviewer: This is all unfolding in Lahore?

SA: Around Lahore. It's fifteen miles [about 24 km] out of Lahore—very rural at that time. When I said the school's going to be co-educational and English medium, everyone said, 'They'll lynch you, you're mad!'—so the madness doesn't stop.

Interviewer: Tell me about both the gender issue and the medium of instruction.

SA: It's so strange. I've found a totally different world out there. Nobody protested, either about the gender issue or the language. I knew they were not going to. Today, we are running 716 schools across Pakistan. We have an enrolment of over 2,30,000 children in our schools. That first school grew very quickly, and today, has 2000 girls and boys. CARE's own schools in rural areas embrace co-education, right up to class ten and class twelve in some schools. Even though so many years have gone by, people still ask, 'And you actually run co-educational schools? You mean up to class two? To class three?' Then I say, 'No. It's all the way up to class ten and twelve, and nobody protests.' So, these are myths that people have created. I've been told that people don't want to educate their girls in Pakistan. In turn, I always ask why I don't come across these parents? Why don't I find the girls who don't want to be educated?

Interviewer: The schools now are all over Pakistan?

SA: They're all over. We recently adopted our first three schools in Balochistan, which was a huge step. A vast majority of our schools are in Punjab. We built another school and then another school in the early years of CARE. Everything was filling up. In our first school, we soon had to start running a double shift. We also built more classes quickly, but it wasn't enough. Within a couple of years, we had 1000 children in there. Today we run more than 100 schools in full double shift.

Interviewer: So, tell me about English. When you started, you must have experienced difficulty—finding teachers. The children presumably spoke Urdu or Punjabi, I gather, not English?

SA: I found that children quickly pick up whatever you teach them, in whichever accent. I would stand in the schools myself every morning. It's just a matter of training. I found that people learn by example, and from what they hear. It's true there were no teachers, but it wasn't so difficult to find them in the long run. For instance, while looking for teachers, I found a carpenter who'd done ten years of school and a retired soldier who had done ten years of school. We just trained them. Somehow, everyone was motivated.

Interviewer: These people were repurposed into teachers, in some ways?

SA: That's how you find teachers. Anyone who's done ten years of school can become a teacher. That's how we started. We weren't going to find graduates in that area. Children came in all ages and sizes because there was no education in that area at all. Again, I found that the older children were learning faster, so we allowed them to keep jumping classes. We were very involved with every child. I always worried because I thought that the poor do not have ten years, and ten years is a ridiculous amount of time to spend on basics. We would closely observe every child. In some cases, whole classes jumped, from class four to class six or from class five to class seven, depending on their proficiency levels. These double-promoted classes ended up doing way better than the regular ones.

Our first graduating class was in 1995, which was just five years after opening our first school. We had excellent results. All the children cleared their matric [matriculation exams taken in the final year of school or college], which doesn't happen nationally. The national result at that time was somewhere around 30 per cent. Then, of course, we started a little college there, because everyone came back and said, 'Now you need to start a college.' I said, 'No, I will only ever do schools.' The whole village came back a month later and said, 'Where are the girls going to go? You better start a college.' Then I understood and said, 'You're right and I was wrong.' We started a college right there and then. The girls and boys started studying.

Interviewer: Because the girls would find it difficult to go to college?

SA: They thought so in the beginning. Yes, at that time, it would have been difficult and public transport is not so good in rural Pakistan. Eventually, I came across some amazing developments. The people were so eager to progress. Our first girls from that village school very soon went to some of the best colleges in Pakistan. As they started graduating, and as they got good enough marks, I realized, by 1998 or 1999, that our children were getting good marks, but couldn't go to college because they didn't have the money. We set up a scholarship fund to put bright children through college. That's how it started. Our first girls were enrolled in Kinnaird, which is the best girl's college in the country. Our girls are also in Government College University, which is a co-educational institute, and among the best colleges in the country. None of the parents thought it was wrong to send their girls to colleges in Lahore, even co-educational ones.

Learnings from Seema Aziz: Never accept broad stereotypes about gender relations. Norms and expectations are always more complex.

5(h)

Rosario Bazán

Rosario Bazán is co-founder and general manager of the Peruvian agribusiness group, Danper Trujillo. Danper began operations in 1994 as a Danish–Peruvian joint venture and is now one of Peru's largest agricultural companies. The company has been recognized for its commitment to society and for its emphasis on the employment of women.

Interviewed by Andrea Lluch in Lima, Peru, on 27 May 2017.

Interviewer: Agribusiness is one of the sectors, especially in Latin America, receiving much criticism for its shortcomings in environmental impact and concern for employees. What has your company done that is different?

Rosario Bazán (RB): We have been able to innovate; we are breaking new ground. The way in which Danper treats its workers aims to have an impact on their living conditions, helping them to acquire technical competencies as well as leadership abilities. In other words, we contribute to our workers' education, providing the training required to enhance their leadership capability. They use that leadership capability inside the organization, and teams grow and become enriched thanks to that leadership, which is based on knowledge and aptitude. However, that leadership does not stay at the company when workers go home. They don't say, 'Okay, I leave my uniform here, along with my leadership abilities and the good practices I have learnt. I leave everything here, and go home without all that.' Every day, workers carry with them what they have learnt, and they use their skill set at home and in their communities. Then, suddenly, those communities have new leaders, who expect and demand that the local administration provides their communities with the basic services they need to develop, because they know they are worthy, and their communities should have the same good, decent development services that their company provides for them. That's the interesting part, that's what's truly disruptive. Our company supports them because we also work with local communities, our surrounding communities. We go with their grassroots organizations' leaders, their mayors to petition together to the local or central government, because these towns can no longer be excluded. We press public officials to urgently use the taxes that companies and workers pay to invest in these towns. What for? To improve workers' and their families' living conditions. Companies cannot do it on their own—therein lies the great need to build bridges among private companies, communities and government agencies. Over the past twenty-three years, we have clearly seen that the communities where Danper has an impact have become progressive, because workers take and transfer leadership competencies to their communities, and they want to drive progress in their communities, and they start working on securing basic services. Thus, little by little, we improve our people's living conditions.

Interviewer: How important is the promotion of gender equality in your mission?

RB: We live in a sexist society. But I have witnessed how, over the years, because we have been able to provide job opportunities for women, women have seized those opportunities as a unique possibility to break away from the vicious cycle of poverty. Why shouldn't we offer opportunities for women to become the masters of their own destiny? I have seen them work very hard, fully committing to their jobs and becoming very professional at them—often without any formal education. There are no illiterate workers at the company now, though there were some when we started. The company has a partnership with the state to operate a small school within our firm, so that people who have not completed their schooling can finish their education in the company. These women understood when I said, 'Okay, so you haven't completed your primary or your secondary education, but you are the best artichoke peeler, so you're the best professional in this process.' They couldn't believe that we regarded them as professionals even though they hadn't finished school. That's what it's all about.

Interviewer: What has been the social impact of investing in the education of women?

The self-esteem of the women rises as we give them room to grow. Many of these women are household heads, and their income has made it possible for their children to get an education—an opportunity that they never had themselves. That's extraordinary. The question remains, where does the balance sheet show these accomplishments? Nowhere. Balance sheets and financial statements only show net profits, EBITDA, gross margins—just figures. Where does all of this show? The wonderful result of the social balance sheet comes from gender equality.

In a country such as Peru—and I've witnessed this first-hand—every time women take a step forward, society moves forward as well, because the income that women make helps them to feel free, to become independent. They can speak up. In many cases, they are no longer victims of domestic violence, because, before this opportunity to earn a living, these women used to depend 100 per cent on their husbands' income, and they had to beg for that money to invest in their children's healthcare and education. Now, when they secure their own livelihood, their self-esteem increases. They feel valued, and a virtuous cycle unfolds. As they feel appreciated, they are willing to study, to learn, to acquire the skills for the company's new processes. It is wonderful. They invest what they make on their children. After twenty-three years, I bear witness and have

been blessed to talk to many of these women, and, when I ask
them, 'So, how are your children doing? Have they finished
high school?' they reply, 'Mrs Rosario, my son attended Lima's
Agricultural University and graduated as an agronomist—not
only that, just so you know, he's already working at Danper.'

I happened to visit a mango processing plant, and a woman
came up to me and said, 'Mrs Rosario, we have a very severe
inspector who keeps demanding more and more from us. He's
young, and we know that we need to perform, but sometimes
he doesn't understand.' So, I told her, 'Well, you know that we
tell inspectors to be demanding but reasonable and respectful.
Who is it?' This is a true story. She replied, 'That young man
over there,' and I said, 'Okay, I'll go talk to him . . .'. 'One more
thing, madam—he's my son.' Imagine just how proud that
worker felt having her son overseeing that processing line as a
result of her income from a job at a company like ours.

Learnings from Rosario Bazán: Facilitating the education of
women lifts the whole of society up.

6

Promoting Inclusion

India is a notably unequal society in which the differences between the haves and the have-nots is still quite striking. Many advances have been made in recent years. More rural children are going to school. More toilets have been constructed in villages. Cell phone usage has sharply expanded, serving as a leveller of sorts. Yet, the top 1 per cent of India earns over a fifth of the country's income, compared to around 11 per cent in 1990. The richest 10 per cent of Indians own 80 per cent of the country's wealth. According to the latest World Bank data (which in the case of India is for the year 2011), India's Gini coefficient (a statistical measure of inequality in income distribution, in which 100 represents perfect inequality and 0 perfect equality) is 35.70, which makes the country a very unequal society. India fares better than China (38.5), United States (41.4) and South Africa (63) by this metric, but still the country is palpably unequal, compared not only to western Europe, but also to many countries in Africa and neighbouring countries such as Pakistan (31.6) and Bangladesh (32.4). According to data generated by the US-based Knoema, a private data tech company based in New York, India's Gini co-

efficient had risen to 47.9 by 2018, which was close to China
(51), and considerably worse than Pakistan (36.2), Bangladesh
(39.5) and the United States (37.8).

The interviews in this chapter examine how business
leaders have responded to the challenges of the many have-nots
to be found in India, and in many other emerging markets.
Inequality is about more than income, it is about access. As the
Covid-19 pandemic has again demonstrated, access to quality
healthcare is both essential and far from guaranteed, even for
the middle class. Devi Shetty, the founder of a chain of tertiary
hospitals, initially focused on cardiac care, talks about how he
has helped drive down the cost of heart surgery for all to one of
the lowest levels in the world, but he also notes how he faced
other challenges of inclusion. Building on the theme of the
previous chapter, he found that families were more willing to
pay for operations for baby boys than baby girls, leaving him in a
moral dilemma, which he has sought to counter with flexibility.
This is the sort of problem unlikely to be encountered in the
West and one that demands a day-to-day managerial response
in India.

Shetty's story is one of multiple examples of the point
that while serving the needs of the excluded is the ethically
right thing to do, making it happen is far more complex and
challenging. Ratan Tata, the chairperson of the giant and
highly respected Tata Group between 1991 and 2012, discusses
another attempt at inclusion that went badly awry. Tata explains
that the plan for a small car arose from observations of families
of four or five people on two-wheelers in the rain and in the
night, and his concern for their well-being. The problem was
in the execution, and it turned out to be a lot more difficult to
be inclusive than had been envisaged. As Tata recalls, there was

an unexpected delay in the roll out caused by political problems in West Bengal, which forced the building of a new plant in Gujarat. There were failures in marketing. Ultimately, though, Tata believes that the Nano project was undone by earning the reputation as India's cheapest car, while even poorer consumers wanted something that gave them status. The lesson is that inclusive strategies demand the sensitive and dignified treatment of those being included. The fact that this lesson had to be learnt by one of India's oldest and biggest business houses is perhaps testimony to the limited attention given to the base of the pyramid by Indian big business.

As liberalization began in India, rural craftspeople were among the most disadvantaged of the have-nots. In her interview, Laila Tyabji, co-founder of the NGO Dastkar, also addresses the challenges of helping the have-nots. While her vision was clear—rural craftspeople could flourish if their wares could sell in urban markets—connecting urban demand and rural crafts was a huge task. What kind of crafts would urban consumers pay for? How could they persuade the diverse universe of rural craftspeople living on the margins of survival to make them? Tyabji recounts in detail how she helped a group of villagers, who had been displaced by the creation of a tiger park, find a new income source in crafts. By visiting the villages and observing, she saw skills and products that the villagers had no idea could be monetized.

If Tyabji can be seen as engaged in informal education— teaching rural craftspeople what urban consumers would buy—Runa Khan, the founder and executive director of the Bangladesh-based NGO Friendship, undertook the Herculean task of bringing formal education to the inhabitants of the floodplain sediment islands in the Ganges delta in Bangladesh.

There is little doubt that the provision of education is a hugely important tool for greater inclusion in societies. The challenge for Khan was how to do this for a population of people who moved houses nearly fifty times in their lifetimes, and about which so little was known that even their total numbers may have been anywhere between 4 million and 10 million. Khan moved incrementally to create schools, train teachers and experiment with pedagogy. She moved beyond the rote learning found so often in government schools to incorporate a code of ethics into the curriculum, believing that values were as important as numeracy and literacy skills. Throughout Khan emphasizes the importance of quality, believing that 'the poor cannot afford poor solutions'. While Khan is discussing providing the poorest of the poor people with rudimentary services, this is exactly the same point made by Tata in the context of the lessons learnt from the failed Nano project.

We end our selection, appropriately, in a country where the exclusion of most of the population was the law of the land for decades. This is apartheid-era South Africa, where the white minority denied all the other ethnicities in the country the vote, and much more. Peter Wharton-Hood was a senior executive of Standard Bank, one of South Africa's largest banks, and in the interview he discusses the journey taken by the bank to facilitate the government's policy of Black* Economic Empowerment. Once again, the clear impression is that to achieve this goal

---

* 'Black' is a term used by some communities, and sometimes by all persons of colour, to describe themselves. It is a term which now had a long history in having been reclaimed and reappropriated by persons of colour and is in widespread mainstream usage. Its usage in this chapter is not pejorative; is not intended as a racial slur; and is not intended to cause offence or to hurt the sentiments of any individual, community, section of people, group, race, caste or religion.

was a lot more complicated than flicking a switch. The bank's leadership really had to lead, including overcoming the fears of their white middle management that they would be forced out and replaced by Blacks. Yet, as he emphasizes, there were huge gains to be made, as diversity drove greater innovation. It was not straightforward to serve Black communities. The four main banks in South Africa had to innovate. They established 'Mzansi Accounts' as a low-income transactional banking account that made banking more accessible to previously unbanked communities.

6(a)

Devi Shetty

Devi Shetty is a cardiac surgeon, and the founder and chairperson of Narayana Health, a chain of hospitals in India that first focused on cardiology and cardiac surgery, and now provides all forms of tertiary health. Since its founding in 2001, the cost of heart surgery at Narayana Health has fallen to being the lowest in the world without sacrificing quality. Shetty initiated the 'micro health insurance scheme' along with the government of Karnataka, which currently insures more than 40 lakh poor farmers in the state. Shetty received the Karnataka Ratna in 2001, the Padma Shri in 2004, and the Padma Bhushan in 2012.

Interviewed by Tarun Khanna in Boston, Massachusetts, on 10 October 2017.

Interviewer: What happens when a very poor patient walks into your hospital and cannot afford to pay? How do you think about that?

Devi Shetty (DS): There are a lot of emotional things involved in this. Let me put it this way. I always introduce myself—when people ask me what my job is—I tell them my occupation is heart surgeon, but the job is putting a price tag on human life. It is really true. Not only me—all the surgeons in developing countries—we are putting a price tag on human life.

A typical kid of mine is a little baby in a mother's lap. I examine the kid, and I tell the mother, 'Look, your baby has a hole in the heart. He requires a heart operation.' The first question the mother asks is, 'How much is it going to cost?' If I tell her, 'It's going to cost, say, $1200 [approximately Rs 78,000] or $1500 [approximately Rs 97,500]'—which she doesn't have—that is putting a price tag on the kid's life. If she comes up with the money, she can save the child. If she has no money, she's going to lose the child. This is the reality. You can always try to justify it, saying that it's not my job to find the money for the operation. I am a surgeon. I can operate. But, then, they have nowhere to go.

So we talk to the family. We have a separate division which spends time. Always, it's very simple. If it is a boy . . . we know with great difficulty, the family will arrange some money. If we tell them it's going to cost $3000 [approximately Rs 2.23 lakh], they will not arrange the money, so we bring it down to maybe $1000 [Rs 74,000] or $800 [approximately Rs 59,000], whatever. If it is a girl child, we make sure that before they leave the building, we have finished—we arrange the money and do the operation.

Interviewer: Because there's a bias towards male children in Indian society?

DS: Huge bias. So they don't have the money, but we give them hope that if you come up with this much money, we will arrange the rest of the money. Everyone has a sphere of influence. All these people are working for somebody. So when you talk about an amount which they do not have, but it is possible to— with great difficulty—come up with, they can manage it in two months or three months, because most heart surgeries are elective procedures. So we help them, and in no time, they come up with the money. We keep their address. We keep in touch with them.

And we have a large pool of donors, and they keep funding these operations. There is this organization called Have A Heart Foundation in Bengaluru, which is made up of regular people running shops in commercial complexes of Bengaluru. They sponsor 100 heart surgeries a month. We have done more than 12,000 to 13,000 heart surgeries with their benevolence. Like this, there are so many organizations. One good thing has happened—when the economy of the country was liberalized, good people became rich.

Interviewer: This is back in 1991?

DS: Yes, in 1991. When good people become rich, money gets utilized for good causes. So raising money in India today for this kind of cause is not a problem. I can confidently say that we have never refused a single patient with a curable heart condition . . . because they couldn't afford the surgery. It's not because of me. The ecosystem that we created makes it possible.

Learnings from Devi Shetty: Unequal access to healthcare is a curve, but it is one that with flexibility, imagination and philanthropy can be countered.

6(b)

Ratan Tata

Bloomberg

Ratan Tata is one of India's most iconic business leaders and was the chairperson of Tata Group, an Indian public multinational conglomerate based in Mumbai, between 1991 and 2012. He joined the family-owned company, which dated back to its foundation in Mumbai in 1868 as a Parsi trading company, in 1961. He was promoted to his first management position in the 1970s. In 1991, J.R.D. Tata stepped down as chairperson of Tata Sons, and Ratan Tata was named as his successor. He was a scion of the Tata family but not a blood relative of J.R.D. Tata. During his time leading the Tata Group, Ratan significantly increased revenues and profits, acquired foreign brands including Tetley, Jaguar Land Rover and Corus, and conceptualized the Tata Nano Car. In 2000, Ratan was awarded the Padma Bhushan, and in 2008, he was awarded the Padma Vibhushan. He remains head of Tata Trusts.

Interviewed by Tarun Khanna in Mumbai on 27 April 2015.

Interviewer: Can we talk about Nano because it was such an interesting episode in so many ways? What are your reflections now at this point in the attempt to build that particular product for the mass market? What did you learn from the design process, the marketing, the development of the entire business system?

Ratan Tata (RT): It was a tremendous learning exercise in terms of what we did right, what we did wrong, and what external circumstances existed, which contributed to this. As I have said many times, the idea of having a new, affordable family transport came from watching families of four or five on two-wheelers in the rain and in the night, and feeling that this was a dangerous form of transport. And we went through several evolutions of trying to make the two-wheelers safer, going to three-wheeled transport, doing something that was akin to an autorickshaw but more car-like until we finally landed on a small car.

The price point was, by happenstance, fixed by the *Financial Times* of London, I think, through a statement that they made, and I decided we could refute that or take that as a task. I chose the latter, and I think with the disbelief of my people, who thought that this guy is crazy. But we took this as a task, and we set about designing a car, not a half-car, not a car that was not painted or a car that looked different, but a regular car with roll-up windows, and air-conditioning as an option. As a people's car, in three stages of trim. Up until then, this was a terrific exercise. We achieved what we set out to achieve. The service of those cars was supposed to be done by young unemployed technicians, whom we would train as service engineers, give them a Nano, and they would have a territory that they would serve—almost taking service to the home, rather than car owners coming in to us.

And after making the first 1,00,000 cars, we were going to have small assembly plants where, again, we would have young entrepreneurs whom we would train—and we would also train their manpower. We would oversee their quality assurance, and they would have satellite operations. These would interact with the service people. So it was maybe a bit of a dream, but the goal was giving employment beyond the conventional form of manufacturing cars. There were many challenges to that. For example, you had to create kits that you would provide to these assemblers. There were issues like you can't weld a painted body part, so we had different forms of adhesion. It was a really good exercise, almost verging on the kinds of experiences you go through in space exploration of dealing with problems that arise.

As all of us know, I think, a month before we would've been online in the marketplace, a West Bengal political leader called Mamata Banerjee mounted her offensive against our plant. Without going into those details, it led us to pull out of

West Bengal a complete car plant on the verge of going into production. And we moved, as it turned out, to Gujarat. It took us a year to re-establish the plant, to build it afresh. In that year, we lost a lot of excitement for the product. When we announced the product in Delhi, we got, I think, within the next week or so, 3,00,000 orders with full cash payments, and we became a banker suddenly. We were giving back interest to the people who wanted a car, but the car was not to come at that time. We had, over a period of time, people starting to want their deposits back, a loss of interest, and maybe some degree of disbelief, that this was just something that you launched on a platform but that it wasn't really a workable project. Competitors had a great time spreading those kinds of stories. But then, those were somewhat beyond our control.

Where we made our greatest mistake, in my view, is, when the car did come out of Gujarat, everybody had become quite complacent with the 3,00,000 orders, etc., that we dropped all these non-conventional plans. And we pushed the car through our regular dealerships. They weren't really keen or interested in selling a low-priced car with low margins, and they really caused a lot of damage by trying to sell everybody up if they came into the showroom, and this is not what you want.

The other mistake we made was we allowed the car to be titled as the cheapest car in India, instead of the most affordable car, or to not talk of its price as its only attribute. What we did was we created a stigma about the car. So people thought, 'I don't want to be seen in that, my neighbours will think I can't afford a more expensive car.'

Those two issues, I think, were the greatest mistakes we made. We had initially planned to go into the rural areas and sell the car like a motorcycle got sold, on the market day, to work the registration, insurance. The owner could [leave] with the car. We never did those kinds of things because our dealers weren't interested in taking that kind of trouble. And then it was too late.

The momentum had gone. Today, we're looking at relaunching the car with more bells and whistles, and capabilities. But the car is now ten years old, and while we're seeing more and more on the road, still the incremental number is very, very small. So we failed to really market the people's car that we had initially conceived.

Interviewer: That's another interesting issue in India, which is for maybe half the population that needs products and services at a particular price point. Getting the market to work for you in support of those goals has proven to be quite difficult. And you have the isolated success. Is that a statement that you would agree with, or is that overstating it?

RT: My own assessment is that the market is very demanding of such products. It's a very sensitive market in the sense that if you have a calamity, you can't give second-hand clothing or yesterday's food. No one wants to be seen or categorized as getting a handout. So whatever one does, one mistake that one makes, of trying to show that we're doing it for the person who can't afford to get something else, is the wrong approach. You can get the price there, but you have to market the product as being just as good as everything else.

The Nano should've been viewed as something that could be in a garage that has a Bentley on the one hand, and a Nano to go to the market—not something that is known as the cheapest car. That's one of the mistakes we made. So I think the base of the pyramid is keen to have its own place and status in the hierarchy of the consuming public, which one needs to respect more than we have been doing.

The second thing I think is that we have a tendency in India to start and scale up as we go. And I think the way that this goes is you have a big splash, you come out with a certain volume as you do in the West, and you market it and you saturate the media—or now the social media—with advertising. You make it the thing you have to have. I think India is quite prone to that. Online marketing has shown that in the acceptance of the digital environment and the satisfaction of having something delivered to you at your house that you pay for in cash. They're quite willing to make a whole transaction online. I would've been the greatest disbeliever of that three or five years ago, but it's true.

Learnings from Ratan Tata: The base of the pyramid provides a wonderful potential market, if you understand that consumers are discerning and need to be treated with respect.

6(c)

Laila Tyabji

Chhaveesh Nokhwal

Laila Tyabji is co-founder and chairperson of Dastkar, an NGO dedicated to working with craftspeople across India to promote the revival of traditional crafts and develop an urban market for them. Throughout her career, Tyabji has also been an active public figure—advocating for the preservation and promotion of traditional crafts, as well as working to promote religious tolerance as a Muslim woman in India. In 2012, she was awarded the Padma Shri.

Interviewed by Prithwiraj Choudhury in New Delhi on 23 August 2018.

Interviewer: You were one of six purposeful women who in 1981 founded the non-profit Dastkar to support traditional craftspeople. Can you tell us how this happened?

Laila Tyabji (LT): We started Dastkar in a very informal way, thinking that it was something we were going to do a few days a month in our spare time. We were all working women, and we felt that craftspeople—they needed design and product development, they needed access to urban markets, they needed access to credit and finance, they needed appropriate raw materials. And so we thought that from our varied experiences—because all of us came from very different backgrounds and work experiences—we could give this information in a very informal way, and we never thought that it was going to become an all-India organization working with over a lakh craftspeople in twenty-five Indian states.

It happened in a very organic, not particularly planned way. And I think that's perhaps one of the reasons that it succeeded and continued—because it responded to situations rather than coming up with a very set complicated plan and expensive infrastructure. Because when you work with craftspeople there is no step one, two, three, four—each community, tradition and craft is so different. The craftspeople may all have a combination of these different needs, but they come in different orders. Priorities are different. Sometimes somebody is making a wonderful product in the middle of the Bastar forest, and all he needs is a marketing platform. But on the other hand, you might have a group of tribal women who have been organized by some nuns in Odisha who have no idea of what they should make for the metro market, and the nuns themselves have no idea of design and product development. They are often unaware that instead of teaching them crochet and knitting, there are some wonderful local skills that can be tapped into, and which would be much easier to sell in the urban market as unique products. So there are so many things to consider. Every time we visit a potential project, we try to go with a very open mind and explore the local skills there. We look at what people have been traditionally doing, so that we don't fall into the cliché of what the local NGO or government department thinks is the right thing for them to do.

Interviewer: You talk frequently about how part of your mission is to create a link between the rural producers and the urban consumers. What made you confident in this market, and how did you go about establishing this link?

LT: Well, I think that I was always convinced there was a market for something authentic and different. At that time, all of us were in our early thirties, so we were our own consumers. We knew what we would like to see, and we knew what we didn't like: the stuff that was being made and put in government emporiums or whatever, and how boring and static it was. From our own travels, we knew the kind of skills that were there and how they could be transformed. And so we were quite confident that if we got this stuff together there would be a market. The thing was to convince the craftspeople that craft could be sustainable! We had an advantage when we started because we didn't have any overheads of our own. We were working out of our homes on a voluntary basis. So we were able to price the products according to what we felt their potential was. There were things that were quite honestly, in the early days, fairly tacky—still in the process of being upgraded and having value added. But we knew that if we could have quite a small markup, and if we could make it interesting to look at, it had potential. We were also very lucky that in India, the market is so multi-layered and there are customers for every price range, and of varying aesthetic sensibilities, as well.

Interviewer: One thing that will probably strike a chord with many entrepreneurs is the fact that you went with imagination and a real sense of need to make this connection. But you didn't have a manual of steps as you said, right? So can you tell us maybe a couple of stories, one where this approach worked really well and maybe an example where it didn't work well?

LT: I think that's important, because when you read stories of entrepreneurs, they usually only discuss all the things that went very well. And it sounds like such an effortless journey—'I started from nothing and I ended up becoming the head of a big corporation'. Actually, it's more important to list the things that were the problems—mistakes and challenges—because that's what you learn from. And so yes, we went with an open spirit, but we were not totally without a plan in our minds. We had listed all the different things that craftspeople needed, and those that prevented them from being successful. And it's just the order in which you address them—keeping in mind that there's a whole basket of services they require, but that not all of them need all the things together, and that you should be flexible enough to juggle these around a bit.

Dastkar's a really big success story. We have had quite a few! There was SEWA Lucknow chikan [a type of hand embroidery using cutwork and shadow work], the Sandur Lambani craftspeople, Dastkar Andhra and Berojgar Mahila Sewa Samiti. We work now with about 700 different artisan groups all over India.

But I suppose the one that encapsulates all of this is the Dastkar Ranthambore project, where, in 1991, Valmik Thapar—the conservationist and tiger expert who was very involved in creating the Ranthambore Tiger Park in Rajasthan—approached Dastkar and asked us to come and do something for the villages and women who had been displaced from the park area. A lot of people don't know that to create the tiger sanctuary, fourteen villages were removed from the area and literally dumped elsewhere. Some bureaucrat must have taken a thumbtack and pointed at blank places on the map of the district—not thinking whether there was water, whether there was access to roads, or local schools or hospitals . . . whether there were any civic facilities. Most importantly, these were agrarian people. They were either herders or agriculturists. So to be suddenly shifted away from a green forested area with water and foliage and fodder to these blank spaces was naturally very traumatic. Valmik thought that Dastkar could maybe come and do something, create some livelihood opportunities for the women. So we went down—my colleague Pramada Menon [a leading women's rights activist and executive director of Dastkar from 1993 to 1997] and I initially—we went to these villages and we got the local pradhan [community leader] to organize meetings. The initial reaction was very hostile. They all had just had this experience of being shunted out of their homes and environment, and of the government making promises of compensation, etc., which had not been adequately met. I remember one woman saying to us, 'You have to fill our bellies before you start asking us about what we can do.' And they, also—because as I said, most of them were herders or farm workers—they had not really crafted things with their hands. Unlike many places in India, they had not traditionally been craftspeople. When we asked them, they were very dismissive, and said, 'Look at our hands, we work in the fields, do you think we can make anything?'

So then I did what I, personally, would hate someone to do to me. I went into their homes and dived under their beds and made them open their trunks and cupboards. I said, 'I am sure you have some things here which you make.' And of course, because they were so poor, they did make a lot of things out of recycled material and scraps: there were quilts, there were little toys, there were some baskets from reeds and palm leaves, the local guys made jutties [closed-toe shoes] from the hides of dead animals. It was all very crude, and they were things that they made just for their own use, but they had the potential. You could see that there was something distinct and with character. So I took something, and I said, 'Okay, here is this little quilt you have made from all these old scraps. Now, I will give you some cloth, and you make me a small cushion or a small child's quilt or something, and you can earn some money.' But every time we went back after three or four weeks, to see progress and motivate the community, I found that they hadn't done anything. They just didn't trust us, and they didn't believe that we would really come back to do anything. They'd had so many disappointments.

So I thought that the only way to achieve anything was for me to take a room in one of these villages and just live there until I could get something going. So I rented a little room, and I settled down in it. I put up a lot of photographs of all Dastkar's projects—a potter and a woman embroiderer and a weaver, etc., and I took my needlework along with me, and I sat in the middle of this room in the middle of the village. And obviously everyone came rushing to see who is this mad behenji [respectful term for elder sister] from Delhi, and what is she doing sitting in our village. So then I would tell them the story of the photographs. I said, 'See, that is Giriraj, he was a potter and he used to sit on the corner of the road and now he is making so much money and he is travelling to Bombay and Calcutta and all these big cities and selling his stuff,' etc.

So after these stories, they would ask me, 'What are you doing?' I would be stitching away. I was doing patchwork because I felt that patchwork was the entry point, because it was familiar to them. I had brought all these little coloured squares of fabric, and I was stitching them together. I would say, 'Oh, I am making a cushion cover, do you want to try?' And they would take it up and they would stitch—obviously huge baggy stitches, very crooked, and they didn't even know how to sequence the colours—e.g., red, yellow and green, and then you have to do red again. It was all very ad hoc. But at the end of the day, when they produced these little odd-looking things, I used to give them some money. And they would say, 'What is this?' And I'd reply, 'Well, you have made a cushion cover, we are going to sell it in Delhi.' So for them, it was a huge thing, you know. And the word spread like wildfire: that there is this lady from Delhi and she is sitting in Sherpur village and she is giving work and she is giving money. And in a few days that room was bursting at the seams with women coming and saying, 'We want to learn, we want to do this.'

I went down to the village square where there was a little tailor sitting making some stuff, and I said, 'Listen, you have to come and help me because I am getting flooded, I can't cut enough pieces fast enough.' So he joined us, and twenty-seven years later he is still part of the project! Initially it was just the two of us together, then there was another young woman who came to watch, and she is now our coordinator in Ranthambore. So, to cut it all short, by the time those three weeks that I spent on that first trip were up, we had a collection of quilts, we had some namda rugs which the menfolk had made, we had some jutties and chappals [types of footwear] that we had designed with the local leather karigars [artisans]. And these products were interesting because we were using local materials, dabu block prints and tie-dye, and they looked colourful and fun from a distance. Of course, if you looked up close they were not very well finished. But because we were able to decide what the markup would be, we put just 5 per cent or 10 per cent, and they sold. Just because they were different. We took I think about Rs 23,000 worth of stock back to Delhi, and it all sold. Dastkar had a shop, in those days, in Hauz Khas village. The excitement when I went back to Ranthambhore and I gave the women the money! And frankly, since then, the project has just blossomed. The women's work has become much more sophisticated. They make mobiles, stuffed toys and all kinds of garments, home furnishings and accessories. The project is autonomous and their turnover last year was over Rs 2 crore. They do very complex patchwork patterns these days, but they laugh and say that actually it was more difficult for them to make those early pieces, when they were doing crude 6-inch squares, than now, when they are doing these tiny intricate triangles and stars. And that is actually the answer—that you have to fit your solution to match the skill level of the craftspeople. One of the mistakes that a lot of designers make is to work with only the most highly skilled person in the community, and then be very frustrated because the sample is beautiful but when the order comes, it's nothing like the original. So I think that, once again, this is a fundament of Dastkar—match your solutions with both the needs and the potential of whom you are working with.

Interviewer: That was a great example of a story that worked. Can you share—as an early entrepreneur, there must have been stories that were disappointing?

LT: You know one of the disappointing things is that the numbers of craftspeople don't grow. I am happy to say that, by and large, most of the Dastkar projects we worked on have become sustainable economically, but they have not had that kind of impact in growth, where say a group of fifteen craftspeople has grown to 100 or more. There are some, of course—for example, Lucknow, where we started with twelve women and there are now over 7000. I think it's important to see why in other instances such small growth happens. And one reason is, of course, that we have failed at convincing craftspeople that there is a future. They want to hold on to whatever little success they have achieved, and they don't want to share it with more people, because they don't think there is real market potential. That is obviously a failure in our ability to communicate.

The other thing, a mistake that we made in the early days, was that when you enter a new community and you are interacting with the crafts women or men, there are always a couple of really bright-eyed people who get what you are saying. It's very tempting, particularly if you are new at the game, to say, 'Okay, these are the obvious group leaders,' and address everything to them and appoint them in a leadership role where they will run and oversee everything. You don't realize that they themselves are not aware of the democratic, equal organization which you are visualizing. So they then become, very often, exploitative middlemen themselves. One thing we have learnt now is to go a little more slowly and talk to everybody, even if it means saying the same thing over and over again in simple ways. Trying to get a group of people together, each aware of their specific role and responsibility, rather than one dominant leader.

The other obstacle is, who are you working with? Our most successful projects have been the ones where we have more or less started from scratch and built the leadership—built the organization as we did in Ranthambore, or as we did in Kashmir with Nayi Kiran. If one is working with a long-established NGO that has been working with those people, which has a certain set mindset, then it's very tough. And it's particularly tough to then introduce the participation of craftspeople in decision-making and issues like wages or production or whatever. Many of the old established NGOs are very conservative—they often come from a background of social work or Left-wing politics—who feel that 'marketing' and 'design' are rather dirty words.

Learnings from Laila Tyabji: Including the rural poor requires close attention to communities, and a willingness to listen to everyone.

6(d)

Runa Khan

Yann Arthus-Bertrand

Runa Khan is the founder and executive director of Friendship, an NGO founded in 2002 that supports remote communities in Bangladesh. Friendship pioneered floating hospitals, provides integrated services for climate-impacted communities, and delivers educational services. Friendship has also been active in the Rohingya crisis, when the Myanmar military persecuted and forced large numbers of Muslims to flee to Bangladesh.

It became the second largest healthcare service in refugee camps.

Interviewed by Prithwiraj Choudhury in Dhaka, Bangladesh, on 17 December 2019.

Interviewer: In 2002 you started Friendship, an NGO, in Bangladesh. The community you began working with are known as the char dwellers. Can you tell us more about the char dwellers?

Runa Khan (RK): The char live in areas that have always had climate impact. These were the most difficult areas in the country to work in because Bangladesh is a country that is made of silt; it's the second largest deltaic plain in the world. The point is the demography fifty years ago, the population living there was two persons, three persons, they had enough land on which they could cultivate, here today and there tomorrow, and yet have a reasonably good livelihood. That has changed over the last thirty to forty years. Demography has multiplied. And it's just that the population pressure doesn't allow life there to really dwell, they really cannot live there any more, but they have to, simply because there is no land in Bangladesh. People cannot just move.

So, the char people started living there because of poverty. They kept going down and down the poverty line. They started having differences with the mainland. People would not marry their daughters into the char community. They would take a girl from the char community and marry her, provided the girl came with land. So there was this difference which did not really exist anywhere else in Bangladesh: class difference. It started happening in the chars, and it was extremely difficult to provide services. Now access to services, I don't have to go through that. You know very well the importance of access to services. You are healthy, you have an economic impact. You are educated, you have an economic impact, you have a social impact. All this happens. So when you do not have access to any services and those services which even when provided, don't actually work, you need to change your modality. It was all right when there were 100 people there. It's not all right when you have 10 million people living there. This is life within the char community, and this is why it is so difficult. People are moving forty-eight times in their lifetime. So, they do not have either opportunity or hope. How can mankind survive without both? And this is the reason why people were not willing to give money and aid to work in these areas. They were sure service access would not work. Nobody wants to give money to work in an area where nobody else has been able to work dependably. Therefore, I think this was a big challenge.

Interviewer: At a conceptual level, what is different in a classroom where you have thirty kids versus 150 kids? How do you explain the difference in the teaching method, the pedagogy for such a diverse group?

RK: In a smaller class, a teacher can listen and teach one-on-one. They can listen to the child and the problems of the child and deal with each child individually. They can also aspire to reach a certain goal with the child. If you have the same methodology for every student, not all will understand. So your methodology has to change, and this is something people don't like to accept. They don't want to step back and think of a totally different approach, and this is where innovation comes in. When you are talking about innovation, innovation for the sake of innovation actually means nothing. For the masses, innovation is about the way you put things together and in the end it should be able to deliver what is needed, in a way that can be understood and used by them even when you are not there. The masses should be able to absorb what you are giving them. So, this is like stepping back from a thirty-student class, totally revamping the delivery mechanism and also the goal, because you cannot hope to reach 100 with the same goal.

In the case of the Friendship schools, I realized that in our working areas, we have, if you take the whole working area of about 250 km along the river, we have millions of people. 4.2 million [42 lakh] was a figure that we kind of guessed— there are no records as such and you cannot get 100 per cent statistics. There are approximately 4.2 to 10 million [42 to 100 lakh people], depending on how much area you take, living along the riverbanks. It was really quite impossible to have conventional schools there, simply because the river Brahmaputra or the Jamuna is 30 km when in spate during summer. The islands are being broken, remade, restructured, moved, changed, you cannot have a fixed structure. Teachers, anyone who has done high school, did not want to remain on these islands. They would migrate. So, who do you have for teaching? And then if you want to have teachers coming from the mainland, as soon as the rains start, you cannot go on those rivers with the boats that are available. So, I knew that I needed to work with the community, I needed to work with whoever was there. I couldn't fight the social system nor could I fight the environment. The schools were all mobile and could be brought down and shifted in three hours by the community. I needed to compromise and I thought, okay, these children do not need to go to big universities and they don't need to be the top, they just need to learn to read and write. So, let's start. Of course, the vision was that one day they will go to these big universities, but we had to go step by step.

So, the first step was at least to give them the ability to read and write. How do you run schools where the person who is the most academically sound has only completed grade five? The whole island had only people who had studied up till grade five, grade six, grade seven. That is your teacher level, academic level. That was reality, so all right. We had to make a totally different modality. Then we took the teachers and we trained them. Class by class, they are brought in and taught for two or three days every month. For three days, the school is closed and teachers are taught and then they are sent back. They are just taught lesson by lesson every month. That teaching level would not ensure admission into a big university in Bangladesh, but at least they would pass the national examination and they would be able to read, write and do mathematics. So I adjusted. Once that became successful, I went to the next step. Let's improve. Let's see how we can better it, and I'm very proud to say that over the last ten to fifteen years, in these seventy to seventy-nine schools that we've got, we had one or two B's, I think one C—and the remainder A's in the national curriculum. So, you see, we brought it down to simplicity and then improved the quality. This is a very simple example of how we changed the modality. Also, we kept the school open for two and a half hours a day as the children have to help their parents in the field. These are the poorest of the poor and some of the most climate-impacted communities on the planet.

Interviewer *It is fascinating the degree of innovation that you have done in the schools, such as the prefabricated buildings and the* *portable library. Can you tell us more about the schools, how many of them you have, and what all you are doing with the school project?*

RK: We started with ten schools and every year we expanded. By 2018, we had seventy-nine primary and seventy-four adult schools. We wanted to expand to middle and high schools, because children needed more.

There are times also . . . when you have to see what the country needs. There was a time when the country had no education system and it needed thousands of schools. But today they need quality. And to make quality I decided to have primary, secondary and high schools. Now we have about 100 primary, secondary high schools and adult centres and another 220 in the Rohingya camps. There's an innate belief that education is what brings hope or can bring hope to a community like this.

So, first the environment, we could not get out of the environmental and social context. How do you fit everything and make it work? This was an environment where schools would break down when the land broke. So we have mobile schools. Not mobile on boats, I don't think that works for me at all, because if you see the chars you will understand, but the island is here today it's there tomorrow, maybe the island is filled with sand, so you have the boat here and you have to cross 5 km of sand to go to their homes. It doesn't work. So, we started building the schools in the community. They could be dismantled in accordance with either the floods or the shifting of the island. We train the school management committee to open and care for the school. The children also help. We find community people whom we train to become teachers. They have a link to the community. They have of course more credibility in the community, and we take them not on their academic qualifications but on their human traits. For example, the typical question we ask them is, 'If before an exam, a parent brings you a chicken, are you going to take it or give it back?' So, questions like that show human qualities, ethics and character. I think it's extremely important, because it is this dedication and commitment which is going to see the children through such a hard academic environment, not just the academic qualifications of the teacher or the children's results. For teaching primary school, you don't need rocket science, and we would train the teachers to teach.

We cannot afford a library in each school, so we have about fourteen trunks which go from school to school, our mobile libraries, we have full editorial boards also for newsletters every month. You cannot imagine the way they can write! Then we started adult schools for the parents, so that they could understand the value, and now we have seventy-four adult learning centres, where parents who didn't know how to hold a pencil are able to write a letter to the government in nine months' time when they leave school. So, we make a package deal.

For me one of the most important things is the code of ethics that Friendship has put into the curriculum. In the olden times in schools we had religious studies or they had civic education or ethical studies. But those are out of the curriculum today and I really think it's a pity. The code of ethics of Friendship builds character and teaches beyond academic learning. Academics is extremely important. It has its space and it has a place in the world. It's not the highest requirement needed for life and living. If these children study up to grade ten, but have a character that is strong, disciplined, good, if they have values, you are making them into human beings and you are making them into good citizens and we need that. So we have to instil this code of values. It's very simple. Everyone in this world has a value system within them. What we do is we nurture them systematically as a lesson every day. So one month is a month of honesty and we tell them about honesty, what is honesty, stories, we hear from them what they have done, and the next month is dedicated to compassion, empathy, tolerance, and people internalize this. Now we have this throughout Friendship at every meeting in office or at the community. So 5,00,000 people, 6,00,000 people that we serve every month, they speak about ethics. It's extremely important, because very often values—every organization has values, every company has values—but very often it is the limiting factor for growth.

For Friendship it is the opposite. Every decision and every idea can come only if it's within the framework of that value. I cannot imagine somebody coming to me and saying we need to do this, but it might have a gender problem, never. It cannot happen. They will come to me saying we need to do this, and this information will only be thought of if it is based on our values. Values are not the limiting factors but the essence of why we do something. This is one of the core differences in how we work with values.

Interviewer: And I'm guessing that hiring the local community folks solves the problem of absent teachers, but you mentioned that the priority now is not only to have schools, but to have quality schools. So what are you doing to enhance the quality?

RK: I think we are training them as better citizens with this value and so the quality of education . . . in the last national primary exam, we bagged all, 100 per cent of the national merit-based scholarships in those regions, 100 per cent of the government scholarships came to Friendship schools. So, you see, it's a balance. For inclusive growth we need academics, teachers who are dedicated, environmentally friendly schools with a curriculum which makes them better human beings. Then improve the weaknesses, for example, we have English lessons. The English pronunciation of many of our teachers is not good. So we have had teachers coming from Europe who recorded the English lessons. We give in class with our limited budgets little recorders and the children are learning English straight from someone who can speak proper English. We have games, editorials for magazines. We are now thinking of even linking schools internationally.

Interviewer: What steps can be taken to create positive and lasting change for the char dwellers?

RK: The poor cannot afford poor solutions. You give your handout clothes to them. You give them bad medicine. You give them a cup that is broken. You are keeping them—you are mentally keeping the poor at that level. You give them something that is beautiful. You give them art. You give them excellent healthcare. You give them the best education you possibly can. Then they start having hope and that's where the change can come in. People can live in poverty, but they cannot live without dignity and hope. That is what you have to bring to them, if you want deep impact to happen.

Learnings from Runa Khan: The poor require the best education that can be provided, as dignity and hope are key to their future.

6(e)

Peter Wharton-Hood

Marinda van Zyl

Peter Wharton-Hood was the former group chief operating officer and group deputy chief executive of Standard Bank Group, and former global chief operating officer of Deutsche Bank. He was born and graduated when South Africa was ruled by a minority white government that enforced a policy of ethnic separation called apartheid, which denied the majority Black population as well as ethnic Asians and others the right to vote, discriminated against them in education and healthcare, and engaged in human rights abuses. He entered the business world just as the leader of the African National Congress, Nelson Mandela, was released from nearly thirty years in prison in 1990. In 1994 apartheid ended and South Africa finally became a democracy, albeit the wealth largely remained in the hands of the minority white population. Wharton-Hood built his career as the country sought to provide more opportunities and power to the majority of its population. He joined Standard Bank, which had a storied history in the country, in 1997 and was involved in many efforts to make its management more diverse. In August 2020, he was appointed group chief executive of Life Healthcare Limited, the largest Black-owned hospital in South Africa, and the second largest private hospital operator in the country.

Interviewed on Zoom by Euvin Naidoo, in Boston, Massachusetts, and Johannesburg, South Africa, on 8 March 2021.

Interviewer: During the 1990s and 2000s, Standard Bank embarked on a journey of inclusion of the banks that had been largely excluded from commercial banking because of the apartheid regime in South Africa. You were a white South African executive, a male, in a position of power. How did you go through the transition to Black Economic Empowerment?

Peter Wharton-Hood (PWH): To summarize Black Economic Empowerment, it's probably best to start with the problem. The problem statement was a new democratically elected government, majority Black, a country, majority Black, business controlled by white people and the senior executive structures across companies in South Africa filled with white men. So one looks at the halls of power in commerce, and you see they're dominated by an extremely small minority. So the notion of making commerce accessible to a broader base of executives, and providing the opportunity for a broader base of executives other than white males to be in positions of authority, to earn salaries, and to be able to command the future of institutions, to my mind in summary is Black Economic Empowerment. It's not about one-off deals where people of colour made money. It is a much longer-term drive to see equity delivered to underlying structures in industry, in commerce, in decision-making structures.

Standard Bank's leadership position on the topic is by and large attributable to the drive and determination and vision that our then-chief executive Jacko Maree had on the future of the country. He made it absolutely clear to all of us that Black Economic Empowerment was not only an absolute essential so that we could get the transition right, he said it was necessary so that we could have balanced working environments and sustainable working environments for us going forward.

There was another catalyst in the mix, in that the drive to present charters between government-inspired direction and underlying industrial participation in the change led to the mining charter negotiations, which you will recall were impactful on the direction that the industry took, and our own financial sector charter, where we as senior banking executives embraced the responsibility to change—and change across a range of dimensions.

The underlying financial sector charter was not just designed to place Black people in jobs occupied by white people. It was far more sustainably driven towards an outcome that allowed us to see better lending practices. Because if you think back to the opportunity and access that Black people had to being able to borrow money from white banks or white-run banks in the late 1990s, it was very, very difficult. Banking was nearly inaccessible. Banking infrastructure didn't go anywhere near the townships that you referred to in the painting behind me. Banking was typically concentrated around white neighbourhoods, white clusters and white business.

So one could see that the drive was to make banking affordable and make banking accessible and making access to loan finance more accessible to more people in the population, which even led to the expansion of the bank's balance sheet. The practice of conforming to the drive by government to see a more equitable society was not only right, it was smart, because it led to better banking, it led to bigger markets, bigger balance sheets, more accessible banking, at better pricing.

We even designed a transaction product called Mzansi. The four banks, the big banks, collaborated with the permission of the minister, because it was not to be seen to be cartel-based pricing. The coalition of banks designed a product which together would take the infrastructure of the then-big banks and make it accessible to millions of customers at very, very affordable fees.

So you had a unique set of circumstances that started to present itself in the South African market, where poor customers had better access to electronic banking than the most sophisticated banking markets outside of South Africa—better electronic banking than Europe, better electronic banking than the US—and it was driven by this catalyst not to make money, but to do what was right within society. It was hard work, but the clear statement of intent to create a sustainable working environment for all, based on principles of equity, led to a most magnificent work experience, and as a leader, taught me skills that would only become apparent in the European context much, much later on.

Interviewer: How did you have a conversation with your leadership team—and you were leading a large part of the bank—to say we have to give up power. You have to allow previously disadvantaged South Africans in.

PWH: In the first instance, it was met with complete fear. We can speak candidly about the topic, and I appreciate the sensitivities around the use of language and sentiment that gets expressed. But middle-aged white males were terrified, in the sense that they just saw their livelihoods disappearing. That was an incorrect articulation of the outcome that was really being sought. This wasn't: retire middle-aged white executives in Standard Bank and repopulate with inexperienced young Black executives who are going to do their job. That was neither the sentiment nor the way that it was explained. But it was the initial reaction, and understandably so.

The reality as to how one had to orchestrate the transformation at a workforce level was to be pretty sanguine that you had to do it over a period of time. But you couldn't answer the immediate question. When someone said speed up, you couldn't say it's going to take time. The correct answer was the progression that was promised had to be delivered.

So what we were obliged to do was we had to figure out who was up for retirement, when they were going, who was going to replace them, and understand that the need to replace from outside of the existing succession plan had to be carefully factored in as to how you then ran the organization. So the longer-dated planning built the platform, and good management placated the fear in the short term.

But what it ended up with was a very detailed operational plan. Yes, we had quotas of people of different designations, different gender and disability that needed to be reflected in the working structures over a period of years. And every time we were questioned, it was about being able to show the plan and the promise, but also back it up with the delivery to date, so that your plan was in actual fact credible. It took a monster amount of planning, and that planning still persists globally as organizations continue to transform. The lesson learnt is transformation wasn't just a dictate in order to be able to satisfy legislative requirements or the instructions of the board. Transformation is a smart thing to do.

With the benefit of hindsight, I can see that diverse teams are just much, much more competitive—not with each other, but they present much better answers to complex problems. And I can say now and candidly, if you took an all-male white banking team and asked them to figure out the strategic plan of any division of any bank and its usefulness over the next three years, Euvin, I guarantee you they won't be able to come up with the best answer. Why? Because you need different views around the table in order to be able to understand the underlying complexities, and you need to be able to understand how different stakeholders view your institution and the likelihood of them wanting to do business with you. You can only do that if you've got a diverse skill set. That doesn't mean you find a Black consultancy to come in and give an all-white male executive team a briefing on how they think things should be done. It just doesn't work. You need an organizational complexity that is representative of a diverse enterprise in order to succeed.

As I later experienced in my European experience, diverse teams are just much more fun to work in. Me arriving in the workplace and having eleven other Peter Wharton-Hoods to deal with every day would be mind-numbingly boring. I wouldn't want to go to work. You get the same view from the same clones giving you the same answers to the questions all the time with no argument, no additional insight, no different experience, and you expect it to make a multinational, multi-competitive answer. It just doesn't happen. So diversity leads to a very, very rich working environment, and I think that our government in 1994 and the progression thereon did us a huge favour as executives. We learnt the lessons early on and the benefits of getting it right.

Learnings from Peter Wharton-Hood: Inclusion enables the creation of diversity in a business, which brings enormous benefits.

7

Creating Value Responsibly

What is the responsibility of business leaders in a capitalist economy? This question has been asked for a long time, and there still remains no consensus and much controversy. Famously, eighteenth-century Scottish economist Adam Smith in his book *The Wealth of Nations* (1776) suggested that simply by pursuing self-interest the 'invisible hand' of the market would deliver benefits to all society. Two centuries later, in 1970, American economist Milton Friedman, who taught at the University of Chicago, insisted that 'the social responsibility of business' was just 'to increase its profits'. A second major critique of social responsibility came from Friedman, who argued in an article in the *New York Times Magazine* that 'the social responsibility of business' was to 'make as much money as possible while conforming to the basic rules of the society'.

There have also been powerful voices arguing that business could not simply focus on profits for owners, and that a 'visible hand' by business was needed to help society. In *The Gospel of Wealth* (1889), American steel magnate Andrew Carnegie maintained that the right to make profits was key to incentivizing capitalist enterprise, but that business leaders had a responsibility to use their wealth to promote social good. He gave away almost all his personal fortune (worth $10 billion or Rs 1,000 crore in 2021) to establish the Carnegie Foundation for the Advancement of Teaching in 1911. In the same period, some American and European employers began providing extensive welfare benefits for their employees. Today, in the wake of the 2008 financial crisis and the growth of inequality everywhere, there are constant renewed calls for business to be responsible and pursue social purpose, although what these terms actually mean is unclear. This chapter will look at prominent examples of business responsibility in India and elsewhere. They provide concrete examples, role models and lessons.

Historically, India has developed a particularly strong cohort of business leaders who believed that business had a purpose beyond making profits for owners. Large, old private sector firms—Tata, Godrej and Bajaj—were heavily engaged in corporate social responsibility [CSR] and philanthropy long before the 2014 law that mandated large companies to spend at least 2 per cent of their net profits on CSR. It has been observed that the subcontinent has a long tradition of charitable giving rooted in a belief in karma, which dictated that good deeds were rewarded in better lives, and practices such as *zakat*.

Responsibility is much more than charitable giving, however. The following selections provide some inspirational—and entrepreneurial—examples of forms it can take. The first interview is by Anil Jain, CEO of Jain Irrigation Systems. Jain Irrigation operates in the frontline of many of the most serious social and ecological challenges faced by India. There are millions of destitute farmers and huge challenges with the availability of fresh water. Jain discusses how his firm pioneered a technological solution in the form of pipe irrigation. He reveals the policy and infrastructure challenges behind India's water problem. Water is treated as a public good and not priced, a situation that politicians had no incentive to change. This depleted the water table. Due to the absence of a credible research or knowledge generating organization, Jain Irrigation took on the responsibility of training farmers itself.

Taking responsibility might be costly, financially and in management time, but there is no simple trade-off with profitability. Anand Burman's Dabur has flourished with the growing enthusiasm for natural and Ayurvedic products. However, this did create a new set of problems. The booming market meant natural herbs and other natural products such as sandalwood became increasingly scarce. In his interview, Burman shows how the company responded by growing its own saplings and training a new generation of farmers to grow the herbs.

Responsibility has also taken the form of filling the gaps left by the public sector. This is the theme of the interview with Anu Aga. She describes her discomfort with the state of public education in India, a discomfort supported by numerous studies. India has achieved universal primary school enrolment, but the quality of the education is poor, notably in rural areas. Aga stresses the key role of education in lifting people out of poverty and argues that business has a responsibility to help. This involves financial contributions, but Aga argues that it is not simply a matter of money. It matters how money is spent. Her own focus is on improving teacher quality. Aga's views were widely shared by responsible business leaders in other regions. Dubai's Fadi Ghandour, one of the Gulf's most prominent entrepreneurs and founder of the shipping and logistics giant Aramex, identifies improving education as the way to create more sustainable societies. In particular, he is concerned that the region—like India—has a 'youth bulge', which must be seen as an opportunity rather than a social problem.

The many acts of individual social responsibility still leave us with the question whether they can make a difference in securing system-wide change. The examples of people like Jain, Burman, Aga and Ghandour provide role models for others. However, María Emilia Correa, a Colombian entrepreneur and co-founder of Sistema B, a Latin American organization promoting new economies and B Corporations, is part of a movement to achieve a system-wide change in how capitalism works. She encountered the B-Corporation movement, founded in the United States in 2006, which sought to create a new governance structure that mandated boards to consider ecological, financial and social performance equally. She and her colleagues took the idea to Latin America, under the new name of Sistema B, and transformed it from the original American model by deciding not just to focus on changing governance structures, but to engage with other stakeholders, including policymakers and educators, in a dialogue about how to change the way business works. There was a reorganization of the entire movement in 2020. B Lab US became a local organization, while B Lab Global was created to act as a truly global organization to pursue system-wide change. There are currently over 3500 certified B Corporations in more than seventy countries. India only has seven such companies—the first, eKutir, was certified in 2016. There are likely to be more.

7(a)

Anil Jain

Jain Irrigation Systems Ltd

Anil Jain is vice-chairperson and CEO of Jain Irrigation
Systems. In 1963, Bhavarlal Jain, Anil's father, founded the
family business, which began in kerosene trading and moved
on to selling pipes to farmers for irrigation. The company
recognized that the amount of usable water in India is depleting

and that pipe productivity was unable to drive a profit for farmers. In response, Jain began promoting drip irrigation. In the early 1990s, Anil took over from his father as CEO of Jain Irrigation Systems. Jain has also started Jain Good Agriculture Practices (Jain G.A.P.) Package, which provides farmers with agricultural know-how.

Interviewed by Gunnar Trumbull in Mumbai on 11 December 2017.

Interviewer: *Your firm pioneered contract farming in India. What is the importance of contract farming for farmers?*

Anil Jain (AJ): We have around 120 crore small farmers in India, and 140 million hectares of land under cultivation—which is one of the largest in the world. Thus the average land availability per farmer is only about 3 acres or 1.3 hectares. They do not have proper infrastructure or connectivity to markets. Today, even after all these years of Independence, Indian farmers still suffer quite a lot due to low prices, because they do not have access to the market, holding capacity, knowledge about what to plant or when to plant, and everybody brings their harvest to the market at the same time, so the prices collapse. And this unfortunately and sadly leads to farmers' suicides in India, which in the early 1960s saw the heartening wave of the green revolution and started producing more wheat and more rice to feed the nation and stop dependence on imports. That happened between the 1960s and 1970s, and that was a great achievement. Today, India always has about 50 to 60 million tonnes of foodgrains stored in warehouses, so that they can be given out to people during a drought or famine period. But the producer—the farmer—does not get the benefit. The country got food security, but the farmer's income security didn't come through. That is why contract farming is extremely important and necessary in India. And we as a company, over the last two decades, have done a lot of path-breaking work in this field.

Interviewer: How did your company pioneer drip irrigation?

AJ: At that time, we used to sell pipes to the farmers for irrigation. That made us realize the seriousness of the water table going down and down. We also realized that the pipe productivity was unable to fulfil farmers' needs. Farmers were still not earning enough profit, leave alone being prosperous! We were trying to help them—selling them some pipes, for example—but that was not enough. Hence, we were looking for a technology or a product or a solution that could address these issues. So, you see, our entire journey since my father started— and as we have continued—has always been in response to the customers' needs. We have never thought, 'This is what I want to manufacture, and therefore somebody should buy it.' We have always worked on the basis of the farmers' needs and tried to fulfil them. When we were looking for that technology, we [went] to the US—to Fresno, California—to see an exhibition on drip irrigation technology. When we came back to India, we wanted to promote this technology amongst the farmers. But then the farmers were paying neither for water nor for energy. Mostly, it was free. But drip irrigation saves you both, right? It saves water, energy and fertilizer. Still, the farmers said, 'Why should we buy it?' They were just merrily pumping out whatever water they had because the pump cost was very small. Drip irrigation would have cost them at least ten times more than what they would spend for the pump because of the filtration requirement. So we had to take a very difficult route in order to make the farmers take an interest in drip irrigation.

We had to convince them that if they used drip irrigation, it would improve their production, they would get better quality produce. Now, that was very difficult to prove, without demonstration. That is why, in the late 1980s, we were the first company—and even today we are the only company in that sense—to set up a research, development and demonstration farm, where farmers can come and see what is actually being done, and how it can be done. But then, some farmers started saying, 'Oh, you guys are a corporate firm, you can do whatever you like. But would that happen on my farm?' So we had to build the entire agricultural extension and training team. Today, our company has almost sixty people with agricultural doctorates, agricultural scientists, and more than 1000 agricultural graduates and postgraduates. We built this team that would actually go into the fields and teach farmers how to do irrigation properly. Now, when we started giving this knowledge, we additionally realized that merely doing irrigation right wouldn't guarantee success. Farmers also had to do other parts of agriculture in the right way. And that is how, ultimately, today we have evolved a large body of work—what we call the 'Jain G.A.P. Package'.

Jain G.A.P. helps farmers, gives them knowledge, handholds them from sowing to harvesting, and also post-harvesting. We teach farmers what they should be doing. It's like a code that they can follow and succeed. So as an organization, we started to embrace concept selling. Our tagline was, 'More Crop Per Drop'. Along with that, we started giving farmers all this knowledge—apart from the hardware, we had to actually give them the software about how to do agriculture right. And that is how we succeeded, because when they started seeing that the farmers who'd tried it were getting more produce and prosperity, they started believing in it.

But at the same time, we also convinced the government that if farmers would invest in drip irrigation, they would be consuming less water, less energy and less fertilizer. So it is in their interest that farmers should shift from flooding the whole field to doing drip irrigation. And so, the government—starting in the state of Maharashtra—started providing capital to the farmers in the form of a grant or a subsidy. That goes on even to date in some areas of some states, which helped farmers in that initial period.

It was not straightforward to get started. In 1987–88—before economic liberalization in India—when we started drip irrigation, we needed to import that technology. We didn't know how to manufacture it. We went to a US company and an Australian company, called Hardy Irrigation, to get the technology, and we negotiated hard with them, and so on. We had to pay, I think, about $50,000 [Rs 6.5 lakh] as a one-time technology fee, and then we had to pay a 4 per cent or 5 per cent royalty. The director general of technical development raised an objection to the idea of bringing drip irrigation technology to India, saying, 'We have been transporting water for thousands of years without this technology. Why do you want to import this technology when India already has it? Why should we spend our hard-earned $50,000 [Rs 6.5 lakh] in foreign currency on this issue?'

Interviewer: What is the importance of managing scarce usable water resources?

AJ: India has about 17 per cent of the world's population, but we have only 4 per cent of the world's freshwater resources.

In fact, even that is depleting rapidly because whatever water becomes grey or polluted cannot be reused properly. So usable water is actually reducing, while you really need to produce more, and therefore, we have been focusing on the issue of water use efficiency. That's why we use drip irrigation on the farm, because you can improve the water's efficiency. The government stores rainwater—because we have only one season of the monsoon rains—but that is transported through open canals. Therefore, a considerable amount of that water is lost through evaporation and percolation. Upstream farmers get the water, but downstream farmers do not get the water. There are all kinds of things that can go wrong. For example, if you have silt in those canals, then you can't use them to their full capacity.

So over last two or three decades, we have worked with the government on this new concept of using pipe conveyance (rather than canals) and then drip and sprinkler systems. You have to provide irrigation to crops every day. Plants, like humans or animals, need that input every day, not once every three weeks. Earlier, farmers would typically use up almost 90 per cent of their available water. With a drip irrigation system, they use hardly 33 per cent. So with the same amount of water, you can double or triple your irrigated area. Now there, the government role is larger, because their job is to provide, to create the infrastructure. And slowly but surely, I think, they have started realizing that this is the right way to do it, and things are beginning to change on the ground. But again, some of these things have been done for centuries, and so people still tend to question us, 'Who are you to come and tell us to change so much?'

Interviewer: How does your company regard your responsibility to stakeholders?

AJ: There are a few things we insist on whenever we have new management come in. Most importantly, we encourage thinking about 'why are we here?' For a lot of people, doing business is merely coming in, doing some transactions, making some money, and that's it—it's transaction-based. But our business is relationship-based.

We are creating shared value, that's the purpose, that's why and how we exist. So, we like to see that the new management teams are also aligned to this thought process. Once that basic thought process—why you come to work every day—is clear, I think the rest of the culture automatically follows. If you want to create shared value for all your stakeholders, then you must ensure that everything is done right. I will give you an example—this whole concept of CSR.

There is now a law that you need to provide some 2 or 3 per cent of your profits to CSR. Our company made that a part of its constitution twenty years ago. Now, it is not about compensation—that you do not do your business righteously and then do some good work just to say, 'See how much we care about society!' Our thinking was, why not do everything right from day one? So that you don't take away anything from anyone, you don't destroy the environment, you don't make a distinction between the people you employ. So we insist that all our people believe in every single dealing they do—whether it's with our own people, whether it's with the customer, a bank or supplier—and maintain a certain standard. The value system then easily follows. We ultimately say that we should be fair to every stakeholder.

Learnings from Anil Jain: Business leaders should reflect on why their firms exists, and the answer has to be more than simply generating profits for shareholders.

7(b)

Anand Burman

Chhatra Singh/Dabur Ltd

Anand Burman is chairperson of Dabur India Limited, a leading consumer goods company based on Ayurveda, a traditional system of natural medicine that treats people according to—in the language of Ayurveda—the three doshas of vata, pitta and kapha. The company was founded in 1884 by his great-great grandfather, Dr S.K. Burman, a doctor living in Kolkata who specialized in Ayurvedic medicines. Anand is part of the fifth generation of the family business, joining first as the manager of research and development in 1980. In 1986, he joined the company's board, the same year Dabur became a publicly traded company, and in 2007, he became chairperson.

Interviewed by Suraj Srinivasan in New Delhi on 21 December 2017.

Interviewer: How did you make a successful consumer products business from traditional Ayurveda?

Anand Burman (AB): We as a company are in the consumer healthcare space largely based on Ayurveda. We are also in the personal care space where we tried to bring in as many tenets of natural products as we could into what we sell. So, for example, Ayurveda has many uses. I mean, I take that back—Ayurveda has many directions on how you can keep your teeth healthy, how to maintain your dental hygiene, etc. So we translated that into what we have today as the Dabur Red Toothpaste, and it has been a runaway success because it works. You put clove and tomar seed oil into your mouth, and it really takes care of your gums. And if something works, the customer will buy it. So we used to have red tooth powder using a very similar formulation, and we converted that into red toothpaste, and today we are the number three toothpaste in the country—very close to being number two.

Interviewer: What is the science of Ayurveda?

AB: Ayurveda is a very, very old science. It treats patients, or treats people, according to their doshas—vata, pitta and kapha are the three doshas. It treats patients accordingly. So if you are treating people according to their doshas—and I am stretching a point to a certain extent—you are essentially talking about personalized medicine. I mean, that is the first form of personalized medicine that existed a couple of thousand years ago. So it's not something that is all froufrou or hand-waving, or something like that. This is hundreds of years of experience, certain recipes or certain formulations have been made in a certain way and again, certain ways in which you are supposed to administer those formulations, and certain ways in which they are supposed to be taken. Now, if you actually look at the science behind this whole thing, which we started doing several decades ago, there were two components we focused on: number one, what scientific backing there actually was for what we were claiming, and number two, how we were making these products, and how we might standardize them so that every batch that is made is made according to the same recipe, and everything is uniform. We came across several issues that we are still trying to remedy.

Interviewer: How did you secure sustainable cultivation?

AB: Ayurveda is based a lot on natural products—herbs—which were originally sourced from the wild. And what we were finding was that the quality and the availability of certain herbs was on a steady decline. So we started doing something about it. We set up two nursery greenhouses, one in Nepal and one in India, where we grow our own saplings and seedlings . . . and give them out to farmers. We teach these farmers how to grow this stuff, and we do a 100 per cent buyback from them. And in that programme, we have about 3000 acres under cultivation—

of herbs and medicinal plants, which we buy back from the farmers. This is not our land, it's the farmers' land, or it could be gram sabha land, or it could be the forest department's land where they allow the local tribespeople to grow this stuff within the forest without cutting down trees.

So the other thing that we found was things like sandalwood was getting more and more difficult to come by. So we recently started our own plantation of sandalwood trees in Madhya Pradesh, and that's working out brilliantly. Within these plantations, we grow other medicinal herbs for our own use. So we have now arrested that decline of quality and availability to a large extent. But there is still a whole heck of a lot more that needs to be done. There are more plants to be cultivated. So far, we have concentrated on rare plants which are on the CITES [a multilateral treaty to protect endangered flora and fauna] list of the United Nations. Stuff that is freely available—like amla, wild amla or the like—there is no point in running after those plants. It's very important to run after those that are in decline. I can think of several plant species that we have cultivated either in Nepal or in India, where, because of what we have done, the availability worldwide has increased significantly.

Learnings from Anand Burman: True sustainability includes not only selling sustainable final products but making sure the whole value chain is sustainable.

7(c)

Anu Aga

Thermax Ltd

Anu Aga is former head of Thermax, an equipment manufacturer. The company that eventually became Thermax Global was founded in 1966 by A.S. Bhathena, Aga's father, as a hospital equipment company in partnership with a Belgian company called Wanson (Babcock Wanson since 1990). Aga inherited the leadership of the family-owned company in 1996 after the sudden passing away of her husband, Rohinton Aga. In 2004, Aga stepped down as chairperson and was succeeded by her daughter, Meher Pudumjee. Since then, Aga has served as the chairperson of the Thermax Foundation and supports other philanthropic activities, including NGOs such as Akanksha and Teach For India.

Interviewed by Geoffrey Jones in Mumbai on 14 February 2017.

Interviewer: *Why should corporations invest in social responsibility?*

Anu Aga (AA): I always feel that corporates owe it to the community to share some of their profits, and especially in India where there are glaring problems staring at us that we need to do something about. In my personal life, I decided to do something towards philanthropy because I had a son who died at twenty-five. He believed that a substantial part of what we earn should go to social causes. In fact, he wanted 70 to 80 per cent of what we earned personally to go to social causes. After he died, I decided to look for a credible NGO and found one. As the company stabilized and started making profits, although it was not in any way compulsory, good companies and people whom I respected, like Azim Premji or Tatas or Bajaj or Birlas or Godrej, did give quite a lot to social causes. So in a small way my board was ready and willing to give. I think we started with 1 per cent, went up to 3 per cent before it became compulsory. And because I had come across a wonderful, dynamic lady called Shaheen Mistri who was passionate about the quality of education, we became interested in the cause of primary education for the underprivileged. We created the Thermax Foundation, and we support an NGO called Akanksha, which runs twenty-one schools on a public-private partnership model with the municipality in Mumbai and Pune. Thermax Foundation supports five schools in Pune and from our personal funds (we give 30 per cent from our yearly income from Thermax dividends) we look after Teach For India, which is a growing organization. Both of these look after quality of education, which unfortunately in India is deteriorating every year. Through our foundation, we train municipal teachers to be more effective and efficient.

Interviewer: What is wrong with public education in India, and what is the responsibility of business?

AA: There is an NGO called Pratham that does a survey every two years. The government pays lip service to education, and teachers have to, at times, pay the people in charge to get into the system, and if you have to pay a large sum to become a teacher you have to pay that back. So you sometimes have a surrogate teacher in the villages who takes care of the teaching while you have another job. There are teachers who are trained in institutes that do not have any actual training—the institutes just charge a certain amount and dole out the degree two years later. So if such malpractices continue, education is bound to suffer in quality. There are many reasons, but teacher training institutes are in very bad shape and there is a lot of corruption in education as in other sectors.

I think that, beyond providing funds, businesses can talk about this situation and make people aware of it. NGOs like Akanksha, Teach For India, Azim Premji's organization and many, many others are doing excellent work to show that there is a way to give quality education. Through Teach For India our hope is that one day, through our fellows who dedicate two years of their lives to teaching in municipal and low-income private schools, we can change the system because unless the system changes, just reaching out to a few thousand children is not the answer in India. We have demonstrated that by improving quality we can change the lives of our students. Seven of our Akanksha children have been selected by Pune-based United World College and their university education abroad will be taken care of. One day we hope that they will come out of poverty, come out of the slums, and help again in this endeavour to improve the quality for the rest of the children.

I am delighted that my fellows of Teach For India—we recruit about 500 each year—are dedicating their lives and 60 per cent to 65 per cent continue in the social sector after they finish their time with Teach For India. We recruit 5 per cent to 7 per cent of the fellows who apply to Teach For India because we want teaching to be an aspirational profession. These fellows could have lucrative corporate jobs and wonderful perks and positions but they are shunning that and instead dedicating themselves to the social sector. So my optimism rises when I interact with them, when I see them, and I feel India has a wonderful future if we can have more and more people like these joining the social sector.

Learnings from Anu Aga: Business has a responsibility to help improve the quality of education in India given the poor state of public education.

7(d)

Fadi Ghandour

Fadi Ghandour

Fadi Ghandour is the founder and former CEO of Aramex, a Dubai-based courier company, and is a leading entrepreneur in the Gulf. Aramex began in 1982 as a small start-up courier company in the Middle East, and eventually came to compete with global giants such as FedEx and DHL. Ghandour also engaged in activities outside of Aramex, including supporting higher education and community empowerment in the Middle East. In 2004, Ghandour launched Ruwwad, a non-profit, which operates in Egypt, Lebanon, and Palestine, and offers university scholarships to promising young people in exchange for their involvement in community service. He is also a founding investor of Maktoob, the first Arabic–English email provider, which was sold to Yahoo! in 2009, and a founding investor of Souq, which was acquired by Amazon in 2019.

Interviewed by Geoffrey Jones in the United Arab Emirates on 4 July 2017.

Interviewer: What is the responsibility of business to society?

Fadi Ghandour (FG): I feel extremely passionate about the region of the Middle East. That goes back to my family experience—to my father, to the way we grew up, to caring about society, to feeling that we should have a positive impact on society. Then, when Aramex became the organization that it is today, I understood very well the impact it had on society. I started thinking about this in the early days, but as Aramex stabilized and became a profitable and powerful brand, and influential in many ways, I understood the power of the private sector and entrepreneurs, and I understood the power of how we affect society—positively or negatively.

Because Aramex was a positive story, I saw how positively it affected youth, young people who wanted to become entrepreneurs. They took us as their role model. I wasn't building it to become a role model. I was building it to be a stellar organization, a beautiful organization that hires fantastic people that take it to new places. But then I suddenly realized the fantastic attraction it had for people, and then realized the impact on society. It became the issue of whether the business of business is only business—you know, Milton Friedman and his idea that it's only business. While I adhere to that concept in some ways, I believe that we have to be activists for positive change, specifically in volatile societies—in emerging markets. All emerging markets are volatile in one way or another—politically, economically, financially.

So what does a capable company do when it lives in a society in flux—or possibly in flux? Do we go out and say, 'You know, we need to actually be active on the ground to make sure that—for selfish reasons—there is stability on the ground to build a business.' I'm not going to just say, 'I'm going to benefit from somebody else's influence on society so that I can build my business, and if it doesn't work, I'll pack my bags and leave.' No. This is our hometown. The youth that are graduating from our colleges are people who we want to employ. Their well-being is connected to our well-being. Society's well-being is connected to our well-being.

Interviewer: How can business empower youth?

FG: Aramex changed the face of sports in Jordan in the very early days. We built and operated a basketball club that recruited kids from the age of five years old all the way up to winning the national championships in basketball—completely non-profit until today. It's their twenty-fifth anniversary today, the Aramex basketball team. It's called Al Riyadi. It changed the face of the game—hiring amateurs—even paying them some wages, hiring them in the company, these sportsmen. They had a career post sports. Because you can't make money in sports in amateurs. We changed it. Later, that's what we did in Ruwwad, our community organization. We didn't want to only give money to NGOs and to social entrepreneurs. We wanted to be social entrepreneurs on the ground, helping youth become empowered in marginalized societies.

For me, the issue of youth is where I felt that I could have the most impact, because youth, entrepreneurship, jobs, employment—this is what I do. Being an entrepreneur and a businessman you're in the business of hiring people. I wanted to do things that I could have an impact on—impact meaning direct impact. I needed to feel that I was doing something. And when I say, 'I', it's the organization—we were actively doing it.

The biggest challenge in the region—and maybe globally today—is, what do you do with young people who are graduating in droves from universities? They call it, in the region, the youth bulge. Look how derogatory that word is—calling your future generations a bulge, or a challenge, or a problem, rather than thinking of them as an opportunity.

You know, a young society is an opportunity. Europe would kill for a young society. Even China would kill for a young society. Japan has negative growth in its population. We have a population that is 50 per cent, 60 per cent under the age of twenty-five. That's a massive resource. But also, if it doesn't get channelled in the right way—if it doesn't get the opportunities, if it doesn't get the education, if it doesn't get to feel that it's part and parcel of society—it will create havoc in society. That's why you saw the Arab Spring, and that's why you see issues in Iraq today, you see issues in Syria, you see issues in Egypt.

Even in stable countries, governments, the private sector, and the people are worried about the stability of society. At the core of it is the young population that is feeling a sense of

despair sometimes because they do not have the opportunities.
That's why we focused on youth in marginalized areas, because
that's where we're needed most. And the idea of it was to be
experiential in everything that we do. We are in the business of
character building.

*Interviewer: How can business encourage a new generation of
change-makers?*

FG: The organization we created is called Ruwwad. In
Ruwwad—which means 'entrepreneur' in Arabic—we say that
the private sector, or entrepreneurs, have to be active in society
and to be partners with government in developing the areas that
they're capable of developing, or are passionate about. Ruwwad
is now active in Jordan, Egypt, Lebanon and Palestine. We give
scholarships to universities for people that cannot afford it, in
return for four hours of volunteer work in the society that they
live in. We create workshops for them every weekend to discuss
and have a serious dialogue about the issues that they confront.

Why? For two reasons. One, we want these people on the
margins to feel that they're earning their scholarship. It's not
charity. I am giving you the opportunity. I'm paying you to go
to school, enabling you to go to school, but you're giving me
your time. Time is as valuable as anything—as you know. And
in your time, you're actually addressing a challenge in society.
So you feel a sense of ownership of the issues in society.

That's what volunteerism is about. It's saying, 'Even if the
state had forgotten us, if we are living on the margins—this is
our home, this is our neighbourhood. Do we go and address
the challenges of our neighbourhood and solve them, or do we
sit and complain and say, "You know, people forgot us, and we

have no chances?".' No, go. This builds character and provides the soft skills needed to have a sense of initiative, to have critical thinking, to work in teams, to address the challenges.

We are complementing what you don't get in universities today. The education system globally is under challenge, but, specifically in our region, it's a conveyor-belt system. You read the books, take the exams and graduate. Here's your certificate. Congratulations. The minute you exit the walls of the university, who cares about what happens to you? But when you've gone to Ruwwad you're going to be a person that has experienced serious dialogue about serious issues. You're going to have volunteered. You're going to have mixed with men and women in the same place and felt that work environment. You're going to have met many people of influence in society—they come and give talks in Ruwwad platforms. You're going to have experienced things you don't experience in the class. So you are much more ready for life after education, after school.

We don't claim that we want to change all of society, but we are also believers that there is a certain bunch of people, a few, who are change-makers that can influence the rest of society. And we feel that, the people who are influencers, they must be from society, and in society, and within society. They're not parachuted from outside. They're the sons and daughters of that street, of that neighbourhood. When they do things, the neighbourhood will listen to them much more than anybody parachuted from outside. There's trust with them. The government might not be there when you wake up one morning, but your neighbour will.

Learnings from Fadi Ghandour: Youthful populations should never be seen as problems. Rather they are opportunities.

7(e)

María Emilia Correa

María Emilia Correa

María Emilia Correa is co-founder of Sistema B, which promotes system-wide change to capitalism based around the concept of B Corporations. With an early interest in nature conservation, Correa was inspired after attending the United Nations Earth Summit in Rio de Janeiro in 1992 to explore ways business could help save the natural environment. She held several positions in civil society organizations focused on helping business to become more sustainable, and in business, including working for Natura Cosmetics in Brazil, a company well known for its commitment to sustainability. In 2012, she and three other Latin Americans persuaded the American founders of the B Lab movement to let them transfer the concept to Latin America. The creation of Sistema B, a more ambitious version of the original concept, was the result.

Interviewed by Andrea Lluch in Boston, Massachusetts, on 8 May 2019.

Interviewer: Why did you move from the corporate world to purpose-driven entrepreneurship?

María Emilia Correa (MC): At one point in my life, I felt that, despite the fact that a lot of progress had been made, because the business sector had taken significant strides, we weren't moving forward with the relevance or the speed the world needed. When you look at the challenges faced by the planet, the climate crisis, the world's inequality, the destruction of biodiversity, the loss of indigenous peoples' ancestral knowledge, you realize what is really at stake. These are all global challenges that we all— every single person on the planet—face. We used to believe that public issues fell under the government's purview: if a river is contaminated, the government should build a treatment plant nearby to clean the river, or we should create a foundation to help clean the river. It is now dawning on us that we are all confronted with these problems, even the people inside business companies. Thus, the notion that we all need to find a way to be part of the solution to our problems is very inspiring and very challenging at the same time. In recent years, companies have adopted a very limited vantage point, focusing solely on maximizing shareholders' financial income. That is certainly our topmost priority, yes, but it is not the only one.

I started to feel that the business sector's amazing ability to accomplish worldwide results hinges on the market, a planet-based platform that could join governments and civil society organizations—not replace them but join efforts with them—to secure global solutions. Yet, that promise remains unfulfilled today because the business sector's contribution proves very irrelevant as compared to the size of our problems and relative to its own capabilities. Feeling uneasy, about ten years ago I chose to step away from the corporate world and became a purpose-driven entrepreneur who wanted to build companies that truly addressed social and environmental issues.

Interviewer: What attracted you to the B Corporation movement?

MC: I have spent my entire life looking for ways to make it possible for a company to be able to secure results that yield both profitability for shareholders and well-being for people and nature. Nowadays, we are organized by law in such a way that fiduciary responsibility forces business leaders to focus primarily on financial outcomes. This accounts for a significant constraint that very often leads non-financial interests—that is, social and environmental issues, both long-term issues by nature—to clash with this short-term decision system that the world orchestrated barely fifty years ago. Also, the solution to social and environmental problems lies outside the company, and we have consistently focused on company issues. Thus, we now need to find a way to raise non-financial interests to the level of financial interests, so that companies can bear a positive impact outside. It's a huge challenge. In the search for a solution, three of my co-founders of Sistema B in Latin America and I—came across B Corporation.

The B-Corp status is a solution created by three entrepreneurs in the United States. These American entrepreneurs said, 'Let's ask shareholders, who own the equity, to broaden the fiduciary mandate. They are the only ones who can do that, apart from the law.' So, B-Corps are companies whose shareholders have broadened the fiduciary mandate to advance society's goals and to protect nature. That commitment is introduced into the company's articles of incorporation, so that it becomes legally binding—that is, mandatory. You see, you often hear that people are starting to mistrust companies. Why do we mistrust business companies? Among many reasons, because companies tell us, 'We are very worried about water issues. This year we are going to focus on water conservation.' Then, the next year, they say, 'No, saving water is no longer a priority. Now, we are going to work on early childhood literacy.' Later they say, 'No, we are not going to do anything because we didn't have enough profits to work on those problems.' As a result, people outside the company are at a loss: they don't know what to think or believe. The upside of making this commitment legally binding is that it ensures the company's long-term, steady commitment.

This small change, broadening the fiduciary mandate, brings some amazing consequences, as it expands the room for innovation. The question we now ask, 'How do we build a world where—in my lifespan, the world population has gone from 2 billion [200 crore] to 7 billion [700 crore] people—we can feed and provide good living conditions to 7 billion [700 crore] people with the Earth's limited resources?' A tremendous innovation dilemma. These are the innovation questions we need to take to the companies. How do we do that? By securing shareholders' permission to work with a long-term vision. B-Corps provide a solution by enabling the business sector to expand its structure in order to genuinely become part of the long-term solution.

Interviewer: Why did you change the original American model when you transferred the concept to Latin America?

MC: My colleagues and I said, 'Let's bring this scheme to Latin America because it provides an amazing solution.' We four friends forged an agreement with the people who created B-Corps to take the idea to Latin America.

We called the organization we created Sistema B, because from the beginning we envisaged a system-wide approach rather than simply a focus on persuading firms to become B-Corps. It is systemic because we sought to gather multiple communities: business leaders, B-Corps, investors and the wider community to join forces to build an economy where success is measured by people's and nature's well-being and not just profits.

We need opinion leaders to think in a different way, and academia to teach a different way of doing business. Seven years ago, when we started working on Sistema B's ideas of bringing purpose-driven companies to Latin America, literally thousands of university students approached us, saying, 'We are interested in this. We want to work at purpose-driven companies.' If you look at the statistics, you'll see that a vast majority of millennials want to work at these types of businesses. However, universities were not talking about it. At first, we all went to universities to deliver lectures, but I soon realized that this just sparked dissatisfaction. We came with these ideas, this inspiration, and stories about fascinating companies that motivate people, but these notions did not resonate in the classes. Students felt frustrated because they wanted to hear about these concepts, but their regular classes continued to be filled with the ideas that their grandparents had heard about fifty years ago.

In response, we created Academia B to invite faculty members to join Sistema B, to participate in conversations with business leaders, public officials, neighbouring communities, indigenous peoples, social activists, and everyone trying to build a new economic scheme. This is a fascinating research field, but it should also become embedded in classes. At this time, 1500 academicians from thirty-five countries have come together in a network created to convey these ideas via so-called 'experiential training', as an increasing number of students don't want to sit in class idly—they want to get out there and engage in this incredibly exciting movement as part of their education experience.

We have also discovered that more educational tools are needed, because when professors take these issues to their schools or their classes, they find that most cases and books do not focus on Latin America, and largely deal with traditional companies and conventional issues. Academia B has supported and funded nearly 100 research studies on this phenomenon in Latin America. Some of these studies have already been published in renowned journals. We have organized academic seminars and round-table meets, and we already have a significant group of academicians in the region and around the world who are working on this topic.

Learnings from María Emilia Correa: Making business more ecologically and socially responsible will require a system-wide approach including investors, the community and educators.

Acknowledgements

This book has been a collective effort, and we would like to thank and celebrate the contribution of others. Morgan Spencer was the research associate on the CEM project during the years when many of the interviews were undertaken, and she has played a key administrative role in bringing this book together. Her successor, Makena Binker Cosen, has been a tower of strength in the last stages of the book. We are hugely grateful to her for the work she had done for this project. HBS's India Research Centre in Mumbai, led by executive director Anjali Raina, has been central to the endeavour. Anjali and her former and present staff, including Namrata Arora, Rachna Chawla, Malini Sen and Rachna Tahilyani, advised on the selection of interviewees and masterfully handled the complicated logistics of making the interviews happen across South Asia. They also read and made many helpful comments on a first draft of this book. We would also like to thank Esel Çekin of HBS's Middle East and North Africa Research Centre and Goulam Amarsy, president of the HBS Club of the Gulf Cooperation Council, for their facilitation of the interviews in Dubai used in this book. Pippa Tubman Armerding of HBS's Africa Research

Centre facilitated the Africa-based interviews used in this book. We are very grateful for the assistance of Cheng Gao, Nataliya Langburd Wright and Tiona Zuzul, past and present doctoral students, on research papers, cases and conference presentations related to the CEM project. The authors would like to express their gratitude to the Division of Research and Faculty Development at Harvard Business School for their consistent financial support for the CEM project out of which this book emanated over the years.

While we undertook in person many of the interviews used in the book, the CEM project has been a collective endeavour in which many past and present Harvard Business School faculty generously gave their time to undertake interviews. We have included interviews made by some of them in this book. We would like to extent our heartfelt thanks to Prithwiraj Choudhury, Srikant M. Datar, Rohit Deshpande, Joseph B. Fuller, Nien-hê Hsieh, Andrea Lluch, Euvin Naidoo, V.G. Narayanan, Meg Rithmire, Sudev J. Sheth, Suraj Srinivasan and Gunnar Trumbull.

We would also like to express our gratitude to our spouses and children for their forbearance and support.

Geoffrey Jones and Tarun Khanna
Boston, August 2021

Appendix

Additional Reading

While the CEM interviews, from which we have drawn the material in the chapters of *Leadership to Last*, were carried out by multiple Harvard faculty, our selections of these interviews are undoubtedly motivated by our own academic and other perspectives and, inevitably, our biases. Both to make these more explicit, and to point to additional writings or materials either one or the other of us has created for those who find our approach compelling, we have put together brief descriptions of a selection of books, articles and an online course below. Since the CEM database is a free, publicly accessible database to promote teaching and research, we also list peer-reviewed academic papers that are based directly on the video and text of the CEM interviews.

Materials Conceptually Related to *Leadership to Last*

Trust: Creating the Foundation for Entrepreneurship in Developing Countries, Berrett-Koehler, 2018
Tarun Khanna

Entrepreneurial ventures often fail in the developing world because of the lack of something taken for granted in the developed world: trust. Over centuries, the developed world has built customs and institutions such as enforceable contracts, an impartial legal system, and credible regulatory bodies—and even unofficial but respected sources of information such as Yelp, which publishes crowdsourced reviews about businesses, and Consumer Reports, the American nonprofit consumer organization dedicated to independent product testing, that have created a high level of such ambient trust. Rather than become casualties of mistrust, smart entrepreneurs in the developing world adopt the mindset that, like it or not, it's up to them to weave their own independent web of trust—with their employees, their partners, their clients, their customers, and society as a whole. Most entrepreneurs profiled in *Leadership to Last* would, somewhere in the interview, emphasize trust with one or other of an ensemble of stakeholders.

Profits and Sustainability. A History of Green Entrepreneurship, Oxford University Press, 2017 (also available as an audiobook)
Geoffrey Jones

Business investment in sustainability is often assumed to be a new phenomenon. It isn't. This book traces green business in organic food, renewable energy and other sectors back to the nineteenth century. Indian agricultural practices are shown to have been a major source of inspiration for the early organic agriculture movement in Europe and elsewhere in the West. The book demonstrates how entrepreneurs created new markets and industries, and drove innovations in sustainable practices, even at times when most consumers and governments marginalized the entire subject. This process was time-consuming in most cases and required long time-horizons. Yet these endeavours were costly—win-win outcomes were few and far between and they were insufficiently widespread to prevent the continued deterioration in the Earth's environmental health.

'The Alternative Business History: Business in Emerging Markets', *Business History Review* 91, no. 3 Fall 2017, pp. 537–569.
Gareth Austin, Carlos Davila and Geoffrey Jones

The lens of Western countries is often used to explore the business history of emerging markets. Yet a growing literature identifies contexts that are different from developed markets. These regions experienced long eras of foreign domination, dealt with extensive state intervention, faced institutional inefficiencies, and experienced extended turbulence. Many characteristics of the Indian experience seen in this book turned out to be found in other emerging markets too. This context drove different business responses than in the developed world. Entrepreneurs counted more than managerial hierarchies, immigrants and diaspora were often critical sources of entrepreneurship, informal and sometimes illegal forms of business were commonplace, diversified business groups rather than the multi-divisional became the major form of large-scale business, corporate strategies to deal with turbulence were essential, and radical corporate social responsibility concepts were pursued by business leaders.

Entrepreneurship in Emerging Economies, 2015 (with adaptations over subsequent years).
Tarun Khanna
Free massive open online course (MOOC) on edX: https://www.edx.org/course/entrepreneurship-in-emerging-economies

A six-week self-paced set of video-based lectures and exercises illustrating principles of entrepreneurship in emerging economies, built around the idea of institutional voids (see description below of *Winning in Emerging Markets*). The course has been taken by more than 6,50,000 learners across 200 countries.

'Contextual Intelligence', *Harvard Business Review*, September 2014.
Tarun Khanna

Conditions of economic development and of institutional maturity, educational norms, language, and culture vary enormously from place to place, making so-called 'best practices' tricky to transfer from place to place. Scholars once thought that technical knowledge of best manufacturing practices (to take one example) was sufficiently developed that processes simply needed to be tweaked to fit local conditions. More often, it turns out, they have to be reworked quite radically— not because the technology is wrong but because everything around it changes how it will work. There's nothing wrong with the tools we have at our disposal, but their application requires contextual intelligence: the ability to understand the limits of our knowledge and to adapt that knowledge to a context different from the one in which it was acquired. Our profiled entrepreneurs exhibit, unsurprisingly, an on-the-ground familiarity with their contexts that allow them to learn from and adapt global models to their own circumstances, and also to contribute their experiences to global knowhow.

Winning in Emerging Markets, Harvard Business School Press, 2010
Tarun Khanna and Krishna G. Palepu (with Richard Bullock)

Conceptual introduction to the idea of institutional voids as a structural way to think about emerging markets. Absence of specialized intermediaries that we take for granted in more mature economies—e.g., risk capital providers, talent search firms, valuation experts for intellectual property, and a continuum of other specialists—are, in fact, a double-edged sword for entrepreneurs. In the first instance, would-be entrepreneurs must find financially viable business models that navigate around the constraints posed these voids, by the absence of such specialists. But equally, the voids themselves are the source of entrepreneurial activity. The actions of virtually every entrepreneur profiled in this book can be seen through the lens of the particular set of institutional voids to which she is adapting or whose existence she is ameliorating.

'Bringing History (Back) into International Business', *Journal of International Business Studies* 37, no. 4, July 2006, pp. 453–468.
Geoffrey Jones and Tarun Khanna

This is the first academic collaboration between Geoffrey Jones and Tarun Khanna, dating back some 15 years. In this much-cited conceptual piece, we argue that the field of international business should evolve its rhetoric from the relatively uncontroversial idea that 'history matters' to exploring how it matters. We discuss four conceptual channels through which history matters. First, historical variation is at least a worthy complement to contemporary cross-sectional variation in illuminating conceptual issues. Second, historical evidence avoids spurious labeling of some phenomena as 'new', and by so doing may challenge current explanations of their determinants. Third, history can allow us to move beyond the oft-recognized importance of issues of path dependence to explore its roots. Fourth, there are certain issues that are un-addressable, including issues of causality so dear to social scientists, except in the really long (that is, historical) run.

Studies Using the Materials Generated by the CEM Project

'Business Investment in Education in Emerging Markets Since the 1960s', *Business History* 63, no. 7, September 2021, pp. 1113–1143.
Valeria Giacomin, Geoffrey Jones, and Erica Salvaj

This article uses a sample of the CEM interviews to show that more than three-quarters of such business leaders invested in education as a non-profit activity. The article explores three different types of motivations behind such high levels of engagement with education: values driven, context focused, and firm focused. The article identifies significant regional variations in terms of investment execution, structure, and impact. In South Asia, there was a preference for long-term investment in primary and secondary education. In Africa and Latin America, some initiatives sometimes had a shorter-term connotation, but with high-profile projects in partnerships with international organizations and foreign universities.

'Drivers of Philanthropic Foundations in Emerging Markets: Family, Values and Spirituality', *Journal of Business Ethics*, 2021. Valeria Giacomin and Geoffrey Jones

This article uses the CEM interviews to argue that many of the foundations founded by business leaders in emerging markets including India are motivated by a specific type of ethics called 'spiritual philanthropy'. It is suggested that business leaders in emerging markets are more directly exposed to dire social, educational and health deprivation than their counterparts in developed countries. As a result they are less inclined towards grandiose world-making, and their foundations are more focused on delivering immediate benefits to communities in their home countries, motivated by implicit or explicit spirituality.

'Emboldening and Contesting Gender and Skin Color Stereotypes in the Film Industry in India, 1947–1991', *Business History Review* 95, no. 3, Autumn 2021, pp. 483–515.
Sudev Sheth, Geoffrey Jones and Morgan Spencer

This article uses interviews with actors and directors for CEM and other oral history projects to examine colourism and sexism in Indian cinema between Independence and the start of liberalization. It shows that Bollywood shared Hollywood's privileging of paler skin over darker skin, and its preference for presenting women in stereotypical ways lacking agency. It was left to parallel, and some regional, cinemas to contest skin colour and gender stereotypes.

Machine Learning Approaches to Facial and Text Analysis: Discovering CEO Oral Communication Styles, *Strategic Management Journal* 40, no. 11, November 2019, pp. 1705–1732.
Prithwiraj Choudhury, Dan Wang, Natalie A. Carlson, and Tarun Khanna

This study demonstrates that Machine Learning (ML) techniques can be applied to video and textual data form the CEM interviews to extract quantitative information that can be used in management studies in a way that meaningfully augments the informative content of more conventionally accessible information.

'Business, Governments and Political Risk in South Asia and Latin America since 1970', *Australian Economic History Review* 58, no. 3, November 2018, pp. 233–264.
Geoffrey Jones and Rachael Comunale

This article uses CEM interviews to identify variations in the nature of political risk perceived by business leaders between different emerging markets, and how firms differed in their responses. Excessive bureaucracy emerged as the biggest source of risk for South Asia, including India, while macroeconomic and policy turbulence was the largest perceived risk for Latin American business leaders. The study shows interviewees in South Asia frequently reported attempting to stay away from highly regulated industries, while many interviewees in Latin America sought to form closer ties or working relationships with incumbent administrations.

'Overcoming Institutional Voids: A Reputation-Based View of Long Run Survival', *Strategic Management Journal* 38, no. 11, November 2017, pp. 2147–2167.
Cheng Gao, Tiona Zuzul, Geoffrey Jones and Tarun Khanna

Although emerging markets are typically characterized by underdeveloped institutions and frequent environmental shifts, they also contain many firms that have survived over generations. This study explores how firms in weak institutional environments are able to persist over time. Drawing on the CEM database, the authors combine induction and deduction to propose reputation as a meta-resource that allows firms to activate their conventional resources. Reputation is seen as consisting of prominence, perceived quality and resilience. A process model is developed that illustrates the mechanisms that allow reputation to facilitate survival in ways that persist over time.

The Impact of Globalization on Argentina and Chile: Business Enterprises and Entrepreneurship, Edward Elgar Publishing, 2015. Geoffrey Jones and Andrea Lluch (eds.)

This book explores the contrasting business histories of two neighboring but very different Latin American countries as they experienced turbulence and shocks over the course of the twentieth century, drawing heavily on the first set of CEM interviews. Both economies relied heavily on the export of commodities to the developed world. In times of economic boom and fast globalization, this created wealth, although institutional failures resulted in gross inequality. However, reliance on global markets also made businesses very vulnerable to shocks far from their borders and beyond their control.